The Low-Carb Cookbook

Over 200 great recipes for everyone

who wants to eat well *and* lose weight,

with diets like *Protein Power,*

The Zone, and *Dr Atkins*

Fran McCullough

Foreword by Michael R. Eades, M.D.,
and Mary Dan Eades, M.D.

thorsons

Thorsons
An Imprint of HarperCollins*Publishers*
77–85 Fulham Palace Road,
Hammersmith, London W6 8JB

The website address is: www.thorsonselement.com

and *Thorsons* are trademarks of
HarperCollins*Publishers* Ltd

First published by Hyperion, USA, 1997
Published by Thorsons 2003

1 3 5 7 9 10 8 6 4 2

A catalogue record of this book is
available from the British Library

ISBN 0 00 714790 2

Printed and bound in Great Britain by
Clays Ltd, St Ives plc, Bungay

Contents

Acknowledgements

I like to think that Doctors Michael and Mary Dan Eades have actually saved my life — certainly their low-carb diet has brought my formerly high blood pressure, high cholesterol and high triglycerides into the normal range, and dramatically reversed my ominous health profile. I can't thank them enough.

I'm grateful to my wise agent, Irene Skolnick, and my unflappable editor, Rick Kot, who made this book happen in record time. Big thanks to Lisa Kitei, who 'got it' right away and put her great enthusiasm to work for the book.

Even with all this support, and the unflagging spirits of my husband, David, who had to literally eat the mistakes, this book wouldn't exist without the help of my endlessly generous cook friends: Bruce Aidells, Colman Andrews, Jo Bettoja, JoAnn Clevenger, Doe Coover, Elaine Corn, Susan Costner, Alice Doyle, Suzanne Hamlin, Ken Haedrich (my dessert guru), Diana Kennedy, Deborah Madison, Norma Marshall, Priscilla Martell, Michael Roberts, Alice Rosengard, Martha Rose Shulman, David Soohoo, Martin and Sally Stone, John Taylor, Sylvia Thompson, James Villas, Eileen Weinberg, Faith Willinger, Barbara Witt, Diane Worthington and Rob Wynne.

Finally, thanks to Irwyn Applebaum, for his brilliant sense of timing in setting me free to finish this book.

Foreword

April 22 and 23, 1996, were red-letter days in the annals of nutritional medicine. It was on these days that a group of internationally renowned experts met in Dallas to focus on the topic of the role of dietary fat in human health and disease. Many of them concluded that the low-fat, high-complex-carbohydrate diet had been a dismal failure in addressing the problems of obesity, cardiovascular disease and diabetes. These leading researchers had spent years investigating all aspects of fat's role in health and discovered that many of the dietary truisms we've been taught to accept uncritically in the last two decades are in fact not only incorrect but actually dangerous in their implications for our health. For instance, no doubt remains that the low-fat, high-carbohydrate diet raises triglycerides – a type of fat found in the blood that was once thought to be a harmless bystander, but is now turning out to be the single best predictor for heart disease risk. No doubt remains that the low-fat, high-carbohydrate diet lowers the level of HDL – the so-called good cholesterol that protects against heart disease. And although it's true that the low-fat, high-complex-carbohydrate diet has accomplished a modest lowering of LDL cholesterol (the so-called bad kind) levels, as it turns out, even this apparent benefit evaporates under closer scrutiny. Although the levels do fall a bit, the LDL particles that remain are smaller and denser and therefore more prone to cause heart disease — in effect, a much stronger negative factor than a somewhat higher LDL level.

But as useless as the low-fat, high-carbohydrate diet has proven to be for cardiac risk, it's an even bigger flop as a treatment for obesity or diabetes. During the last decade — the heyday of the low-fat diet — the American nation has become substantially fatter (by a third) and the incidence of adult-onset diabetes has *tripled*.

Such dismal statistics come as no surprise to us, since we've seen the same results in disappointed low-fat dieters who've come to our practice. During the last decade, we've devoted our professional lives to treating these disorders nutritionally. But we have not used the standard low-fat, high-carbohydrate approach. We tried that model very early in our medical careers and met the same high rates of failure that frustrate doctors and patients today. So we stepped back and took a fresh look at what works biochemically and what simply doesn't. That led us to develop the Protein Power programme, which we've used successfully to help thousands of patients in our clinical practice reclaim their health as well as lose weight.

The approach we take is to control the hormone insulin, which not only causes the fat cells to store fat but also has a key role in high blood pressure, vascular disease and diabetes. Of the three dietary elements — protein, fat and carbohydrate — only carbohydrate increases the production of insulin, which then sets off these adverse effects in people with hyperinsulinaemia (insulin resistance). And curiously enough, the *only* way to cut back on insulin production is through diet, by cutting back the carbohydrates, the very sugars and starches emphasized on the low-fat diet. The several low-carbohydrate diets differ a little in specifics, but they all restrict carbohydrates to achieve their health benefits and weight loss.

Given our success in bringing down our patients' cholesterol and triglycerides, controlling their blood sugars, virtually reversing adult diabetes and helping people to achieve weight loss who had failed again and again with the low-fat diets, we are amused when nutritional 'experts' trot out worn clichés in an effort to discredit our higher-protein, moderate-fat, restricted-carbohydrate approach. Among these tired warnings are that a low-carbohydrate diet will damage your kidneys and weaken your bones, and that all the weight you lose is simply water that will be gained right back. While our own experience belies these myths – in ten years of practice with thousands of patients, we've never seen a single person develop kidney damage or weak bones (and we check their blood regularly to be sure) – even the peer-review medical literature abounds in work that disproves them.

Dr. Miriam Blum laid to rest the myth that higher-protein diets damage the kidneys in a classic paper published in the *Archives of Internal Medicine* in 1987. Her research team identified adult subjects who currently ate and had eaten a high-protein diet – including meat of all kinds – for most of their lives and matched them by age and sex to a second group of adults who were long-term vegetarians. The second group (who had been vegetarians for an average of 13.3 years) consumed very little protein, and what they did eat was entirely of vegetable origin. The team then measured the natural 'age-related decline' in kidney function (a condition that unfortunately occurs in all humans as we age) and found that there was absolutely no difference between the two groups across the entire spectrum of ages. This study shows that eating meat or eating a diet of high protein

carries with it no risk of damage to normal, healthy kidneys. A much more recent study by the German research
team of Remer and Mantz, published in the *Journal of
Nutritional Biochemistry* in 1995, showed that weightlifters
who consumed excessive amounts of protein actually ex-
perienced *improved* kidney function.

Similar studies have disproved the argument that protein causes osteoporosis. According to this theory, increased protein intake should cause increased acidity of
the blood, as a result of an elevation of protein breakdown
products. To maintain the proper acid level, the body
must therefore 'neutralize' the acid excess by leaching
calcium out of the bones to act as the buffer. The calcium
would then pass into the urine, at the expense of the
bones. In fact, Dr Herta Spencer considered the fore-
most calcium research expert in the world, has published
a number of papers showing absolutely no correlation
between meat consumption and loss of calcium in the
urine.

Some medical writers have suggested that the low-
carbohydrate diet increases uric acid levels in the blood –
a major factor in gout – but in fact the diet *lowers* uric acid
levels.

We, our patients, a growing number of doctors of all
specialities and millions of dieters are convinced of the
safety and efficacy of a low-carbohydrate nutritional regimen. The most common reason that people do abandon
this programme is not that it damages their health, or
fails to correct their problems – quite the contrary. One
of the statements we hear most often from patients com-
ing into our office is: 'The only time I ever really lost
weight and felt good was on a high-protein diet.' When
we inquire why they abandoned a regimen that by their
own admission worked, they usually reply, 'I just got tired

of eating nothing but meat. And I just didn't know what else to cook.' How can one follow a nutritional programme of any kind for the long term without variety in texture, in flavour and in food choices? To say the least, overcoming this monotony has been a challenge.

Since the publication of our book *Protein Power* in early 1996, we have been besieged by readers wanting more how-to advice on low-carbohydrate meal preparation. They've discovered the same thing we have: there's just not much information out there on the practical aspects of maintaining the low-carb lifestyle. We made a foray to our local book shop and encountered a plethora of books on vegetarian cooking, fat-free cooking, high-carbohydrate cooking, and fat-removal modifications of virtually every kind of ethnic cooking in existence. All in all, we found 617 different titles on some aspects of low-fat cooking, but not even *one* low-carbohydrate cookbook. Not a single one! Over the years we've gathered recipes from patients, friends, the Internet (an active low-carb newsgroup creates and exchanges recipes) and from our own experimentation and modification of published recipes that we've adapted for low-carbohydrate cooking. With such slim offerings available, we even included a mini-cookbook in *Protein Power*, but space constraints limited the number of recipes we could offer.

Finally, however, comes Fran McCullough to the rescue, offering us a tour de force for low-carbohydrate cooking. Fran is uniquely qualified to this task. She is a fabulous cook herself, with a discriminating palate, an inventive mind and a love of good food; she has several previous cookbooks to her credit; and she has edited award-winning cookbooks by other authors. Most importantly, she herself has lived a lifelong battle with her weight and the health issues related to it. She has walked the walk, and knows firsthand the culinary dilemmas that bedevil people trying to adapt to a low-carbohydrate life in a high-carbohydrate world. And what she offers in *The Low-Carb Cookbook* is more than just a collection of recipes – it's a complete primer on how to modify your kitchen, stock your cupboard, alter your cooking methods and change your life to accommodate your new dietary regimen. She's packed her book full of helpful ideas and suggestions for navigating the minefield of carbohydrates. Because of her own health problems and sensitivity to carbohydrates, she's acutely aware of the way that even tiny bits of carbohydrate can add up to sabotage good intentions. She understands that carb grams are much like long-distance phone calls – each one costs only a few pennies, but at the end of the month, the bill can be outrageously high. Her own struggle has helped to define this book and make sticking to a lower carbohydrate regimen a snap. She's packed *The Low-Carb Cookbook* with complete and easy-to-understand instructions on how to prepare exceptional dishes, from appetizers to soups and salads to main meals, snacks, and desserts – everything you could need to cook well for yourself while at the same time preparing meals that will satisfy your family and will be impressive enough for entertaining friends.

Fran also loves to travel, and her journeys have given her a familiarity with cuisines around the world. Many of her delicious recipes reflect these rich influences. Her knowledge of speciality ingredients is encyclopaedic. When we travel, we always check with Fran for tips on local specialities that will fit into our eating plan.

With *The Low-Carb Cookbook* boredom will never again be a valid excuse for straying from the path of low-carbohydrate righteousness. Thanks, Fran!

– MICHAEL AND MARY DAN EADES

Introduction

As I have almost every year, I spent most of 1995 dieting. But this time there was a big surprise: for the first time in a lifetime of try-and-fail yo-yo dieting, I know that the weight loss I've already sustained (over 60 pounds) will continue and that I'll end up sometime soon as a normal-weight person who is no longer at the mercy of food. Finally, I got it. It's not that I've solved an emotional problem centred around food – although simply being fat and failing over and over again to solve the problem certainly creates major anxiety – but rather that I discovered I have a metabolic problem, specifically an insulin problem. And now I know what to do about it, with a new way of eating so simple and so enjoyable that there's no question of losing control. The only question is how to adapt this new way of eating to the rest of my life – which is how I came to write this book.

I'm sure my diet history will be familiar to anyone who's been overweight. Weight Watchers was a great struggle, and then the few lost pounds would come right back. The liquid diet was easy and worked like crazy, though it left me with a strange 'wasted-but-still-fat' look. But after four months of liquid dieting my hair started falling out around my shoulders, and I panicked. When I came off the diet, all I wanted to eat was sugar and fat, preferably together. I would eat an entire batch of biscuits and then make another one and eat the dough right from the bowl – followed by a walk to keep myself from eating ice cream. My cravings were simply overwhelming and not to be denied. In desperation I turned to a version of the old Atkins diet, the only diet that ever really worked for me. After my doctors told me I'd ruin my kidneys if I stayed on it (not true, as it turned out), I resigned myself to simply gaining back more weight. Next, I gave low-fat dieting a big try with a famous doctor, whom I loved. First I gained 10 pounds, as I'd been assured I might (not to worry – they'd come off soon), and though it was a lot of fun to eat all that bread and pasta, I didn't really feel good and I didn't lose any weight. And I started to develop gout.

One day my favourite diet counsellor pointed out that there is a typical dieting pattern. She drew a lozenge on a blackboard that showed where anxiety levels typically peaked after regaining weight, then intensive dieting began, then slacking off, and then the anxiety again, etc. I was aware of this cycle, of course, but seeing it so starkly represented had a big effect on me: I knew I had to stop doing this to myself. Either I would solve this problem and lose weight or I'd ignore it and just get fatter.

My first clue to a solution came from a nutritionist who told me I had a big difficulty with carbohydrates. 'Your metabolism just can't handle them,' she said. She put me on a very restricted diet, limiting my carbs to a few green vegetables, rice and apples. This diet seemed right to me, and in fact it worked very well. But the routine was so bleak – a harsh sentence for a cookbook editor who passionately loves food – that I couldn't stand more than four months of it. And my hair was falling out again. On to another famous doctor who put me on his low-carb salmon and salad diet – another success, but then the gout returned. So I began searching for something similar but better, something I could live with that didn't have these alarming side effects.

At that point I got really lucky: into my life walked doctors Michael and Mary Dan Eades with the manuscript for their book, *Protein Power*, for me to edit, and I knew right away that here was the answer. The Eadeses explained that the carbohydrate-intolerance problem is actually a genetic insulin problem, and that it contributes to a cluster of chronic diseases, including hypertension, heart disease, gout and diabetes. I already had gout and occasional high blood pressure, which runs in my family, as does heart disease. My bloodwork looked terrible, with extremely high triglycerides and low HDL, the good cholesterol. I had all the signs of pre-diabetes plus a good 80 pounds to lose. In the course of editing *Protein Power*, I became a convert. Not only does their theory make excellent medical sense, but their diet offers a broad range of foods. Now my blood looks terrific, with model numbers for cholesterol and triglycerides and very low insulin. Beyond that, I have enormous amounts of reliable, steady energy, a new mental clarity and a strong new body with muscles. For those things alone I'd keep on this diet for life.

But there were other surprises: my husband, just to be companionable, joined me on the low-carb diet and promptly lost the 30 pounds he'd slowly put on over the years. Our daughter, a wilderness instructor in her mid-twenties, had been unable to shake an extra 20 pounds despite careful low-fat eating and vigorous exercise. She was intrigued by our dramatic weight loss and tried a modified version of it herself by just cutting out obvious carbohydrates. At the end of a summer of turning away from bread, pasta, potatoes and sugar, she found that the

20 pounds were gone. All of us, of course, have the insulin problem, and all of us will be on some form of the low-carb diet for the rest of our lives.

In the months that followed I watched other people go on the diet for entirely different reasons with equal success. One friend just wanted to lose a few pounds and have more energy; another wanted to recompose her body in the direction of muscles (a great side effect of the diet); another was a panicked, newly diagnosed diabetic. The broad health benefits of this way of eating continue to amaze me.

In the end, I learned the hard way (which may be the only way) that you have to trust your own instincts about your body. Despite my lack of results with it, I stayed with the low-fat programme for far too long because it seemed the entire medical establishment insisted – and still does – that it is the only effective way to lose weight. If you stay tuned to yourself, and keep conscious about what you eat and how you feel, you'll begin to have a sense of what works for you. For me, this is hardest at wonderful dinners where the champagne and wine are flowing freely and after two glasses I simply don't care what I eat. But basically such temptations come up every day, and although my eating is almost automatic now, I still have to remember to watch the boundaries.

When you're trying to lose weight, it's a lot easier if the food on a given diet is very simple and not all that interesting; when you're maintaining your weight for life, though, if the food you're eating is boring, you almost certainly won't stay on the regimen. You can easily fall into a pattern of making boring meals. For instance, protein in the low-carb way of eating is so satisfying that sometimes it's hard to remember to make the side dishes and salads that put the meal together – but that gets tiresome, and such limited repasts will eventually send you off the diet. So make an effort to have regular meals.

Once I understood that I'd been given the tools to solve my weight problem – finally! – I realized that I was going to have to do some serious thinking about what to eat for the rest of my life. As a cookbook editor and author, I'd managed to make food the centre of my professional life, as well as my personal life, and I was losing my favourite part, the carbohydrates. No more wild mushroom risotto, no more pecan pies or chocolate hazelnut tortes or homemade bread or waffles. Granted, when you're dieting you assume you'll give up those things, but not forever. And you also assume you'll go off the diet – but not this one.

Instead, I'd entered an odd new world of food: sometimes I'd pretend I was a cavewoman browsing through the supermarket; anything I couldn't have dragged into my cave wouldn't make it into my trolley. I was so used to dieting in general that things like carrots would just jump into the trolley by themselves before I remembered they're a little pricey in carbs. But slowly I began to get it; I even found myself, as the editor of *Protein Power*, taking phone calls from strangers who wanted to know what to eat. Well, I'd say encouragingly, you could take that piece of fish and do this or that to it and serve it with some spinach that you'd tossed with butter and toasted sesame seeds and . . . Butter! They'd get excited all over again, and so would I – what a great diet!

That was all fine, but I knew I was going to have to come to terms with real low-carb life: sort out the various sweeteners, find some substitutes for the things we were all missing, see what I could do to make real food, delicious food, fit into this context. I wanted everything in one place: I could never remember things like how much the onions were costing me or whether a certain cracker had worked as bread crumbs last time I tried it. I was always meaning to spend a few hours cruising the speciality stores for seasonings that were carb bargains. And if I, with so many resources at my fingertips, had these problems, what about busy home cooks who had families to feed?

There would be holidays and dinner parties and house-guests for breakfast – you don't factor such things into your usual diet, but for your lifetime diet, you must.

In short, I needed this book, so I had to write it, since there was nothing like it on the market. With the help of my wonderful cook friends and a lot of research, I solved at least some of these problems. But in the same way everyone's cooking repertoire changes from year to year, so will our low-carb cooking, as we grow more comfortable with its limitations and more inventive in overcoming them. So I think of this as a primer on the subject – there's a great deal more to come, and I'm eagerly awaiting it.

It can be hard to defend the low-carb diet in the face of such overwhelming endorsement of the opposing low-fat diet on all sides. My kinder friends say things like, 'Aren't you worried that you'll get cancer?' Am I worried that I'll get cancer because I don't eat sugar and starch? Well, no. In fact, there aren't extensive studies that compare the two diets, and there are unlikely to be any anytime soon. (See the Foreword, which recounts the latest science on the subject.) But a good general guideline is to trust your own bloodwork. While the low-fat diet isn't dangerous on its own, if you do have hyperinsulinaemia, it could indeed be dangerous for you.

Finally, I know that everyone has to work out an individual way of dealing with this or any diet – a version that works for him or her. With its emphasis on real food and its de-emphasis on ersatz starches and sugars, *The Low-Carb Cookbook* reflects my way of dealing with it. Of course, it's not the only way, but I hope that with these recipes you'll always look forward to the next meal with the joy of knowing you're going to eat well in all senses of the word.

How We Got Here:
A Little History

Be reassured, I shall map out a diet for you, and prove
to you that there are still a few pleasures left for you
here on this earth where we live to eat. . . . Shun anything made with flour, no matter in what form it hides;
do you not still have the roast, the salad, the leafy
vegetables?

— Jean Anthelme Brillat-Savarin, Meditation XXII on
Obesity from *The Physiology of Taste*, 1825

You may be reading this book because you're already a
successful low-carb dieter who needs help figuring out
what to eat, or because you're thinking about taking the
plunge. You may be unsure of the medical underpinnings
of the low-carb approach, you may wonder how to
choose between the various versions of the diet, you may
think you'll never eat a good meal again — but read on; all
of these questions have answers.

The very idea of a low-carbohydrate cookbook seems
startling in this era of low-fat eating — which has necessarily meant low-protein as well, since meat, poultry,
fish, eggs and cheese, the major sources of protein, also
contain fat. As we've struggled to follow the government's low-fat recommendations, we've actually increased our carbohydrate levels, consuming more pasta,
grains, bread, beans and fruit, just as prescribed by the

model of the nutritional pyramid. Because there are only
three basic elements of food – fat, protein and carbohydrate – when one element is reduced, another must go
up. In the case of the low-fat diet, since both protein and
fat are down, the only alternative is for carbohydrates to
take up the slack.

Although we don't think of them that way, the hun-
dreds of low-fat cookbooks on the market are in effect
high-carbohydrate cookbooks. While most people scarcely
think about carbs at all, for those who do tend to gain
weight and have the family constellation of hereditary
health problems associated with obesity – heart disease,
high blood pressure, diabetes – the sugars and starches
that make up carbohydrates are a big part of the problem.
For them, carbohydrates trigger excess insulin production, which initiates fat storage, vascular damage that can
lead to heart disease, and high blood pressure. In addition, if the pancreas keeps frantically overproducing
insulin to stabilize blood sugar in response to the presence
of more and more carbohydrates, the insulin receptor
cells can become exhausted, developing a state called
insulin resistance. And insulin resistance can easily lead to
Type II diabetes.

For people who have this underlying metabolic disorder, the low-fat prescription has been a disaster, not only
because it doesn't work very well for weight loss, but
also because it actually makes the associated health problems worse. Many dieters make the crucial mistake of
regarding the low-carb diet (low-sugar, low-starch) as
simply a quick fix for weight loss, and once the pounds
are off they return to their old ways of eating – even to
the recommended 'healthy' low-fat diet. But they find
that along with the pounds return the health problems,
including a raised LDL or 'bad' cholesterol level, a

lowered HDL or 'good' cholesterol level, and a dramatic increase in triglycerides, a dangerous blood fat thought to be predictive of heart disease.

Although the low-carb theory may seem new and radical and unproven, it's the basis of our ancient hunter-gatherer diet, and in fact has been the main approach to weight loss for well over a hundred years. The French gourmand Brillat-Savarin observed in 1825 what so many of us have noticed on our own: that certain people seem destined to be fat. The only way around this, he advised his readers, was to stop eating starch and sugar (he also distrusted eggs for some reason) and stick to protein, salad and vegetables – especially radishes, asparagus and celery (all extremely low-carb). He noted that one could eat very well on such a regimen – remember, he was a gourmand. He also recommended wearing a snug belt and drinking lots of water, ideas that have passed into contemporary diet lore.

In our own century, low-carb diets became popular in the 1960s and 1970s, featured in books like *The Stillman Diet*, *The Scarsdale Diet*, *The Drinking Man's Diet* and, of course, Dr Atkins, the all-time bestseller. Though there are differences between them, these diets all restrict carbohydrates more or less drastically and emphasize protein (to maintain lean body mass) and fat. The diets were all wildly successful, partly because they were fun and satisfying and especially because they worked. (Some, in fact, are still in print.) Dr John Yudkin was a true pioneer in the field. Yudkin's regimens were based not on hard science (because no one understood why they worked) but on Brillat-Savarin's system – simple observation. For years it was a diet commonplace to eschew bread, potatoes and dessert and stop worrying about calories.

In the 1980s, around the time Dr Dean Ornish began to publish his work on heart disease and the minimal-fat diet, however, the thinking moved in a new direction. Protein and fat became suspect, and the low-carb diets were seen as dangerous — bad for the kidneys and bad for the blood vessels. Though there are now plenty of studies to refute these allegations (see the Foreword), the low-carb diets fell into disfavour and the low-fat regimen won the official endorsement of the government, not to mention the media. Suddenly there were 'bad' foods that could kill you — eggs, butter, red meat — and forget the salt. When cholesterol hysteria hit hard, we chose margarine. Entire industries sprang up around these dietary principles, and some extraordinary careers were made touting them. But little by little the programme has begun to fall apart.

In the spring of 1996 Dr Walter Willett of Harvard, a leading researcher in the field, remarked at the Second International Conference on Fats and Oil Consumption in Health and Disease that it was time for the scientific community to acknowledge that the results of the low-fat prescription had been a disappointment. According to the latest government statistics, for the first time, more than half the American population is overweight, and extreme obesity has doubled in the last ten years — the era of low-fat. Dr Tim Byers of the University of Colorado says, 'It's been clear for several years that Americans are getting fatter, and it's accelerating.' Meanwhile, the overemphasis on cholesterol has begun to be corrected, and even the reputation of much-maligned eggs has been rehabilitated — thanks to discoveries that they don't have as much cholesterol as originally thought, and that most cholesterol is in fact made in the body itself, not ingested.

The ratio of HDL to LDL has come to be seen as a much more important index of vascular health than the total cholesterol number, and the triglyceride level and its relative ratio to HDL looks as though it's going to be even more critical. Margarine has been revealed as not only a fake food, but a dangerous trans fat. Salt isn't much of an issue anymore, and even red meat has some positive benefits in its stearic acid content. But consider this: if it's true that 25 percent of the population has a metabolic problem with carbohydrates (which is just a guess on the part of the medical experts), that's an even larger percentage than the group that's salt-sensitive – and it's on their behalf that we were all supposed to stop using salt. Couldn't the government just as easily have recommended a low-carb diet for everyone to be sure that we were as protected as the salt-sensitive people?

Merely posing this question points up one of the great fallacies in making dietary policy: there isn't a single diet that's right for everyone. Legislating diet was simply an experiment that didn't work for one of the target groups in the population it was meant to address: the unhealthy overweight. While the low-fat diet works well for people with normal metabolisms who just eat a little too much and exercise not enough, it's been dramatically demonstrated that the rest of us need something else. And something else was waiting in the wings: the new generation of low-carb diet books.

Right at the epicentre of this group is the same old Dr Atkins, much reviled by the medical establishment but much beloved by his desperate readers. Although he fell out of the media's sights in the eighties, his loyal readers continued to pass the word, and in 1996 his new book sold over a million copies. Hard on his heels came the Hellers, authors of *The Carbohydrate Addict's Diet*, *Healthy for Life* and *The Carbohydrate Addict's Lifespan Program*. The Hellers focused on the addictive nature of carbs but tried to help their readers ingest as many carbs as possible in a scheme that gave over an hour a day to pleasurable eating of just about anything. In *Healthy for Life*, they drop the one-hour prescription but add more carbs in general for very slow weight loss, a system they recommend over Atkins's speedy results. Barry Sears's *The Zone* (and its sequel, *Mastering the Zone*), another stunning bestseller, isn't really geared for weight loss, but it does recommend cutting the carbs back and balancing them with protein and fat intake to get into the optimum state of performance, both mental and physical. (Note: Despite the white coats on most of these book jackets, not all of these authors are real doctors with real patients.)

Finally there's *Protein Power* by Doctors Michael and Mary Dan Eades, who wrote the Foreword to this book. When the Eadeses discovered that the low-fat diet was not a success for their overweight patients, they returned to the literature to see if there might be a better approach. They were intrigued by the strong history of the low-carb approach and decided to try the regimen, first on themselves and then on their patients. The results were amazingly successful, but they were puzzled about why. Going back to their biochemistry textbooks, they figured out how it worked and why, which meant they could play a little with the parameters of the diet and give their readers more carbs – more healthy carbs, not more sugar and starch.

Essentially, say the Eadeses, all carbohydrates are basically sugar – that's what they're broken down into, and that's how the body receives them. For people with the metabolic disorder we've been talking about – hyperinsulinaemia or Syndrome X – *any* form of sugar, whether it's a bar of chocolate or bowl of rice, triggers an outpouring of insulin, the master hormone without which no fat is stored. The more carbs you eat, especially simple sugars, the more insulin pours into your bloodstream, and the more fat you store (assuming you have consumed more calories than you've burned). Through some very elaborate mechanisms explained in *Protein Power*, excess insulin initiates a cascade of health problems: you make more triglycerides, more bad cholesterol, have higher blood pressure – and you're likelier to develop gout and diabetes. As the Eadeses point out in their book, the diet the government wants you to follow gives your body a full two cups of sugar a day to handle – fine if you don't have the genetic tendency to the insulin problem, but a true disaster if you do.

How do you know if you're a candidate for this diet? Your family history is a good guide: if obesity, heart disease, diabetes, gout and high blood pressure run in your family, there's an excellent chance you have this problem. If you are overweight and can't overcome it with a simple diet and exercise programme, this is probably the reason why. You can have your fasting insulin level tested; anything above 10 is abnormal for men and most women, though some women test normal despite having hyperinsulinemia. According to the Eadeses, a high triglyceride level all by itself is almost enough to diagnose hyperinsulinaemia.

But try Brillat-Savarin's idea: just observe yourself. Do you crave sweets? Once you start eating bread, or pasta or dessert, is it hard to stop? Do you actually feel better, free from cravings and energy swings, when you cut the carbs back? (Give yourself a week to test this, since it will take you several days to start producing the right enzymes to digest your new diet.) Remember, if this is in fact your problem, it's a health problem as well as a weight problem, and it's important to address it for the long term, not just as a quick weight-loss scheme. Diet is the *only* way you can control your insulin output, and it's amazingly effective.

It's always a good idea to see your doctor before you start on *any* regimen – and in this case there's a real bonus, since you can compare your bloodwork before and after and see for yourself what an excellent favour you've done your health. Many a sceptical doctor, including mine, has been won over by the amazing results. If you're taking any medication it's *essential* to check with your doctor, since this diet has such profound effects it can play havoc with your medications.

As Dr Atkins explains, there are many gradations of insulin sensitivity within the hyperinsulinaemia population – some people do very well with cutting carbs back just a little once they've reached their ideal weight; for others, carbs will always have to be kept at a bare minimum for life. The only person who can figure this out is you: once you reach your goal weight, you'll have to increase the carbs bit by bit – 5 grams a week, and then hold for a week – and see how you feel. When the scale begins to drift upwards, you'll know exactly what your level is, and that's where you should try to stay for life.

If you have more than 15 pounds to lose, it's a good idea to read one of these diet books, choosing the programme that seems to make the most sense to you. (See the box on Sorting Out the Low-Carb Gurus, page 17.) Then you'll have a programme to follow and answers to your many questions, which will make the diet much easier to live with for months. You can fit most of the recipes in this book into your programme – just check the level of protein, fat and carbohydrates you require and look for the recipes that match it.

In the same way that low-fat has become a lifestyle choice, low-carb eating will take its place as the diet of choice for those of us with a metabolic problem, because it's essential for our continued good health as well as weight control. Although most of the recipes in this cookbook work perfectly well for the quick-fix weight-loss plans of the low-carb diet books, they're really designed for the long haul, on the assumption that if you're seriously concerned about your health and your weight, you'll need to watch the carbs for the rest of your life. But you'll also need to be able to entertain, to serve holiday meals, to move easily from one season to the next, taking advantage of farm-fresh produce. You'll need to know how to stock your cupboard in this new and unfamiliar way of looking at the kitchen. And you'll probably prefer to avoid eating bizarre diet versions of familiar foods. Because I'm a cookbook editor and author myself, it's very important to me to eat well, and to serve food that's as much like traditional good food as possible while staying within the diet guidelines. That's my mission here: simple food, real food that works to solve some of the problems of cutting back the carbs.

Does taking the low-carb leap mean you'll never eat another doughnut, another plate of pasta, another slice of your own birthday cake? Of course not – life is too cruel, and these foods are too wonderful to forswear them entirely. A little treat every now and then works wonders (but *only* every now and then), and a special occasion becomes truly special when it involves an indulgence. Once your insulin is well under control, you'll probably notice that an occasional piece of cake – once or twice a month, say – has no effect whatsoever, possibly because you lack the enzymes to properly digest the sugar.

Sorting Out the Low-Carb Gurus

All the popular low-carb diet programmes agree that excess insulin production is the real problem in weight gain, and they all take a low-carb approach to controlling it, but there are lots of differences in the diets themselves. Here are some of the significant ones, plus their ideas on how to measure out the three major elements of food: protein, fat and carbohydrate. It's useful for comparison to remember that the average Western diet contains at least 300 grams of carbohydrate a day, and the government's food pyramid recommends even more. Do calories count? Not in these schemes, but if you're having trouble losing weight, you may also need to cut back the total calories, which usually means cutting back the fat. The diets have in common a stricter phase for weight loss and a more generous one for weight maintenance.

- Robert C. Atkins, M.D., <u>Dr Atkins' New Diet Revolution</u> (Vermilion, 1999). Dr Atkins is the grand old man of low-carb dieting. His millions of readers have been losing weight on this restricted diet for decades. Dr Atkins insists his patients go into ketosis, a state reached by extreme carb restriction in which ketones – a product of fat breakdown – are produced in abundance. The diet has two phases: induction (15 grams of carbohydrate per day for 2 weeks), followed by a gradual increase of not more than 5 grams per week until maintenance level is reached (i.e. the level of ideal weight). For most people, that's between 25 (below diet level for <u>Protein Power</u>) and 90 carb grams per day, or less than a third of the average Western diet. You can have all the protein and fat you want and almost all the macadamia nuts you can afford, but Atkins never allows sugar or starches like potatoes and pasta. He also frowns on alcohol.

- Dr Michael R. Eades and Dr Mary Dan Eades, Protein Power (Thorsons, 2000). The Doctors Eades key protein requirements to individual needs in a formula explained in their book. More lean protein is okay; less is not. The intensive weight-loss phase is restricted to 30 grams of carbohydrate per day. (Because the Eadeses calculate the carbs by subtracting the metabolically inactive fibre content of food, their carb allowance is actually quite a bit more generous than Atkins's.) For a long-term diet, the carbs go up to 40 per day after the first three or four weeks. The Eadeses don't worry about fat, except for unhealthy trans fats, and warn that too much rich cheese will stop weight loss. At ideal weight, dieters increase by 5 carb grams per week until they reach the magic number where weight is maintained. Although the doctors acknowledge that some carbs like flour and fructose have more dramatic effects on insulin than others, they basically see all carbs as essentially sugar. They allow small amounts of actual sugar and starch as long as they're accounted for in the carb budget. Their way of counting carbs steers dieters towards fibre-rich, vitamin-loaded vegetables and fruits.

- Rachel F. Heller, Ph.D., and Richard F. Heller, Ph.D., Healthy for Life (Dutton, 1995), The Carbohydrate Addict's Diet (Vermilion, 2000) and The

Carbohydrate Addict's Lifespan Program (Dutton, 1996). He's a pathologist, she's a therapist. The Hellers' first book was a huge amount of fun: as long as you restricted your carbs in the other two meals of the day, you could eat whatever you wanted for dinner, even many desserts, as long as you ate it all within an hour. The strategy was to avoid extra insulin production, which would occur at exactly 1 hour 15 minutes after eating began. That approach has been dropped in Healthy for Life, which lets you have only one quarter of your day's carbs for dinner. But the Hellers still feel that high-carbohydrate foods such as fruit juice and pasta are valuable 'for essential balance' and should constitute at least 50 percent of the diet once you're beyond initial weight loss. This makes for very slow weight loss, if any, but the Hellers think that's sounder in the end. They feel it's unwise to lose more than 1½ pounds a week. Their programme has three different levels of weight loss with a lot of options and add-ons. The Hellers are against alcohol and caffeine on the grounds that they raise insulin levels.

- Barry Sears, Ph.D., with Bill Lawren, The Zone (Thorsons, 1996), and Mastering the Zone (Thorsons, 1998). This long-lived bestseller (and its how-to successor) is based on Sears's expertise in drug delivery. He's figured out how to use food as a drug to manipulate the hormonal system into producing optimal performance, both mental and physical – a state he calls 'the zone'. Elite athletes who use his programme swear by it. Although it's not designed for weight loss, this system does often reduce weight because the protein levels are higher and the carb and fat levels lower than the standard Western diet. Of all these diets, Sears's is closest to the standard low-fat nutritional advice, but the establishment doesn't like his programme any more than the others.

Sears insists that everyone has an exact individual protein requirement – no more, no less – that must be met every day and matched with carbohydrates, eaten together in a system of blocks. Monounsaturated fats form the rest of the diet. In terms of calories, it's 40 percent from carbs, 30 percent each from protein and fat. If you're very small, this way of eating will leave you with very few calories; if you're very large, it will leave you with too many carbohydrates, which will keep you large. If you have a lot of weight to lose, this may be too many carbs for you.

• Oddly enough, all these diets aren't drastically different from the old Overeaters Anonymous diet (OA no longer has a diet), which has been around for years (its fruit-for-breakfast prescription would seem to fit the hypothesis that insulin is better able to handle carbs in the morning):

Breakfast: 1 fruit, 4 ounces of protein
Lunch: 2 cups of vegetables, 4 ounces of protein
Dinner: 3 cups of vegetables, 4 ounces of protein

However, do not, under any circumstances, take a major holiday from your diet. I did this one Christmas for two weeks, thinking I'd just deal with the few pounds I gained later, and it would all be worth it. My weight loss stopped cold, and it took me six months of strict dieting to get back to where I was, never mind to get the momentum going again. Your body has a built-in survival mechanism that actually promotes fat storage once you've come off a diet, and it's frighteningly effective.

So stay conscious, watch the scale, and remember: you're doing this for your good health as well as to lose weight, so you don't want to sabotage all your hard work. A weekend is about the maximum debauchery you can easily handle — just jump right back on a strict version of the diet, consuming as few carbs as you can manage, until you lose the extra weight. And even that will be hard; the Hellers are right — for people with insulin problems, carbohydrates really are addictive.

But the good news is that this diet is a snap to follow, because the terrible cravings for food, especially sweet and starchy food, disappear quickly. You'll have an amazing take-it-or-leave-it-alone attitude about food, you'll drop all the anxiety and guilt and shame you may have felt about it, and you'll feel so good and so energized that sticking with it seems a very minimal price to pay.

The Nitty-Gritty on Carbs

⁄⁄⁄⁄

Starting Out:
What *Is* a Carbohydrate?
And What *Do* You Eat?

A carbohydrate is one of the three basic food elements (the other two being protein and fat), and it's composed of carbon, hydrogen and oxygen. But essentially it's sugar, and that's how your body processes it, which is where the insulin problem comes in. As the *Oxford American Dictionary* notes in its 'carbohydrate' entry, carbs are 'considered to be fattening'. It's easy enough to get rid of the obvious sweets when you're dieting, but carbohydrates also lurk in starchy foods like potatoes, pasta, bread, grains, popcorn, beans and bananas – not to mention raisins, yogurt and many other surprising places. In the low-fat era, these foods have been extolled as the healthiest, and as we've noted, they're fine for people who don't have an insulin problem. But for those of us who do, they're always going to be a problem that we need to control. And in terms of nutrition, they come close to being high-class junk food. The nutritious part of the potato is not the starchy white but the skin – and that you can have (see page 292). The courgette pasta on page 267 has many more nutrients than plain old white-flour pasta.

A rule of thumb is to ditch the whites in your diet — potatoes, pasta, bread — and go for the greens and reds: virtually anything green, plus tomatoes and red peppers. Sugar is completely out, except for tiny amounts that make a big difference in desserts. In this new way of eating, protein, whether it's meat, fish, eggs, poultry, cheese or tofu, is the heart of your meal, accompanied by vegetables and perhaps fruit. (See the chapter titled 'Your New Best Friends'.) And yes, you get to have fat — good fats from nuts, seeds, butter and oils, even cheese. (If you're trying to lose weight, though, too much fat will sabotage your efforts.)

But once you get beyond the delirious joy of having steak and brie all the time, how do you ease into this diet as a way of life? That's what this book is all about — how to stock your cupboards, how to deal with holidays and entertaining, how to satisfy your cravings beyond sweets. (These will disappear in a matter of days or weeks — I promise.)

Does It Matter When You Eat These Carbs?

The Hellers' *Carbohydrate Addict's Diet* suggests eating anything you like for dinner, as long as you eat it within one hour, so your insulin doesn't get overstimulated. My own experience is that their approach doesn't work for weight loss, though it's an interesting way to indulge without paying the piper too much. (Since the Hellers dropped the idea in their latest book, *Healthy for Life*, they've probably come to the same conclusion.) A much better bet is to eat your major carbs for breakfast, as the Eadeses advise, because that's when your insulin is most sensitive, and you won't be launching the craving and bingeing cycle you'd get later in the day. Try this for yourself: see if you can have a banana, say, for breakfast without sabotaging your weight. Otherwise, spread the carbs as evenly as you can throughout the day.

Getting Back What You're Missing

The low-carb way of eating is so inherently satisfying that it may take a while before you realize you're missing anything. You may even forget to eat the vegetables and the occasional fruit, which you do need for both their vitamins and their fibre. But sooner or later you're going to miss one or all of the following textures and tastes. Here's what to do about those cravings:

Crispy

This may be the reason we love French fries and crisps.

- Have just a little: a few potato crisps contain only a few carbs.
- If you don't think you can control yourself, try pork scratchings. They're practically all protein, not fat as you might think, and you can eat a lot of them for no carbs at all. This is the choice for the freakout binge.

If the Diet Isn't Working for You

Everyone hits plateaus, but if from the very beginning you don't feel good eating fewer carbs and more protein, chances are it's because you're sensitive to arachidonic acid – a subject discussed in both <u>Protein Power</u> and <u>The Zone</u>. This substance is found in red meat and eggs. If you're sensitive to it, arachidonic acid can make you feel lousy. If that's the case, you have two choices: either drop red meat and eggs from your diet and see what happens, or add three to four 1000 mg capsules of cholesterol-free EPA oils with each meal when you consume those foods. The EPA solution is such a good fix that you'll feel better within 15 minutes.

Another possibility: your blood type may be a crucial metabolic factor. Get a copy of Dr Peter D'Adamo's <u>Eat Right for Your Type</u> (Century, 1998) and check it out. The diet for type O is low-carb. According to D'Adamo, each blood type has different diet and exercise requirements for optimum health. If you're Type O, though, you're on the right diet: Os are the oldest blood type, and they flourish on a low-carb hunter-gatherer diet. We Os may just be less evolved than the newer blood types, who've adapted to the 'new' agricultural diet (just 8,000 years old, a mere blip in human history).

+ For an elegant crisp, try the frico, page 124, for almost no carbs. Good as these are, they're self-controlling – you can't eat an endless amount of them.

- Corn crisps, page 125.

- Nuts: try one of the roasted nut recipes in the Appetizers chapter.

- Make some fried chicken with a pork rind crust – incredibly crunchy.

- Sizzle a few croutons in olive oil and scatter them over a salad for the crunch factor and just a couple of extra carbs.

- Sizzle a few croutons in some melted butter and stir them into your scrambled eggs.

Creamy

If you find yourself missing mashed potatoes see potatoes, opposite. Creamy in general isn't such a big problem, since you can actually have cream, though mainly for dessert.

- Vegetable purées with cream: cauliflower, broccoli and creamed spinach head the list.

- Quiche and frittatas: although these usually form the main course, a little sliver of either can be served along with dinner as a creamy accent.

- Avocados: whether they're stuffed with, say, prawn salad, or just sliced as part of a salad or mashed into guacamole, these highly nutritious tropical treats are luxuriously creamy.

- Coconut milk: unsweetened canned coconut milk is a good thing to keep on hand for making instant Thai curry sauces, drinks and ice cream.

Potatoes

At a restaurant you can always snatch a few French fries off a friend's plate to get your fix. Beyond that, try substituting cauliflower for potatoes – an amazing impostor. And try small, pointy-tipped sweet potatoes, with their skins left on, which are much lower in carbs than you'd think – about 13 grams.

- Real baked potatoes: eat just the skin and a little of the white (see page 292). These are unbelievably good and satisfying. You won't miss potatoes anymore.

- Cauliflower purée: you can hardly believe you're not having mashed potatoes. Page 302.

- Cauliflower vichysoisse: no one will guess you're not serving potato soup. Page 104.

- Cauliflower potato salad: another completely satisfying masquerade. Page 119.

Bread

This one's tough. Again, the cravings leave quickly. A bite of bread out of the basket at the restaurant may be all you need to remember that it really wasn't all that wonderful. Although low-carb diet programme books are full of ersatz bread recipes, and supermarkets carry low-carb breads, I find them all distinctly unappealing. Much better to buy a loaf of multi-grain bread from a health-food shop and have only a slice or two for breakfast.

Fat-free whole wheat tortillas are great with eggs or as a sandwich wrapper – just 3 carb grams.

Pasta

Now that pasta's become so popular, abandoning it is especially hard. Save it for your birthday, and have the best imported Italian pasta you can get your hands on. Low-carb pasta is surely on the way, but until it gets here, you'll need to make do with squash and greens.

◆ Courgette pasta: this is pretty delicious, and faster than actual pasta. Page 267.

◆ Spaghetti squash: use the basic recipe, page 310, and toss with pesto sauce.

◆ Lasagne: make your favourite lasagne recipe substituting savoy cabbage leaves or chard for the pasta. Just dunk the leaves in boiling water for 30 seconds, then in iced water to make them flexible. Dry them well before using and be sure to butter or oil the lasagne dish so the leaves won't stick, then proceed as usual.

Understanding the Tradeoff System

Once you figure out what your carbohydrate level is — which will depend on which diet system you're using, or your own careful monitoring to see what works for you (i.e. how your carb intake affects the scales) — you can work the specifics of your diet out any way you want to, as long as you're getting enough protein, fibre, and vitamins, or supplementing them. Remember, the carbs are all basically sugar, so these count as treats, even though they don't seem like treats.

If you'd die for a plate of risotto, have a little, and confine the rest of your meal to protein and salad. For any indulgence, just figure out the carbs involved and how to incorporate them into your regimen. A glass of wine may mean much more to you than some peanuts, so drink it and plan accordingly.

My own system of tradeoffs turned out to be something of a surprise: I assumed I'd be saving up for bread or pasta or sweets, but in fact I save my carbs for seasonal fruit and vegetables. When corn season hits I'm in agony, but I figured out that I can have two ears of corn on weekends if I have them for breakfast with some ham or sausage. When crisp, tart apples are in the farmers' market, that's my treat; it's cherries in early summer; apricots when they're great; pears when it's their moment. I love these things so much that I'm willing to have just salmon and salad or some other spartan meal so I can really enjoy them. Other times when a craving hits, I have to have a handful of chocolate-covered coffee beans after dinner.

To make tradeoffs work smoothly, you have to be conscious of what you're eating, and you need to have a good idea of how many carbs are in your favourite foods – which means you need a good carb-counting book (such as Corinne T. Netzer's) that also lists fibre counts, since you can subtract those grams from the total carb count. Of course, you can go on automatic pilot and cut out almost all the carbs, but that's a harsh and not very healthy way to live over the long term. And once you get the hang of it, this is one of the easiest regimens in the world to stay on – easy to figure out and easy to live with. As your hair and skin improve dramatically, your energy burns evenly and reliably, you're no longer at the mercy of food, your body begins to recompose, and your face regains the flattering tiny muscles it lost over the years of dieting, you will have every reason to keep eating this way, and you will.

Hitting the Wall:
The Dreaded Plateau

All diets have plateaus, even the astonishingly effective
low-carb diet. The usual advice to up the exercise and cut
back on the treats is the first line of defence, but when
that doesn't work, you need more help. Here are some
possibilities.

- Check your actual carb level. Write down every
  morsel that goes into your mouth and check it on the
  charts. If you drink a lot of coffee, for instance, you
  could be adding some surprise carbs – a cup has only
  .8 grams (these are beans, remember), but if you
  have six cups a day you're getting almost 5 grams of
  carb, plus whatever you add to lighten it. If you're
  heavily invested in artificial sweeteners, it may come
  as a shock to learn that they all contain a little sugar
  – fractionally less than a gram per packet, true, but
  if you have a lot of them in a day it adds up. You may
  think those little pink and blue packages are free,
  and they are, in moderation, but if you're overdoing
  it you could be sabotaging your diet.

- Consider cutting out all artificial sweeteners, especially if you're drinking a lot of fizzy diet drinks.
  There's a possibility that for extremely sensitive
  people even the sensation of sweetness can trigger a
  release of insulin – the same way that some people
  think that merely stepping into a bakery makes them
  gain weight. It may be true, in the sense that the
  anticipation excites an insulin release.

- Check your thyroid. An underactive thyroid and insulin problems are old comrades, and they could be
  ganging up on you.

My very slow rate of weight loss speeded up once my
deficiency was corrected. I discovered this myself, though
my famous low-fat doctor had earlier diagnosed a goitre
– but told me I didn't need to take thyroxine if I didn't
want to. Since I was completely clueless at the time, I decided not to. But an underactive thyroid is a very serious
problem that often accompanies the metabolic disorder of
hyperinsulinaemia; thyroxine has a role to play in pre-
venting heart disease, infertility and a number of other serious conditions as well. And if you go on a low-carb
regimen, you'll be requiring even more thyroxine from
your body just to deal with the extra protein, so you can
easily become deficient. If you suspect you have an underactive thyroid, consult your doctor.

You can also check for an underactive thyroid yourself
using the Barnes Basal Temperature Method: for four con-
secutive days, before you get out of bed in the morning, put
a glass thermometer under your armpit for 10 minutes
(shifting hormones can skew the reading, so women should
do this beginning the second day of their period). Anything
below 98.2 is low. For further information, the Broda
Barnes Foundation (contact at www.brodabarnes.org), a
non-profit organization that works with doctors and
patients to further the work of Dr Broda Barnes and other
pioneers in the field of hormone research. According to Dr
Barnes, if you have red hair, you're by definition low-
thyroid (due to a missing chromosome).

- Consider adding some supplements: Atkins recommends CoQ10 at the 100 mg level (also good for

your heart and your gums, and widely used in Japan). If you've been off your diet recently, you may need to take chromium picolinate to curb cravings or take a more effective kind of chromium, such as Ultra-Chrome.

- The jump start. Sometimes when nothing will budge, a radically different diet will help. The low-carb gurus focus on a single food group for these adventures in metabolic chaos. Atkins has a Fat Fast – at its most basic, it involves eating only five handfuls of macadamia nuts throughout the day (about 1,000 calories) and nothing else – but warns not to do it for more than five days. Atkins also likes the Fruit Fast: eating nothing but fruit for a few days, especially if you've been feeling fruit-deprived. You'll probably gain a little weight, but you may satisfy your longing for fruit and shake things up when you go back on the diet. The Eadeses like a lean protein fast: try eating just tofu and salad for a couple of days – again, this will be less than 1,000 calories.

- Drink more water. The more you drink, the more you'll lose. You may think you'll spend your life in the toilet, but not so, says Phoenix diet-doctor Donald Peterson; the body adjusts after a couple of weeks.

- If all else fails, just hang in there. Eventually you'll start to lose again, and in the meantime you're getting all the health benefits of the low-carb diet, so don't worry too much about it.

The Sweet Question

This is perhaps the most vexing issue in low-carb cooking. Sugar is clearly out of the question, except in very small amounts, and none of the alternatives is entirely satisfactory, with the exception of SPLENDA® Low-Calorie Sweetener – a mix of dextrose, maltodextrin and sucralose. Sucralose is made from sugar, modified so that it isn't absorbed by the body, and this slightly fluffy sweetener performs nearly the same way in the kitchen that sugar does, although it doesn't caramelize and does make chewy meringues. There's no bitter aftertaste and no known side effects, so there are no restrictions on its use in countries where it's approved, even for pregnant women. A packet of Splenda is equal to 2 teaspoons of sugar and has 1 carb gram. It also comes in bulk form; it's used and measured like sugar. All of the sweet recipes in this book have been tested with Splenda as well as aspartame, and it's definitely the preferred choice. Splenda can be purchased from the Low Carb Megastore either by phone (01933 357755) or on-line (enquiries@LowCarbMegastore.com). If you have questions you can contact the manufacturer via their website www.splenda.com.

The next most palatable sweetener choice is aspartame, a blend of two amino acids that's packaged under the Canderel and NutraSweet brands. Aspartame has a chemical backtaste, but it's minimal. It doesn't perform well in baking, especially if a dessert must stay in the oven for a long time, and it won't caramelize or make meringues easily. It makes rock-hard ice cream unless you add gelatin. Aspartame is best added at the end of cooking, when it has less chance to break down.

Although it has been approved for use, there's been a recent groundswell of paranoia about aspartame. In some studies, it has caused brain tumours in rats and is suspected of causing eye problems. Because it's an excito-toxin, aspartame is also suspected of causing brain damage, especially memory loss. It can decrease mela-tonin and serotonin, which some researchers speculate may lead to increased cravings for, you guessed it, sweets.

Aspartame has been used in this book as the lesser of many evils just on the grounds of taste. If you're worried about the chemicals, swallow the bitter pill and use ste-via. On the plus side for aspartame, it contains PEA, phenylethylamine, a natural amphetamine secreted in the brain during erotic arousal. (See *The Alchemy of Love and Lust*, by Theresa L. Crenshaw, M.D.)

Saccharine is still with us in the form of Sweet 'n Low, but it's strongly suspected of causing cancer and may be banned soon, as it has been for years in France and Ger-many. One teaspoon of saccharine replaces ¼ cup of sugar and costs 5 carbs. Saccharine-fed lab animals get hungry and gain weight. Not a pleasant substance.

You may believe, as so many nutritionists do, that nat-ural sweeteners such as honey and maple syrup and rice syrup are big improvements over sugar, but they're all just sugar in the end, and they all have the same unfortu-nate effect in the body. Fructose, often touted as the best sugar, actually raises triglycerides, a dangerous marker in blood tests.

None of these substitutes manages to perform the same functions that sugar does in baking – which includes browning, and adding tenderness, texture and volume. From both a taste and health perspective, you'd be best off avoiding sugar substitutes altogether, and that's the recommendation here. But human frailty being what it is, we all need a little something sweet from time to time, which means compromise. Or try mixing the various sweeteners to cancel out their drawbacks.

On the horizon is Alitame, 2000 times sweeter than sugar, with no aftertaste. Alitame is not totally heat-stable, and will first appear in food products before it's available to the home cook.

The Low-Carb Kitchen

If you haven't done so already, your first mission is to go through your cupboards, your refrigerator and freezer and remove the following, many of which are staples of the low-fat diet world: rice cakes, popcorn, flour, grains, pasta, crackers, pretzels, powdered sugar, syrup, raisins, flavoured yogurt, jams and jellies, and chocolate. Virtually anything labelled low-fat goes. Keep sugar around for your friends, and for your own use in minute amounts. Flour and cornmeal get used from time to time, but in very small measurements. A handful of rice or beans can be good in soups.

Crossovers from the old diet world — and there are precious few — are cottage cheese, celery, some other vegetables (but not carrots) and some fruits (but not bananas).

You'll be eating lots of grilled foods, salads, hearty soups and stews, stir-fries, vegetables and — for special treats — fried foods and desserts. This food will be fresh, real food, uncomplicated and served with sauces, dressings and marinades, which makes it important to keep a number of seasonings and condiments on hand.

The Store Cupboard

Seasonings and Condiments

SALT: Number One is good salt — sea salt — both coarse and fine. You don't have to worry about salt on these regimens, and it plays such a big role in seasoning simple food (see Bringing Up Flavour, page 207) that it's worth the tiny investment to have good salt around. Best of all is Maldon salt, which has no additives. (Sea salt in the supermarket does contain them, but it's a good second choice.) Look for it in gourmet stores.

PEPPER: You need a peppermill, actually two — one for black pepper (Tellicherry peppercorns are especially good) and one for white. If you're not used to cooking with white pepper, try it; some cooks think it's more delicate than black, some think it's more assertive. It's absolutely delicious and different, and it adds another level of flavour to food.

PAPRIKA: Even regular supermarket paprika is useful and cheering in many dishes, but sweet Hungarian paprika is better yet.

CHILLI: If you can get your hands on some good New Mexico chilli powder, by all means do so, and keep it in the freezer. If all you can get is the chilli mix, get a good one.

CHIPOTLE CHILLI: A smoked jalapeño chilli that will quickly become addictive. This comes three ways: dried, as powder or canned in adobo paste. The canned chipotles should be rinsed and seeded, then spun into a paste in the food processor. The paste will keep for months tightly sealed in the refrigerator. Chipotles are great in mayonnaise and on grilled foods. A pinch of the powder on scrambled eggs is magical.

GREEN PEPPERCORNS: These are delicious with cream cheese on crackers.

HOT PEPPER SAUCE: Essential for both meats and greens.

PICKAPEPPA SAUCE: The taste of Jamaica, and a great pick-me-up for almost any kind of protein for just 1 carb per teaspoon. Pickapeppa has lots of forbidden tastes – mangoes, raisins, tamarind, cane sugar – and it's especially great with ham. Make a little sauce with cream and Pickapeppa. It's also delicious spread over a block of good organic cream cheese, served with crackers.

SESAME SEEDS: Great for tossing on vegetables and salads, making a crust for fish, etc. You can buy Japanese toasted sesame seeds in a jar. Keep sesame seeds in the refrigerator; they turn rancid easily.

BACON BITS: There are several brands on the supermarket shelves. These are real bacon, not hydrolized protein, and they seem to keep forever. Good for tossing into egg salad, chef's salads, cooked greens and scrambled eggs.

LIQUID SMOKE: Look for hickory smoke; this comes in a little bottle that will last the rest of your life.

CAPERS: Those in the know insist on salt-cured capers, which you can find at Italian delicatessens. They need a good rinse or a 15-minute soak to remove the extra salt. The salted capers last indefinitely. Otherwise look for Spanish nonpareil capers, the tiny ones in glass bottles.

ANCHOVIES: These are simply delicious if they're not too salty and aggressive-tasting. Keep them in the refrigerator. Or use anchovy paste in a tube.

SUN-DRIED TOMATOES: These give a lot of value for their carb money – just one piece of the oil-packed variety costs you about 1 carb. Sliver it and you have a lot of flavour.

HORSERADISH: This comes fresh in root form (well, around Christmas it does), but otherwise it's in the dairy section or in little jars on the supermarket shelf – endlessly useful. Cut away any green on fresh horse-radish – it's bitter.

SOY SAUCE: Labels on the bottles claim it contains no carbs, but list wheat and soy on the ingredient list. Whatever the truth is, soy sauce is so useful for marinating steaks and other meats and fish and making stir-fries that it's hardly worth worrying about the phantom carbs. In Asian stores, look for mushroom soy to use in stir-fries.

OLIVE PASTE: Good for tucking into devilled eggs, adding to sautéed greens, spreading on salmon to be broiled, etc.

THAI RED CURRY PASTE: Added to canned unsweetened coconut milk, it makes a great curry sauce. Just a little spoonful is all you need to enliven a stir-fry. Heat gently in oil for several minutes to bring out flavour.

MANGO FAT-FREE DRESSING & MARINADE: This is a favourite condiment that delivers tropical taste and exuberant flourishes to a great variety of dishes from melon and prosciutto to coleslaw, for just 1 carb per teaspoon. Available at some supermarkets. A great secret ingredient.

CITRUS OILS: These come in lemon, lime and orange. They're intense and wonderful; use them by the drop. (Unfortunately, they don't come with a dropper, so just pick one up at the chemist.) Start off with a sampler kit of all three flavours in small bottles. They save a lot of carbs in marinades, vinaigrettes, baking and dozens of other uses. A mint oil that's delicious in drinks is also available.

CANDIED GINGER: Half-inch chunks are less than 3 carbs each. Good minced in or on ice cream.

ROASTED GARLIC PASTE: This staple of the low-fat kitchen has more carbs than you'd like if you use it generously – and roasting a whole head of garlic will leave you with too many cloves to use before they spoil. A better solution is to buy one of the pastes, and just use a little at a time for less than 1 carb per teaspoon. These are better with a little cream added; sometimes they develop an acrid bite, and the cream will smooth it out.

SWEET RED PEPPERS AND SWEET PEPPER SPREAD: Look for brands that contain no citric acid. The spread includes Greek sheep cheese, and it's delicious on grilled aubergine or crackers – less than 1 carb per tablespoon. Use the peppers in pepper soup or for antipasto.

CURRY POWDER: From eggs to chicken salad to soups and stews, curry powder is great to have on hand. A mild, sweetly fragrant curry is the most useful – Ameer from Harrods in London is brilliant, but there are many others.

MAYONNAISE FLAVOURED WITH DIJON MUSTARD: Great for snacks and for punching up and smoothing a vinaigrette. Less than 1 carb per tablespoon.

Or make your own by mixing mayonnaise (2 parts) with Dijon mustard (1 part).

DaVINCI SUGAR-FREE SYRUPS: These are the best I've found to date. They're actually meant for coffee and Italian soda drinks, but they work for fruit, pancakes or almost anything that needs sweetening. You can even make snow cones with them. There are 18 sugar-free flavours, including interesting and odd ones like amaretto, buttered rum, Irish cream, and crème de menthe. Unfortunately, the chocolate is disappointing. Available from the Low Carb Megastore.

CRAB BOIL: These little sacks of intriguing spices are great for seasoning seafood, especially prawn. Just drop them into a pot of boiling water along with a half lemon and some garlic and then add the seafood.

DRIED WILD MUSHROOMS: Best, and most expensive, are Italian porcini. You can either soak these and chop them before adding to soups and stews or just toss them in the food processor and grind them up into powder. If you soak them, save the liquid for soup; strain it first.

Canned Goods

TUNA: A mainstay of the everyday low-carb diet. It's worth seeking out the best tuna on the market, Genova, from Italy, in the gold can. Genova is yellowtail tuna packed in olive oil, and is truly delicious. The brand is pricey as tuna goes, but not as protein sources go — and it's worth every penny. Genova is available in some supermarkets and speciality stores.

SARDINES: If you like sardines, they're also great for this diet. Best are the Norwegian brislings packed in olive oil and Portuguese sardines. These are good on crackers and they also make a good pâté, mashed with a little mayonnaise and lemon juice and a jolt of horseradish.

SALMON: Canned salmon varies from nearly inedible to quite delicious – price is a perfect index.

TOMATOES: Organic tomatoes are the gold standard. Diced tomatoes, which have most of the bitter seeds already removed, are especially useful.

COCONUT MILK: The Thai unsweetened coconut milk in cans is a good alternative to the real thing. Good for ice cream and for making curry sauces. Store any leftovers in a glass jar in the refrigerator for up to 24 hours.

GREEN CHILLIES: Canned whole chillies are very low-carb, about 1 gram per chilli, and they're good in chilli con carne, eggs and stews.

PICKLES: Not sweet pickles, of course, which are very high in carbs, but dills and kosher pickles. Be sure to check the labels – you're looking for pickles that are a great carb bargain, about 1 carb per pickle.

JAMS AND JELLIES: You can find special dietetic versions of these in the supermarket, but I don't think they're very good. I'd rather poke around the shelves looking for a fruit-only spread and then have just a teaspoonful, which will run 3 to 4 carbs.

SYRUP: Try Walden Farms Syrups in chocolate or pancake/maple.

MARINARA SAUCE: These run 12 to 14 carbs per ½ cup.

Shelf Items

SOYA MILK: Good for making breakfast smoothies. Nutrition counts vary, but what you want to avoid is sweetened soya milk, which is more common than you might think.

DRIED EGG WHITE: On the baking shelf at some supermakets, this makes meringues and is a good emergency protein powder.

COCOA: Unsweetened cocoa is a carb bargain at 4 grams for 3 tablespoons.

HOT COCOA MIX: Carnation Fat-Free (but not the one with mini-marshmallows) is lowest in carbs. Add your own cream, and it's pretty good.

CROUTONS: These seem forbidden, but just a few will bring crunch to a salad or – sizzled in a little butter – scrambled eggs. Just 4 carbs for ¼ cup of croutons, which will be enough for two people.

PEANUT BUTTER: As long as you don't overdo it, you can have a lot of fun with peanut butter. Ordinary brands include dangerous trans fats and peanuts that are sometimes rancid, not to mention sugar. Look for a good unsweetened alternative or get your own fresh ground at the health food shop. Or roast and grind your own, page 163.

ALMOND AND HAZELNUT BUTTERS: More delightful nut spreads. Look our for brands in health food shops.

FIBRE RYE OR SESAME CRACKERS: These should always be waiting on the shelf – at just 2 grams for a giant cracker that's also delicious, they're the obvious rafts for impromptu open-face sandwiches as well as the buttered base for smoked salmon. Grind up crackers in the food processor for crispy toppings – mix them with a little grated Parmesan and a spoonful of wheat germ and drizzle melted butter on top.

HOUSE OF AULSEBROOKS: Crackers from New Zealand with pepper or sesame seeds. Very good, and just 3 carbs.

FIBRE-RICH CRACKERS: These seem a little too good to be true; once you subtract the fibre grams, they have 0 carbs. On the other hand, they have a kind of horse-in-the-feed-bucket quality. For pig-out moods, they're a good choice although they are unsalted, unfortunately.

PORK CRACKLINGS: The butt of many diet jokes, these are still pretty useful as snacks and comfort food when you need something crispy, or you just want something to dip into salsa. Pork cracklings have been around at least since the Ming Dynasty (1358–1644) and the Chinese love them (avoid Chinese brands with added MSG). People think they're entirely made of fat, but they're almost entirely protein; check the label. You can crumble a good brand of pork cracklings into stews and hearty soups, as the Mexicans do. Pork cracklings don't last forever on the shelf – check the labels for expiry dates.

CHOCOLATE-COVERED COFFEE BEANS: Lots of companies make these, but most don't give you a carb count. Starbucks does; their beans cost you a little over a gram of carb for 2 beans.

CHOCOLATE-COVERED ALMONDS: A nice, slightly sweet finish to a meal.

PIZZELLE: These big Italian waffle biscuits are crisp and satisfying, great-looking stuck in a dish of ice cream.

They come in different flavours and cost around 4 carbs per big biscuit. In supermarkets.

AMARETTINI: These are the miniature button versions of amaretti, the famous Italian biscuits that come in the red tins. The babies have only 1 gram of carb for 3 little biscuits. Good on their own or crumbled into fresh fruit compotes.

Flours

You might use a little regular flour from time to time but mostly you'll use an instant flour, added by the teaspoon or tablespoon to thicken sauces and stews.

ALMOND AND HAZELNUT FLOURS: These slightly mealy flours are delicious and very useful in baking. Try almond flour made with Spanish 'Marconas' almonds from the Low Carb Megastore (see page 33). You can make your own if you have a flour mill; a food processor will produce oily nut butters, not flours. Refrigerate these flours, tightly sealed.

PEANUT FLOUR: Sometimes available in health food shops and African markets. Good for breading.

QUINOA FLOUR: Sometimes available in health food shops, this high-protein flour is tastier than soya flour for bread making – but still relatively high carb at just under 34g for ½ cup.

SOYA FLOUR: I'm not a big fan of soya flour, and it doesn't figure in any of the recipes in this book – but for the record, it's 13.5 carbs for ½ cup. It tastes better if you toast it briefly in a frying pan.

OAT FLOUR: This is delicious, and of course it has more carbs than we wish it did (24 grams per ½ cup).

Still, if you have to bake something, it's a good alternative to white flour, which has twice as many carbs.

CHEESE POWDER: This product works like flour to bind elements together wherever cheese would work with the other flavours.

CORNMEAL: You'll need a little to make the corn crisp on page 125 and to enrich your chilli. Get the best stone-ground cornmeal you can find and keep it in a glass jar in the freezer.

Fats and Oils

You'll just have to forget that these are the villains of the low-fat nutritional police. They're important for a number of reasons: if you don't have enough fat in your diet, you won't make enough hormones, your immune system will be compromised, your hair and skin will suffer, and you won't enjoy your food very much. Not all fats are good, certainly not margarine (which has been so manipulated that it's a dangerous trans fat), and not highly processed fats like solid vegetable shortening. Oils heated to the smoking point are damaged, as are oils that are fried more than twice even at the correct temperature. But pure oils like olive oil, nut oils and even coconut oil (which isn't dangerous, media hype notwithstanding) are fine. And then there's lard, which has less cholesterol than butter. And finally there's butter.

BUTTER: This superb fat (see box) is just about irresistible, and there's no reason to resist.

To clarify butter for sautéing: You'll be taking out the milk solids, the part that burns. To do this, melt unsalted butter slowly in a heavy pan over medium-low heat, or do it in the microwave. You definitely don't want the butter to boil. Skim off the foam at the top and carefully pour the clear yellow liquid into a clean jar, leaving the milk solids behind. You'll have about ¾ of what you started with. Store the clarified butter in a tightly sealed jar in the refrigerator; it will keep for many weeks. *To make ghee,* the nutty-tasting Indian clarified butter, keep cooking the butter until the milk solids turn golden. Strain the liquid through a coffee filter and store in the refrigerator.

OLIVE OIL: Rich in micronutrients and mono-unsaturated fat. Extra virgin is good for salads and vegetables; otherwise, regular old olive oil is fine. Spanish

What's So Good About Butter?

According to Sally Fallon, author of <u>Nourishing Traditions</u> (ProMotion Publishing, 1995), a lot. Butter is a rich source of the essential fat-soluble vitamins A, D and E, not easily found elsewhere in the diet in a simply assimilated form. Butter has a good supply of the X Factor, a catalyst that helps the body absorb minerals. Its short and medium-chain fatty acids are much less likely to cause fat storage than the long-chain acids in olive oil; they also have anti-microbial, anti-tumour and immune system—supportive functions—especially 12-carbon lauric acid, which isn't found in other animal fats and is the one saturated fat the body doesn't make itself. Butter also contains conjugated linoleic acid, which has anti-cancer properties. It also supplies lecithin, which aids in the proper metabolism of cholesterol and other fats. On top of all that, it has a lot of trace minerals.

Why have we spent all these years eating margarine?

and Greek oils tend to be good bargains. Olive oil is excellent for frying, since it has a high smoking point and tastes delicious. For frying, use the cheapest olive oil.

FLAVOURED OILS: These deliver some carby flavours with no extra carbs. Garlic oil is excellent and saves you the garlic carbs, which aren't insignificant. Or make your own no-carb garlic oil: heat a clove of garlic, crushed, in a cup of olive oil until the first bubble appears. Remove the garlic and let the oil cool. Use it the same day or store it, tightly sealed, for up to 2 days in the refrigerator.

Fresh Food

You'll be eating a lot of truly fresh food in the form of seasonal produce, supplemented by a few frozen products. In the refrigerator at all times should be: celery, spring onions (better carb bargains than storage onions), sweet peppers, cabbage, cucumbers, citrus fruit (oranges, lemons, limes, but mainly for the zest – which you can peel and freeze). Herbs are wonderful for vegetables and salads; you can even make a whole salad out of mixed herbs if you have a garden. Sometimes when you're eating a lot of protein you crave something light and refreshing, and a lot of mint, parsley and chives can do wonders to take a dish in that direction.

In the Refrigerator

MAYONNAISE: Hellmann's – no point in using Light. You can have an instant sauce, a marinade, a crunchy coating for chicken in seconds with this excellent product.

SOUR CREAM: A spoonful or two makes a big difference for very few carbs, and sour cream seems to have an inordinately long shelf life. Don't overheat sour cream or it will curdle.

CHEESE: Good cheeses for snacking are the relatively low-fat ones such as mozzarella and Muenster. Parmesan, Cheddar, feta and blue cheese are always useful. For treats, brie and cambozola and chèvre.

CREAM CHEESE: Exiled from the low-fat kitchen, cream cheese is back and welcome – all ready to be whipped into a cheesecake or spread on crackers with some interesting seasonings for a quick appetizer or snack. Whipped cream cheese is ready to spread, of course.

COTTAGE CHEESE: You want 2 percent or 4 percent-fat cottage cheese, which has fewer carbs. This can be breakfast or served on sliced tomatoes with lots of black pepper as lunch or a snack.

CREAM: It's up to you how much fat you want to use, but cream is luxurious and very useful. You'll quickly notice that single cream has many fewer carbs than the 1 percent or 2 percent milk you may be used to with your coffee.

NUTS: Forbidden though they are in most diets, nuts are welcomed in the low-carb world. You can't eat endless amounts of them, but you can have a few every day, and they're a reliable treat. They're also very good for you, full of essential nutrients such as calcium, phosphorus, magnesium, potassium, folic acid, vitamin E, some of the Bs and antioxidants. It may be because they have long roots reaching deep into the earth that they have such an abundance of nutrients in their tiny packages. Macadamia nuts

Know Your Onions

On low-calorie and low-fat diets, any kind of onion is virtually free, but in the low-carb world you pay a little price for their sweetness. Here's what it costs:

chives: so low in carbs they're considered free
garlic clove: 1 carb gram
shallot: 3 carb grams
onions: 5 carb grams per ½ cup
spring onions: 5 carb grams per cup
leeks: 4 carb grams per ½ cup

If you're trying to lose weight, the carbs can add up. To flavour oil with garlic, use the trick on page 47 (see Flavoured Oils), then discard the garlic. Chives are obviously the winners in this category, especially for salads and garnishes. Spring onions are a good choice otherwise, but for flavouring a stew or other long-cooking dish, choose leeks, onions or shallots.

are lowest in carbs and high in the good fat, POA, palmitoleic acid, which some studies show helps the body metabolize fats and balance HDL and LDL cholesterol; it also helps break down the harmful fats surrounding the liver and heart.

Peanuts are, of course, in the bean family, not the nut clan, but they act like nuts and they have a very similar profile.

If you store nuts properly – tightly sealed in the refrigerator – they'll keep from 9 months (pecans) to a year, so it's a good idea to find an excellent nut supplier and stock up. You can also freeze them, especially macadamia nuts, but the texture suffers a bit.

To toast nuts: put them on a baking sheet in a 350°F/180°C/Gas Mark 4 oven for 5 to 10 minutes, until they start to smell good.

To crisp pistachios that have been refrigerated: put them on a baking sheet in a 200°F/130°C/Gas Mark ½ oven for 10 to 15 minutes, until they start to smell good.

To skin or not to skin: don't buy skinned almonds; the skin protects them, and adds flavour and fibre. There's almost no point in skinning hazelnuts for the purposes of this book, but toasting them will make a big difference.

In the Freezer

FROZEN BERRIES, RHUBARB AND GRAPES: You can provide these yourself when they're in season. Just freeze on a tray and store in tightly sealed bags.

SMOKED SALMON: For instant celebrations, just pull out the smoked salmon, defrost and serve with rye or sesame crackers, butter and a little snipped dill.

BACON: Good bacon is one of the big treats on low-carb diets. Microwave bacon to minimize the formation of dangerous nitrosamines – or eliminate them by buying nitrite-free bacon at the health food shop.

SAUSAGE: Shop around for good brands to keep in the freezer.

VEGETABLES: Frozen spinach and other greens are your best bet.

OTHER FRUITS: Frozen unsweetened rhubarb, peaches and melon balls are useful to have around.

TOFU: Freeze firm tofu right in the sealed carton for up to several months and defrost before using. The colour will change to old ivory, but the texture just improves.

Equipment

You really don't need anything special, but a cutter or V-slicer is useful for making little vegetable shreds for salads, and a citrus zester for making elegant little ribbons of orange or lemon zest. A grill is endlessly useful for low-carb cooking, as is a smoker. An ice cream maker is a major convenience.

The Organic Question

A number of the low-carb fruits and vegetables — strawberries and broccoli, for instance — turn out to be on the list of those vulnerable to pesticide contamination. And of course the main protein sources — meat, dairy and eggs — may harbour not only pesticide residues but also hormones and antibiotics. You can drive yourself crazy trying to sort out these issues. If you can afford to eat organic food, you probably should do so. If you can afford only some organic food, here are some suggestions.

My vote goes to strawberries, broccoli, potatoes (for their skins) and pumpkin. Veal and pork are not raised with hormones, so you don't have to worry about them for that reason. According to Dr Samuel Epstein of the University of Chicago, the American government has never tested a single animal for hormone levels so it has no idea what the actual levels are – but independent tests reveal levels 30 times the normal background levels for cattle. So beef may be the organic choice in the meat department, if you have just one.

Chickens are another story; free-range sounds wonderful, but it does not necessarily mean that the chicken was frolicking on the farm. Look for the descriptions Traditional Free Range or Free Range Total Freedom and choose a brand that consistently tastes good.

Remember that toxins, like pesticides and excess hormones, are stored in fat – if you cut off the visible fat, you'll be removing a lot of them. That's also a good reason to choose organic dairy products such as butter and cheese; as a rule, these also offer significant taste benefits. Organic eggs are a relative bargain and much tastier than the generic product.

As with everything else in the world of food, you'll have to consider the issues and make your own decisions. There are no easy answers, but there's also no reason to worry about all this excessively. Dropping sugar and junk food from your diet will make a much bigger difference in your health than eating all-organic, however desirable that may be.

NOTE: In this book, carbohydrates are counted as they are in <u>Protein Power</u>, which is minus the fibre content. This is a breakthrough, and in fact it's the way nutritionists understand carbohydrate composition: the fibre element is not metabolically active. This means you can eat much more of the fibre-rich carbs – vegetables, certain fruits and high-density crackers and breads – which guides you towards naturally healthier choices and lets you enjoy a lot more carbs than more restricted programmes.

In some cases, soya products particularly, there's disagreement among the authorities about what the actual carb content is. Don't worry about this too much; just go with what it says on the product you're buying.

Appetizers

Of all the courses of a meal, this one offers the most variety to the low-carb gourmet. The traditional titbits of nuts, cheese, olives, prawns, crudités, etc., are all on our approved list. Even those on strict weight-loss diets can have a field day with appetizers, so it seems prudent to keep the carbs as low as possible here and spend them elsewhere in the meal, where they may be more useful.

To minimize the carbs, you may want to offer some cracker alternatives – with a rich pâté, for instance, a slice of daikon or French breakfast radish (or any radish that's not too bitter) makes a perfect base. Cucumber slices are good for lighter fare, such as fish. And radishes with soft sweet butter and a little bowl of sea salt to dip them in are simply terrific (but check to be sure they're not bitter). Cherry tomatoes scooped out with a melon baller and filled with something interesting like herbed goat's cheese are always a hit, at about 1 carb gram each.

It may seem tempting to just put out the old cheese tray, but it really works much better to save it for the salad or dessert course – everyone will be too stuffed to eat dinner if they pig out on several kinds of cheese first. A little cheese is fine, of course, such as little balls of fresh mozzarella marinated in olive oil with garlic, parsley, hot pepper flakes and salt and pepper (serve with toothpicks).

Nuts are also candidates for overconsumption; use one of the spiced nut recipes here, and your guests will be satisfied with just a few, not handful after handful.

As a good host, keep in mind that many of your guests will not only not be on your regimen, they'll be devotees of its polar opposite, the low-fat diet. Be sure you have enough elements that work for both regimens — crudités, for instance — so that everyone will feel comfortable.

ROASTED ALMONDS
WITH SPICES

Just a little hot, these are great with drinks. They'll keep
for a couple of weeks in a tightly sealed container.
MAKES 10 SERVINGS

> **3 tablespoons olive oil**
> **12½ oz almonds**
> **½ teaspoon ground cumin**
> **½ teaspoon chilli powder**
> **Salt to taste**

Per Serving: Protein: 6.7 g   Fat: 21.7 g   Carbohydrate: 3.2 g

In a large frying pan, heat the oil over medium heat,
add the nuts and sauté until they're golden, giving a stir
from time to time. When they're golden, remove them
with a slotted spoon to a bowl, then toss with the cumin,
chilli powder and salt to taste. Spread on a baking sheet
to dry.

ROSEMARY WALNUTS

This much-copied recipe seems to have first turned up in
The Pink Adobe Cookbook by Rosalea Murphy, where it's
made with butter. That's very good, but olive oil is even
better. MAKES 8 SERVINGS

> 2½ tablespoons extra-virgin olive oil
> 2 teaspoons crumbled dried rosemary
> 1 teaspoon salt
> ½ teaspoon ground red pepper (cayenne)
> 6 oz walnut halves

Per Serving: Protein: 7.6 g   Fat: 22 g   Carbohydrate: 2.2 g

Preheat the oven to 350°F/180°C/Gas Mark 4. Mix
everything but the walnuts together and toss the olive oil
mixture with the nuts to coat well. Scatter the nuts on a
baking sheet and roast for 10 minutes.

ROASTED PISTACHIOS WITH MACE AND CINNAMON

Mace is the outer covering of nutmegs – a more delicate version of the same spice. It's too fiddly to shell this many pistachios yourself, so if you can't find shelled ones, just skip it. MAKES 10 SERVINGS

10 oz shelled pistachios
1 teaspoon ground mace
1 teaspoon cinnamon
1 teaspoon sugar
Salt to taste

Per Serving: Protein: 4.7 g   Fat: 4.5 g   Carbohydrate: 5.3 g

In a large frying pan over medium heat, heat the nuts – no oil – until they're golden, stirring from time to time. It will take about 5 minutes. Add the spices, sugar and salt, stir well to combine and remove from the heat. Let the nuts dry on a baking sheet.

GUACAMOLE WITH CAULIFLOWER

This dip-and-dipper combination may seem like a bizarre one, but in fact avocado and cauliflower are classic companions in Mexican cooking. Make the guacamole just before you serve it – or make it up to several hours ahead without adding the coriander and tomato, cover it with a layer of plastic wrap directly on the surface and refrigerate. Bring to room temperature before serving, stir and add the final cilantro and tomato. Surround the guacamole with the cauliflower florets for dipping. SERVES 4

2 cups cauliflower florets

GUACAMOLE:

2 Hass avocados

2 tablespoons chopped onion

1 teaspoon coarse sea salt

1 serrano chilli, seeded and minced

1 tablespoon chopped coriander leaves

**1½ oz diced tomato without seeds or diced
    radishes**

Additional coriander for decorating

Per Serving: Protein: 3.6 g   Fat: 15 g   Carbohydrate: 4.3 g

The cauliflower: drop the florets into a pan of boiling salted water and let cook for 3 minutes. Drain and let cool to room temperature.

The guacamole: roughly mash the avocado in a bowl. Using the back of a fork in a small bowl, mash the onion with the salt until it begins to liquefy, then add the chilli and chopped coriander. Mix this into the avocado and taste for seasoning. Decorate with additional coriander and tomato bits before serving with the cauliflower florets.

ISRAELI GUACAMOLE

The Israelis wisely add some protein to their avocado dip.
Serve this one with spears of Belgian endive for dipping.
(Cut out the bitter cores before you separate the leaves.)
If you can find some imported Italian tuna, that will be
the best. SERVES 8

>   1 recipe guacamole, page 63, minus the coriander
>   1 (6-oz) can tuna, drained and flaked
>   3 Belgian endive

Per Serving: Protein: 8.2 g   Fat: 18.7 g   Carbohydrate: 4.1 g

Mix the guacamole with the tuna and serve in a bowl
surrounded by spears of Belgian endive. Cut them off at
the base so they'll all be roughly the same size.

HAZELNUT CREAM CHEESE SPREAD

This is an interesting change from the common cream cheese spreads — and very useful to have on hand. Stuff celery with it, spread it on rye or sesame crackers, try it with smoked salmon. MAKES ABOUT 12 SERVINGS

2½ oz toasted hazelnuts (don't bother removing skins)

8 oz whipped cream cheese, at room temperature

1 teaspoon ground black pepper

½ teaspoon ground red pepper (cayenne)

2 tablespoons toasted sesame seeds, optional

Per Serving: Protein: 2 g   Fat: 7.2 g   Carbohydrate: 1.1 g

Put the nuts in the food processor and chop — don't let them get too fine or you'll have hazelnut butter. Add the cream cheese and black and red pepper and beat until creamy. Chill for 2 hours to develop flavour. Remove from the refrigerator 1 hour before serving. Scatter sesame seeds over if you like.

Hazelnut Cream Cheese Spread in Cucumber Cups

Use a long hothouse cucumber and score it down the length of the skin with a fork to make skinny stripes. Cut crosswise into chunks at 1-inch intervals. Scoop out the centre of each chunk. Fill the holes with the hazelnut spread, mounding it over the top. Sprinkle with toasted sesame seeds.

CUCUMBER DIP WITH CUMIN

Good for crudités when you can't stand to face another
plate of them. SERVES 8

    1 (8-oz) packet cream cheese, at room temperature
    2 tablespoons double cream
    1¼ oz minced cucumber
    1 tablespoon minced spring onions
    ½ teaspoon salt
    ¼ teaspoon ground cumin

Per Serving: Protein: 3.5 g   Fat: 7.5 g   Carbohydrate: 1.2 g

Mash the cream cheese with a fork until it's soft, then
add the remaining ingredients and mix together well. Let
stand for half an hour to develop flavour.

AUBERGINE AND PEPPER DIP

Known as ayvar (EYE-var) in the Balkans, where it's a defining regional dish, this delectable dip appears in one form or another all over the Middle East. This version, which I learned from Margot Blair, is very easy and very good; it may seem like the cumin is overkill, but it isn't. And you'd swear it has garlic in it, but it doesn't.

Once you have this spread on hand, you'll think of lots of uses for it beyond serving it as a dip (with endive leaves or red pepper strips) or spreading it on rye or sesame crackers or stirring it into scrambled eggs.

MAKES ABOUT 16 SERVINGS

2 red sweet peppers
1 medium aubergine
3 fl oz olive oil or more to taste
½ teaspoon salt or more to taste
1 tablespoon ground cumin or more to taste
Optional additions: 1 tablespoon minced lemon zest
        with 1 teaspoon fresh lemon juice, 1 tablespoon
        chopped mint or basil, a shake of cinnamon

Per Serving: Protein: 0 g   Fat: 4.6 g   Carbohydrate: 2.4 g

Preheat the oven to 350°F/180°C/Gas Mark 4. Line a baking sheet (one with a small lip) with foil and put the vegetables on the foil. Bake for 1 hour. Remove from the oven and let the vegetables cool. Remove the stems from the vegetables but not the seeds (adds fibre).

Put the oil in the bowl of a food processor and add the vegetables. Process until you have a rough purée, adding more oil if necessary. Add the salt and cumin and the other optional ingredients and blend well. Store in the refrigerator for several days – it actually improves in flavour.

ENDIVE LEAVES WITH ROQUEFORT AND WALNUTS

You can put all sorts of things in endive leaves and use them for dippers as well, but this particular combination of flavours is just right. SERVES 6

> **2 heads Belgian endive**
> **½ lb Roquefort or Maytag blue cheese, at room temperature**
> **2 fl oz double cream**
> **Ground black or white pepper**
> **18 toasted walnut or pecan halves**

Per Serving: Protein: 10.8 g   Fat: 21 g   Carbohydrate: 2.3 g

Cut off the bases of the endive heads and separate them into leaves. Trim the leaves so that they're all more or less the same size. You should have 18 leaves.

In a small bowl, blend the cheese and cream together until they're nearly smooth. Mix in a grinding of pepper. Put a teaspoonful of the cheese on each leaf at the base and press in a walnut half on top. Arrange the leaves sunflower style on a round platter, with a mound of toasted nuts in the middle.

Endive Salad

Core and slice the endive and add other sharp lettuces like radicchio and watercress. Thin out the creamy cheese with a little apple cider vinegar to make a dressing, break up the nuts and toss the whole thing into a gorgeous winter salad.

LIPTAUER

This utterly delicious cheese spread originated in Hungary, where it was often made with cottage cheese instead of the traditional sheep's milk cheese. Goat's cheese works well too — try using chèvre, or a mix of chèvre and cream cheese, or even all cream cheese. Serve the liptauer with vegetable dippers: trimmed radishes, spring onions, celery sticks, and sliced green sweet pepper.
SERVES 8

>   8 oz chèvre, or half chèvre, half cream cheese, at
>   room temperature
>   8 tablespoons butter, at room temperature
>   1 teaspoon sweet Hungarian paprika
>   ½ teaspoon ground caraway seeds
>   ½ teaspoon Dijon mustard
>   2 oz minced spring onions
>   ½ teaspoon anchovy paste

Per Serving: Protein: 5.4 g   Fat: 17.2 g   Carbohydrate: .7 g

Mash the cheese together with the butter in a bowl, using a fork. Add the remaining ingredients and mix to combine well. Put the liptauer in a small bowl, cover and refrigerate for 4 hours or overnight to develop flavour. Bring to room temperature before serving.

ASPARAGUS WITH ORANGE
AND PROSCIUTTO

Although asparagus is in the markets all year, it's worth waiting for spring and the real thing to make these delectable spears wrapped in prosciutto. SERVES 8

    4 oz whipped cream cheese
    Minced zest of 1 orange
    16 asparagus spears
    8 prosciutto slices, chilled and cut in half
        lengthwise

Per Serving: Protein: 1.2 g   Fat: 4 g   Carbohydrate: 1.1 g

Mix the cheese and the orange zest together in a small bowl with a fork and set aside to develop flavour.

Snap the ends off the asparagus spears where they break easily. In a large shallow saucepan or frying pan, boil enough water to cover the asparagus. Add salt to taste. Cook the asparagus in the simmering water until just tender – check every minute after 5 minutes. Using tongs, remove the asparagus from the heat as soon as it's done and let it drain on a kitchen towel. Let cool to room temperature.

Spread a thin smear of the orange cream cheese over each prosciutto slice and wrap each one around an asparagus spear in a spiral fashion. Serve right away or chill until ready to serve.

FRIED CHEESE ON GREENS

This may sound like the ultimate forbidden diet food, but
of course it's fine on our diet. Instead of bread crumbs,
we'll be using nuts, which are even more delicious.
SERVES 4

½ lb Gruyère, Monterey Jack or fontina cheese, in
    ½-inch-thick slices
1 large egg
½ teaspoon water
3 oz finely chopped nuts – walnuts, almonds or
    pecans
Oil for frying
12 oz mesclun or other mixed salad greens
3 fl oz lemon vinaigrette

Per Serving: Protein: 23.1 g   Fat: 45.5 g   Carbohydrate: 5.3 g

Have ready a cake rack for drying the cheese slices.
Mix the egg and water in a soup plate with a fork, beating well. Have the nuts in another soup plate next to the
egg wash. Dip the cheese slices one at a time into the egg
wash and then into the nuts, coating them all over. Let the
slices dry for 15 minutes on the cake rack and refrigerate
for half an hour.

When you're ready to serve, heat oil to a depth of 1¼
inches in a frying pan or wok. When the oil is hot but not
smoking and sends up a faint blue haze, add the cheese
slices and fry until golden and crisp on both sides. Drain
on paper towels.

Toss the greens with the vinaigrette and distribute among 4 salad plates. Top with the cheese and serve immediately.

Fried Cheese Log

You can also mix goat's cheese with cream cheese and chopped herbs – chives, mint, basil, parsley – and form it into 4 skinny logs. Refrigerate the logs, then dip them into the egg wash and nuts and proceed as above.

PRAWNS WITH BACON AND CHEESE

This tasty dish turned up in a Mexican seafood restaurant in Santa Fe. It's really a first course, but if you serve it over sliced romaine dressed lightly with a garlic vinaigrette and double the number of prawn packages per person, it's dinner.

SERVES 2 AS AN APPETIZER, 1 AS A MAIN COURSE

4 (2-inch-long) slices Monterey Jack cheese
 (¼ inch thick)
8 extra large prawns, shelled and deveined
4 thick slices smoky bacon

Per Serving (for 2): Protein: 34 g   Fat: 34 g   Carbohydrate: 2 g

Sandwich each cheese slice between 2 prawns and wrap a piece of bacon around the whole package. Secure with toothpicks.

Grill the prawns on a barbecue or under the grill just until the bacon is done, turning over once. Serve on a plate or over romaine salad.

WALNUT PARMESAN LACE CRISPS

These are great little savoury party nibbles: finely chopped walnuts and Parmesan cheese bound by egg white in a lacy network of crunch. The trick is to handle the mixture – you wouldn't call it a dough – very gently, not compacting it, until you put it on the baking sheet. At that point you pat and push it into thin rounds. They'll seem loose, but cooking the cheese and egg white binds them. Serve on a tray with cheese, apple slices dipped in lemon juice and celery sticks. SERVES 8

4 oz walnut pieces
1 tablespoon wheat germ
1 teaspoon fine yellow cornmeal
Pinch of salt
1 oz finely grated Parmesan cheese
1 large egg white

Per Serving: Protein: 6.3 g   Fat: 10.4 g   Carbohydrate: 1.8 g

Preheat the oven to 375°F/190°C/Gas Mark 5 and lightly butter a large baking sheet. Put the walnuts, wheat germ, cornmeal and salt in the bowl of a food processor and chop the nuts finely – do not overprocess. Add the cheese and pulse once or twice to mix.

In a medium mixing bowl, whisk the egg white until foamy. Add the nut mixture to the egg white and toss with a fork to mix. Switch to your hands, rubbing the mixture gently through your fingers to combine; the mixture should remain crumbly.

Using a tablespoon measure, spoon slightly mounded tablespoons of the mixture onto the baking sheet, leaving a little room between each mound. With your fingers, gently press and shape the mounds into thin crackers. Bake the crackers for 8 to 10 minutes; they should turn a shade or two darker, but they shouldn't get very dark. Cool on the baking sheet for 3 minutes, then carefully transfer the crackers to a cooling rack. Cool completely before serving. Store in a covered dish. To recrisp, warm the crackers in the oven for several minutes.

HOT GARLIC PRAWNS

These Spanish-style prawns should be served sizzling hot from the oven with toothpicks for spearing. Use an oven-proof dish just large enough to hold the prawns and attractive enough to serve them in. SERVES 10

1½ lb medium raw prawns, shelled, with tails
    left on
7 fl oz olive oil
6 whole garlic cloves, crushed
Salt to taste
Chopped parsley for garnish

Per Serving: Protein: 13.8 g   Fat: 2.6 g   Carbohydrate: .6 g

Put the prawns in an ovenproof bowl and pour the olive oil over them. Drop the garlic cloves into the oil, add salt to taste and let the prawns marinate in the refrigerator for at least 1 hour and up to 5 or 6 hours. Bring to room temperature before proceeding.

Preheat the oven to 450°F/230°C/Gas Mark 8. Roast the prawns just until they turn pink, about 6 minutes. Remove the prawns from the oven, sprinkle the parsley over and serve immediately with toothpicks.

CHEESE BALLS

Not the giant cheddar balls of fifties holiday parties, these
have a more exotic air. You can roll them in either finely
chopped pecans or finely chopped mint – or both – and
serve them mounded into a little tower on a round or
square plate. If these are cocktail fare, be sure to provide
plates and toothpicks, since the olive oil will drip.

SERVES 8

½ lb mild chèvre
6 oz feta cheese, drained
½ teaspoon ground cumin
¼ teaspoon ground red pepper (cayenne)
¼ cup finely chopped mint leaves *or* pecans
2 fl oz olive oil

Per Serving: Protein: 5.9 g   Fat: 10.5 g   Carbohydrate: .3 g

In a large bowl or in the food processor, combine the
cheeses with the cumin and cayenne. Mix well. Form the
mixture into small balls – about 24 is the right number.
Put the mint or nuts on a plate and roll the balls in it to
cover. Chill on a plate for at least an hour and up to 4
hours.

Remove from the refrigerator and let stand for half an
hour. Arrange the balls into a little tower and pour the
olive oil over. Serve with toothpicks.

MEXICAN PRAWN COCKTAIL

Serve these zesty prawns in a tapered glass or a small glass bowl. SERVES 4

- ½ lb medium or large raw prawns
- 2 diced tomatoes, no seeds
- ½ medium cucumber, peeled and cut in tiny dice
- 1 oz minced red onion
- ½ oz chopped coriander
- 1 avocado, diced
- Jolt of hot pepper sauce
- 4 fl oz Clamato juice
- 1 lime, cut into 8 slices
- Coriander sprigs to garnish

Per Serving: Protein: 6.3 g   Fat: 4.2 g   Carbohydrate: 5.4 g

Have a large pot of boiling water on the stove. Toss in the prawns and cook just until they turn pink. Drain in a colander over the sink. When the prawns are cool enough to handle, shell them, removing the vein. Put the prawns in a bowl, cover, and refrigerate until ready to serve.

In a large bowl, mix everything else except the lime and coriander sprigs. Add the prawns and divide the cocktail among 4 glasses or bowls. Hang 2 lime slices over the edge of each glass and decorate with coriander sprigs. Serve immediately.

THREE THINGS TO DO WITH SMOKED SALMON

SUSHI WITHOUT RICE

SERVES 6

4 oz smoked salmon, presliced

1 Hass avocado

12 sprigs coriander

2 oz cream cheese mixed with horseradish

Per Serving: Protein: 4.5 g   Fat: 8.2 g   Carbohydrate: 1.3 g

Separate the salmon slices into 12 – if there aren't 12 slices, cut the slices you have into 12 equal parts. Halve the avocado; remove the stone and peel off the skin. Cut each avocado half into 6 slices. Lay the salmon slices flat on a work surface. Tuck an avocado slice and a sprig of coriander close to one end of each salmon slice, folding the edges over as necessary to make a little package the size of the avocado slice. At the other end, spread a teaspoon of the cream cheese. Roll the slices up towards the cream cheese end and press together to seal.

SMOKED SALMON PINWHEELS

SERVES 6

4 oz smoked salmon, presliced
6 oz cream cheese with chives

Per Serving: Protein: 4.9 g   Fat: 8 g   Carbohydrate: .6 g

Separate the salmon slices into 12 — if there aren't 12 slices, cut the slices you have into 12 equal parts. Spread each slice with 1 tablespoon cream cheese and roll lengthwise. Cut each log into 4 pinwheels.

SMOKED SALMON CANAPÉS

SERVES 8

1 oz smoked salmon
1 long hothouse cucumber
4 oz cream cheese with chives
Sprigs of dill from 1 bunch

Per Serving: Protein: 1.2 g   Fat: 3.9 g   Carbohydrate: 1.3 g

Cut the salmon into pieces the width of the cucumber. Score the cucumber skin lengthwise with a fork to make stripes or peel large stripes with a vegetable peeler. Slice the cucumber about ¼ inch thick. Spread a dab of cream cheese on each slice, top with a piece of salmon and put a sprig of dill on top.

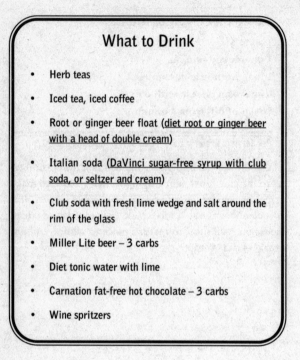

What to Drink

- Herb teas

- Iced tea, iced coffee

- Root or ginger beer float (<u>diet root or ginger beer with a head of double cream</u>)

- Italian soda (<u>DaVinci sugar-free syrup with club soda, or seltzer and cream</u>)

- Club soda with fresh lime wedge and salt around the rim of the glass

- Miller Lite beer – 3 carbs

- Diet tonic water with lime

- Carnation fat-free hot chocolate – 3 carbs

- Wine spritzers

SMOKED SALMON WITH CAVIAR

This fancy restaurant dish is so easy to make — and so impressive — that it's a good thing to have in your repertoire. Serve it with champagne and crackers for a big occasion.

SERVES 8

½ lb smoked salmon
8 fl oz double cream, whipped to soft peaks
2 handfuls of delicate greens — mâche or mesclun
½ oz caviar, black or red

Per Serving: Protein: 6.2 g   Fat: 2.6 g   Carbohydrate: 1.2 g

In the bowl of a food processor, purée the salmon — it should be as smooth as possible. Put the salmon in a mixing bowl and fold the whipped cream into it. Force the mixture through a food mill.

Arrange the greens over a serving plate and mound the smoked salmon mixture on top. Spread the caviar over the salmon mound and serve with crackers.

SALMON TARTARE

Yes, this is raw salmon, and while I wouldn't recommend
beef tartare, salmon is quite safe to eat raw — and entirely delicious. If you're nervous about it, try using half
raw salmon and half smoked salmon the first time. Feel
the salmon all over for stray bones before you chop it.
SERVES 4

½ lb raw salmon fillet, chopped coarsely
1 oz minced spring onions, including some green
½ teaspoon sea salt
Freshly ground black pepper to taste
2 tablespoons olive oil
2 drops hot pepper sauce
½ teaspoon minced lemon zest
2 tablespoons chopped chives

Per Serving: Protein: 11.3 g   Fat: 13.1 g   Carbohydrate: trace

Mix all the ingredients together in a bowl and cover
with plastic wrap. Refrigerate at least 1 hour until ready
to serve. Serve on rye or sesame crackers spread with
butter or horseradish cream cheese.

SMOKED TROUT ON WATERCRESS

This is an ideal starter for a holiday meal, the bright idea
of my friend Barbara Witt. The trout will break naturally
into little chevrons, which perch on top of a zesty salad
dressed with a creamy lemon vinaigrette. SERVES 6

   2 smoked trout
   2 bunches watercress, washed, spun dry and heavy
       stems removed

Per Serving: Protein: 3.9 g   Fat: 15.4 g   Carbohydrate: .7 g

DRESSING
   1 shallot, minced
   ½ teaspoon salt
   2 tablespoons fresh lemon juice
   Minced zest of half a lemon
   6 tablespoons light olive oil
   1 teaspoon Dijon mustard
   2 teaspoons double cream
   Salt and pepper to taste

Take the trout flesh off the bony frame and pull it into
chevron shapes where it breaks naturally. Set aside. Tear
the watercress into bite-size sprigs and set aside in a large
bowl.

Make the dressing: in a screw-top jar, mix the shallot with the salt and lemon juice and set aside for 15 minutes to half an hour.

When ready to serve, add the remaining dressing ingredients to the jar and shake well. Taste for seasoning, then pour over the watercress. Toss well and arrange the salad on serving plates. Arrange the trout pieces on top and serve immediately.

CHICKEN SATAY

This works as an appetizer or a main course — it's so good and so easy that you might want to make it dinner. The chicken is threaded on 6-inch wooden skewers, about 14 of them. Soak the skewers first in cold water for half an hour so they don't burn in the oven, or use metal shish kebab skewers. **SERVES 6 FOR DINNER, 18 AS AN APPETIZER**

3 whole boneless chicken breasts, skin removed
2½ oz roasted peanuts
1 teaspoon mild curry powder
2 fl oz soy sauce
2 tablespoons dark sesame oil
Pinch of chilli powder
Garnish: chopped coriander leaves and a few
sprigs, optional

Per Serving (for 18): Protein: 10.6 g Fat: 5.3 g Carbohydrate: .5 g

Preheat oven to 325°F/170°C/Gas Mark 3. Cut the chicken into ½-inch chunks and arrange them on the skewers evenly. Rest the skewers on a baking sheet covered with foil. In a nonstick frying pan, roast the peanuts over medium heat until fragrant. Let them cool a little and chop them coarsely.

Put the nuts in a bowl and add the remaining ingredients except the coriander. Stir well and pour the sauce over the chicken skewers. Bake for 10 minutes and serve on a platter, garnished with the coriander leaves and whole sprigs.

DEVILLED EGGS, PLAIN AND FANCY

Eggs have been so vilified for cholesterol reasons for so long that lots of people have just forgotten about devilled eggs – but try offering a plate of them; they disappear almost instantly. The basic recipe is for plain devilled eggs; fancy options follow. SERVES 6

> 1 dozen extra-large eggs, at room temperature
> 6 tablespoons mayonnaise
> ½ teaspoon dry mustard
> Salt and pepper to taste
> Paprika, optional

Per Serving: Protein: 12.2 g   Fat: 22.2 g   Carbohydrate: 1 g

Put the eggs in a large saucepan with cold water to cover. Slowly bring the water to a boil. The minute the water boils, remove the pan from the heat. Cover and let the eggs stand in the hot water for 15 minutes – set the timer.

When the eggs are done, put the pan in the sink and run cold water into it. When the eggs are cool enough to handle, tap them against the side of the pan all over to loosen the shells. Let them sit in the cold water until you're ready to peel them.

Remove the shells and cut the eggs in half crosswise. Remove the yolks to a bowl, mash them well with a fork and add the mayonnaise, mustard and salt and pepper. Cut the very ends off the egg-white cases so they'll stand up easily, and stuff them with the egg yolk mixture. Sprinkle paprika over the tops if you like.

Devilled Eggs With Smoked Salmon

Chop 2 slices of smoked salmon and stir into the egg-yolk mixture. Add a tablespoon of drained capers. Top each egg half with a frond of fresh dill.

Per Serving: Protein: 13 g Fat: 22.4 g Carbohydrate: 1 g

Devilled Eggs With Caviar

Top each egg half with a spoonful of red or black caviar.

Per Serving: Protein: 13.3 g Fat: 23 g Carbohydrate: 1.1 g

SALAMI AND EGGS WITH ROCKET

A sort of antipasto, presented on a big platter. Scatter sprigs of rocket over the platter, then tuck in very thin slices of salami, as many kinds as you can find. In the centre, make a mound of hard-boiled eggs or devilled eggs, page 84, allowing 2 whole eggs or 4 devilled egg halves per person. Decorate the eggs with more rocket sprigs. Give each person a small plate and pass the salt and peppermill.

PICKLED HARD-BOILED EGGS

Instead of pitching out the juice from the emptied pickled cucumber jar, fill it with hard-boiled eggs — just be sure they're all submerged in the green liquid. After 3 days they're ready to eat, but they'll keep for weeks in the refrigerator. These are great snacks, but they're also delicious as hors d'oeuvres, cut in half lengthwise and spread with a little sour cream, then sprinkled with salt and white pepper. (Zero carbs.)

NACHOS

No tortillas here, but these are a delicious way to have something close to the real thing. SERVES 2

> **Skins from 2 roasted potatoes, page 292, with as little flesh as possible**
> **1⅓ oz grated Monterey Jack cheese**
> **Half a 4-oz can chopped green chilles**

Per Serving: Protein: 2 g   Fat: 3 g   Carbohydrate: 12 g

Preheat the oven to 400°F/200°C/Gas Mark 6. Sprinkle the cheese and chilles over the potato skins and put them on a baking sheet. Bake for 10 minutes or until the cheese is melted and the potatoes are crispy. Cut each potato skin in half and serve hot.

CUMIN SALT

Delicious with hard-boiled eggs or for dipping crudités
into — cucumber spears, kohlrabi, daikon, etc.
ENOUGH FOR 8 SERVINGS

1½ teaspoons ground cumin
½ teaspoon ground black pepper
Pinch of ground red pepper (cayenne)
2 teaspoons salt

Mix everything together and store in a sealed jar.

TEA EGGS

Here's a recipe to astound your friends. The Chinese have
discovered some very interesting things to do to eggs,
and this is one of the most intriguing. The eggs are hard-
boiled once, and then again, for a very long time, in
spiced tea; their shells are cracked all over to give the
surface of the eggs a beautiful crackled glaze, like old
porcelain. Serve the eggs on a little nest of watercress in
a basket. SERVES 12

> 12 large eggs, at room temperature
> ¼ cup Chinese tea leaves (tea bags from Chinese
>   takeaway are okay)
> 1¾ pints water
> 1 teaspoon 5-spice powder
> ½ teaspoon salt
> 2 teaspoons soy sauce

Per Serving: Protein: 6.1 g   Fat: 5.6 g   Carbohydrate: .6 g

Put the eggs in a saucepan of water to cover and bring
the water slowly to a simmer. Let the eggs simmer, uncovered, for half an hour.

Have ready a bowl of cold water and put the eggs into
it when they come off the fire. Crack them all over very
gently – the shell should stay intact but be cracked all
over in spiderweb fashion.

Bring the water to the boil and add the tea leaves. Let
steep for 8 minutes – the tea should be very strong –
then strain out the leaves. Return the brewed tea to the
saucepan and add the 5-spice powder, the salt, soy and the
cracked eggs. Simmer the eggs gently, uncovered, for one
hour, replacing water as necessary. (Don't worry, the eggs
will be tender inside.) Let cool before removing shells.

GEORGIAN EGG SALAD

This fascinating Russian take on egg salad comes from Darra Goldstein's prize-winning cookbook, *The Georgian Feast*. It's delicious on rye or sesame crackers. SERVES 4

- **4 large eggs, hard-boiled**
- **3 tablespoons unsalted butter, softened to room temperature**
- **¼ oz ground walnuts**
- **2 tablespoons minced fresh dill**
- **2 tablespoons minced fresh coriander**
- **2 tablespoons minced spring onions, white part only**
- **⅛ teaspoon salt**

Per Serving: Protein: 7.1 g   Fat: 17.7 g   Carbohydrate: 1.6 g

Mash the eggs with the butter in a small bowl. Stir in the remaining ingredients and mix well.

PROVOLETA

This Argentinian classic makes a hearty first course or a
delicious lunch – just add a big green salad and a plate of
sliced tomatoes. You can also make it with Parmesan
cheese, for an expensive treat. Whatever you serve with
it, be sure you have red wine.

SERVES 2 AS A MAIN COURSE, 4 AS AN APPETIZER

½ lb provolone cheese
Sage or oregano leaves, chopped fresh or dried
Black pepper

Per Serving (for 4): Protein: 14 g   Fat: 16 g   Carbohydrate: 2 g

Cut the provolone into 2 thick slices. Grill them about
6 inches from the heat until the cheese is golden brown
and soft, just starting to run. If you let it go a minute too
long, you'll have a puddle of cheese (delicious, however).
Put the cheese on small plates, sprinkle with sage or
oregano and grind pepper on top. Serve with a knife and
fork.

TRICOLOUR PEPPER CRESCENTS

These savoury peppers aren't quite soft when they're cooked – they still have a little texture. They're good for a buffet or as part of an antipasto platter. SERVES 6

 3 sweet peppers, green, red and yellow if possible
 3 garlic cloves, sliced thinly
 1 large tomato, seeded and cut in dice
 12 anchovy fillets
 12 teaspoons olive oil

Per Serving: Protein: 2 g   Fat: 10 g   Carbohydrate: 3.5 g

Preheat the oven to 350°F/180°C/Gas Mark 4. Quarter the peppers and remove the stems, seeds and ribs. Lay the pepper crescents on a baking sheet and scatter the thin garlic slices over them, about 3 to a crescent. Top with the tomato dice. Lay an anchovy fillet over the tomato and garlic, and add salt and pepper to taste. Drizzle a teaspoon of olive oil over each crescent and bake them for half an hour.

Let cool to room temperature before serving.

BRIE QUICHE

This is wretched excess, but very delicious. You can serve it on a bed of watercress and topped with caviar for an over-the-top appetizer. Also works for dessert with grapes, snappy apples or pears. SERVES 10

> **4 large eggs**
> **12 fl oz single cream**
> **1 lb ripe Brie, including the rind, at room**
>   **temperature**
> **⅛ teaspoon salt**

Per Serving: Protein: 14 g   Fat: 19 g   Carbohydrate: 2.6 g

Preheat the oven to 350°F/180°C/Gas Mark 4. Separate the eggs. In a mixing bowl, beat the egg yolks with the cream. Chop the cheese in the bowl of a food processor until you have a paste. Add the creamy yolks and combine thoroughly. Pour the mixture into the mixing bowl and stir in salt and pepper to taste.

Beat the egg whites with the salt until stiff and stir ⅓ of them into the cheese mixture. Fold in the remainder with a rubber spatula.

Pour the custard into an 8-inch quiche pan and grind a little more pepper on top. Bake for 30 minutes or until set. Serve at room temperature.

CRACKLINGS

Some commercial cracklings, aka pork rinds, are pretty good but the vast majority are tasteless at best. The real thing is made when pigs are butchered and lard is rendered outdoors in big iron pots stirred with a shovel. But you can also do it at home, and it's a cinch. If you're a porcophile, these cracklings will be sheer Pig Heaven. You'll probably have to order the fat ahead from your butcher.

> **2 lb pork fat, preferably from the loin, in**
> **1-inch cubes**
> ¼ **cup water**

You want as little flesh on the fat as possible, since any meat will turn hard in the cooking process. Cut out any bits of meat that escape the butcher.

Preheat the oven to 250°F/130°C/Gas Mark ½.

In a cast-iron casserole, heat the pork fat cubes with the water over medium heat until the fat begins to melt. Stir the cubes gently a couple of times.

Put the casserole in the oven and give the contents a stir every 20 minutes or so. The temperature of the fat shouldn't go above 255°. The cracklings will be done when bubbles form and the cubes start to float to the surface, after 1½ to 2 hours. Skim them off and drain well in a colander — you want all the fat to be cooked out, and they'll continue to drain after they're cooked.

When the cracklings have finished draining, roll them in paper towels and salt them. They're delicious hot, but also good at room temperature. Try them on salads. You can even bag and freeze them to use later. Save the lard for cooking. As a variation, try dusting the finished cracklings with chilli powder.

Soups

/||\

A hearty soup can of course be a meal in itself, and that's
a very satisfying way to eat – just add a salad and cheese.
It's easy enough to improvise soups by simply sautéing the
basic seasoning elements – onions, garlic, celery etc. – in
a little butter or oil and adding cubes of leftover meat or
sausage slices, then cut-up vegetables. Once all these basic
elements are sautéed, you can just add broth or water and
let it all simmer together for a while, then taste for seasoning. Finish the soup with garnishes – croutons sizzled
in a little butter, tiny cubes of cheese, a spoonful of cream,
olivada, roasted red pepper dice, minced herbs, a sprinkle
of grated Parmesan etc. Simple enough, and yet there's
one big problem: most soups benefit from a thickening
agent, which is almost always starch. Since we won't be
using potatoes or pasta or rice or beans or barley, except
in the tiniest amounts, we need an alternative. Possibilities
include a tablespoon or two of instant flour blended into
the soup shortly before serving or a big dollop of vegetable purée. The purées can include leftovers; likely candidates are broccoli, cauliflower, courgette, spinach etc.
But consider the other flavours in the soup – if the elements would be good together on a plate, they'll work in
the soup. The ultimate thickener is cream, of course, but
there are more interesting possibilities. One that also adds
protein to the mix is beating a couple of eggs together
well, then stirring them into the hot soup with a fork just
before serving to make egg strands.

CREAM OF TOMATO SOUP,
WITH OR WITHOUT CRAB

When too many tomatoes are around in Indian summer, this is the soup to make. Or you can make it with canned tomatoes, which work perfectly well. Either way, it's luxurious. SERVES 6

   3 tablespoons clarified butter, page 45
   3 shallots, chopped
   3 lb ripe tomatoes or 2 (14½-oz) cans diced
       tomatoes
   ¼ teaspoon dried thyme
   15 fl oz chicken stock
   ¼ teaspoon baking soda
   4 fl oz double cream
   Pinch of ground red pepper (cayenne)
   Salt and ground black pepper
   1 tablespoon grated horseradish, optional
   ½ lb picked crabmeat, optional

Per Serving: Protein: 1.2 g   Fat: 13.1 g   Carbohydrate: 7.2 g

In a large saucepan, melt the butter and add the shallots. Cook slowly for 10 minutes or until soft. Cut the fresh tomatoes in cubes and discard the seeds. Add the tomatoes to the saucepan along with the thyme and chicken stock. Bring to a simmer and cover. Cook slowly for 20 minutes.

Turn off the heat and purée the soup in the blender or right in the saucepan with a hand-held blender. Add the baking soda, cream and cayenne. Heat the soup for serving but don't let it boil. Stir in the horseradish just before you ladle it into warm soup bowls. Scatter the crab on top or just finish the soup with a grinding of black pepper and a feathering of cream on top.

CREAM OF MUSHROOM SOUP

This is Mexican maestra Diana Kennedy's way of cooking mushroom soup – it's unusual and unusually good. Not too many soups begin with the instruction to turn on the oven. SERVES 6

1 lb cremini or wild mushrooms
1 tablespoon fresh lemon juice
4 small garlic cloves, chopped
2 tablespoons butter
1 tablespoon safflower oil
Salt and pepper to taste
1 pint chicken stock
4 fl oz crème fraîche, page 158, or double cream
6 tablespoons Madeira
Croutons and snipped chives for garnish, optional

Per Serving: Protein: 3.1 g   Fat: 9.8 g   Carbohydrate: 5.7 g

Preheat the oven to 300°F/150°C/Gas Mark 2. Wipe the mushrooms clean with a damp cloth and slice thinly. Spread them out in a shallow, ovenproof dish in a double layer. Add the lemon juice, garlic, butter and oil to the mushrooms and season lightly with salt and pepper. Bake the mushrooms for about an hour or until they are completely cooked and the juice is thick and dark. Set aside a few mushrooms for garnish and put the rest in the blender. Add the stock and blend until smooth.

In a heavy saucepan, heat the chicken stock for about 5 minutes. Add the cream, stir it in, and cook for 5 more minutes, but don't let it boil.

Put a tablespoon of Madeira in the bottom of each soup cup and add the hot soup. Garnish with the optional croutons and chives and the reserved mushrooms.

SAUERKRAUT SOUP

This is great comfort food on a winter's day, and it's a
meal in itself. And dinner's ready in less than half an hour.
You might want to stir in a spoonful of Dijon mustard at
the table to punch up the flavours. Rye or sesame crackers with horseradish cream cheese and a salad of sharp
greens would be good with this pungent soup. SERVES 4

> **2 oz chopped leeks**
> **6 oz sauerkraut, well rinsed and chopped**
> **1¾ pints chicken stock**
> **4 oz chopped kale, about 4 large-stemmed leaves**
> **1 lb sliced kielbasa, sautéed until golden and**
>   **drained**
> **Salt and pepper to taste**
> **Garnishes: a spoonful of sour cream per person, a**
>   **sprinkle of fresh snipped dill, a spoonful of**
>   **mustard**

Per Serving: Protein: 17 g   Fat: 23 g   Carbohydrate: 8 g

In the same pan you used to sauté the kielbasa, cook
the leeks in a tablespoon of the drippings until they begin
to colour.

In a large saucepan, combine the leeks, sauerkraut and
stock. Bring to a simmer and add the kale. Cook until the
kale is tender, about 10 minutes. Add the kielbasa and
simmer for 10 more minutes. Taste for salt and pepper.
Ladle the soup into 4 deep bowls and pass the garnishes
on the side.

ESCAROLE SOUP WITH MEATBALLS

This old Italian favourite is a meal in itself. You can make the meatballs ahead and freeze them, so you can put the soup together quickly once they're defrosted. Escarole is especially low-carb – if you substitute other greens, such as kale, you'll need to up the ante. SERVES 3

½ lb ground sirloin
1 oz grated Parmesan cheese
¼ cup crumbled garlic croutons
2 tablespoons minced parsley
¼ teaspoon salt
Pepper to taste
1 large egg, lightly beaten
2 oz plus 1 oz minced onion
3 tablespoons olive oil
2 garlic cloves, minced
5 cups shredded escarole, rinsed and dried
1¾ pints chicken stock
Hot red pepper flakes, optional

Per Serving: Protein: 30 g Fat: 23 g Carbohydrate: 9 g

Make the meatballs: in a mixing bowl combine the meat, half the cheese, the croutons, parsley, salt, pepper, egg and 2 oz of minced onion. Mix well with your hands and divide into 24 little meatballs.

In a Dutch oven or other large, heavy pot, heat 1 tablespoon of the olive oil over medium-high heat. When it's hot, add the meatballs – half at a time – and sauté until they're golden brown all over. Remove the meatballs to a plate.

Add the remaining olive oil to the pot along with the additional ounce of onion and cook over low heat, stirring frequently, until the onion is soft. Add the garlic and cook for another couple of minutes. Stir in the escarole, cover and cook until it's wilted, about 3 minutes. Add the stock and the meatballs, bring to a boil, then simmer uncovered for about 3 minutes. Serve in warm soup plates, sprinkled with the remaining Parmesan and pepper flakes.

COLD CUCUMBER SOUP WITH MINT AND LEMON

A good soup to make when the dog days arrive and it's so hot you don't want to cook – or for that matter, eat too much. The soup goes together in minutes and can be made in the morning. Add prawns and you have a complete meal. If you're serving the soup for company, you might dice the cucumber finely instead of grating it; remove the seeds first.

SERVES 4 AS A MAIN COURSE WITH PRAWNS, 6 AS A FIRST COURSE

1½ Knorr chicken bouillon cubes
15 fl oz hot water
8 fl oz yogurt (not low-fat or fat-free)
8 fl oz sour cream
1½ medium cucumbers, peeled and grated (about 1½ cups)
Grated zest of 1 lemon
Juice of 1 lemon (2 tablespoons)
2 tablespoons chopped fresh mint leaves
2 tablespoons snipped chives or minced spring onions
Dash of white pepper, optional
1 lb cooked shelled prawns, optional

Per Serving as first course: Protein: 2.7 g   Fat: 9.3 g
Carbohydrate: 5.8 g

Per Serving with prawns: Protein: 29 g   Fat: 16 g
Carbohydrate: 10.5 g

Dissolve the bouillon cubes in the hot water and let cool. In a large bowl, whisk the stock with the yogurt and sour cream until smooth. Add the cucumber and everything else but the pepper and prawns, if using. Cover the soup and refrigerate for at least 2 hours. Whisk again before serving and taste for seasoning. Serve the soup with a grinding of white pepper on top and divide the prawns among the bowls.

BLT SOUP

Yes, you can make BLTs wrapped in a big romaine leaf or a tortilla and they're very good if messy – but this interesting soup from Deer Meadow Vineyards in Virginia is a whole different take on the subject. **SERVES 4**

4 slices smoked bacon
1 tablespoon butter
2 oz chopped onion
2 oz chopped green sweet pepper
2 oz chopped celery
2 garlic cloves, minced
1¾ pints chicken stock
1 medium tomato, diced
Chopped or shredded romaine or rocket
4 fl oz cream
Salt, pepper and hot pepper sauce to taste
¼ cup croutons for garnish, optional

Per Serving: Protein: 7.7 g   Fat: 17.4 g   Carbohydrate: 6.8 g

---

Fry the bacon crisp and crumble it when cool; set aside. In a soup pot, melt the butter and sauté the onion, green pepper, celery and garlic over medium heat until tender. Add the chicken stock and bring to a boil. Lower heat and simmer for 10 minutes.

Just before serving, add the tomato, romaine, crumbled bacon and cream. Mix well and season to taste. Heat gently and serve, topped with croutons if you like.

VICHYSSOISE

No, it's not potato vichyssoise, but it tastes amazingly like it – and has all the richness, the smooth texture and the satisfying quality we love about vichyssoise. If you serve this to guests, they won't guess it's not made with potatoes. Try adding 2 teaspoons of curry powder with the onion for a lively version. SERVES 6

2 tablespoons olive oil
1 medium onion, chopped, about 4 oz
1¾ pints chicken stock
½ large head cauliflower
4 fl oz double cream
8 fl oz single cream
White pepper
Snipped chives
Snipped dill

Per Serving: Protein: .5 g   Fat: 17.6 g   Carbohydrate: 3.6 g

Heat the oil in a large soup pot and add the chopped onion. Cook, stirring from time to time, until the onion is soft, about 5 minutes. Add the chicken stock and bring to a simmer.

Meanwhile, chop the cauliflower into small pieces – the food processor is fine for this – about the size of croutons. Add the cauliflower to the broth, cover and cook until tender, from 5 to 10 minutes.

Purée the soup in the blender in 2 batches. Let cool for ½ hour, then add the cream, whisking in. Add white pepper to taste.

Chill for at least 2 hours, blend again before serving, and add a grinding of white pepper and a scattering of herbs to each bowl.

MEXICAN CHICKEN SOUP

This earthy soup is the one to make when you want a fast, comforting one-dish meal on a cold or blustery day. Of course it's better with homemade chicken stock, but canned works fine here. The secret ingredient is the chipotle chilli, see page 36. SERVES 4

1½ tablespoons olive oil

½ medium onion, chopped

2 large garlic cloves, minced

1 small carrot, minced

2 medium courgettes, diced

1 bunch Swiss chard leaves, cut into ribbons and
    chopped

1¾ pints homemade chicken stock or 3 (13-oz)
    cans low-sodium chicken stock

2 large boneless whole chicken breasts, cut into
    bite-size pieces

2 canned chipotle peppers, rinsed, seeded and
    minced

Salt and pepper to taste

4 oz Monterey Jack cheese cubes

1 oz chopped coriander leaves

½ avocado, diced

1 lime, cut into wedges

Per Serving: Protein: 46 g   Fat: 39 g   Carbohydrate: 14 g

In a large saucepan or Dutch oven over medium-high heat, warm the oil and when it's hot add the onion. Cook, stirring frequently, until it's soft, about 4 minutes. Add the garlic and stir for 1 minute.

Add the carrot, courgette and chard and cook, stirring, for another minute. Add the stock and bring the soup to a boil, then lower the heat and simmer for 8 minutes, or until the carrots are tender.

Add the chicken pieces and the minced chipotle peppers and cook for another 5 minutes or until the chicken is cooked through. Season to taste with salt and pepper.

To serve, divide the cheese cubes among four deep soup bowls, ladle the soup over, and garnish with coriander and avocado dice. Pass a dish of lime wedges to squeeze over the soup at the table.

ROASTED PEPPER SOUP
WITH FETA CHEESE

You can make this soup with either the roasted peppers on page 297 or jarred peppers or your own oven-roasted peppers. SERVES 2

12 oz roasted red sweet peppers
8 fl oz chicken stock
1 garlic clove, pressed
½ teaspoon oregano
8 fl oz double cream
Salt to taste and lots of black pepper
2 oz crumbled feta cheese
Additional oregano to garnish

Per Serving: Protein: 5.9 g   Fat: 50.5 g   Carbohydrate: 6.7 g

Blend the peppers with the chicken stock in a blender or food processor. Put the mixture in a heavy saucepan and heat gently with the garlic and oregano until it comes to a boil. Reduce the heat and simmer, uncovered, for 5 minutes. Add the cream and bring to a simmer. Taste for seasoning. Pour into deep soup bowls, crumble feta cheese on top and sprinkle with pepper and additional oregano.

SWISS CHARD AND COURGETTE SOUP

A delicious soup made from two of our vegetable heroes.
The recipe comes from Diana Kennedy; the chilli garnish
is the only hint of its Mexican origin. SERVES 6

    2 tablespoons butter
    ¼ lb Swiss chard, leaves roughly chopped, stems
            chopped finely
    3 tablespoons finely chopped white onion
    2 garlic cloves, chopped
    ½ lb courgettes, in very small cubes
    1⅓ pints chicken stock
    Salt and pepper to taste
    Optional: 2 fl oz double cream; finely chopped,
            hot, skinny, green chilli, to taste

Per Serving: Protein: 1.1 g   Fat: 4 g   Carbohydrate: 3.6 g

Melt the butter in a heavy saucepan over medium heat
and add the chard stems, onion and garlic. Cook, stirring
constantly, over a high flame for about 5 minutes. Add
the courgette and the chard leaves along with 8 fl oz of
the stock. Cover and cook over a medium flame until the
vegetables are just tender – about 10 minutes.

Put half the vegetables and 4 fl oz of stock in a blender
and blend until almost smooth. Repeat with the remaining vegetables and another 4 fl oz of broth. Heat the
purée in the saucepan with the remaining broth; add salt
and pepper to taste. Bring to a simmer and cook gently
over a low flame for about 5 more minutes. Add the
cream if desired, blend thoroughly, and pour the soup
into warm bowls. Garnish with the optional chilli.

NAPA CABBAGE SOUP WITH TOFU

This fast, clean-tasting soup is the creation of Martha
Rose Shulman, who's famous for her low-fat recipes. This
one can be vegetarian if you make it with vegetable stock
instead of chicken stock. SERVES 6

1¾ pints chicken stock (canned low-sodium
    is fine)
1¾ pints water
1 lb (½ medium-size head) napa or savoy cabbage,
    shredded
6 spring onions, including the firm green, sliced
    thinly
1 garlic clove, minced
2 tablespoons soy sauce
2 tablespoons dry sherry
2 teaspoons grated fresh ginger
½ lb firm tofu, cut into thin slivers
1 tablespoon cornflour, dissolved in 2 tablespoons
    water
2 large eggs, beaten
Salt and pepper to taste
⅓ cup chopped coriander, for garnish

Per Serving: Protein: 10.2 g   Fat: 5.7 g   Carbohydrate: 6.4 g

Combine the stock, water, cabbage, spring onions, garlic, soy, sherry, ginger and tofu in a large soup pot. Bring to a boil. Reduce the heat and simmer for 10 minutes, or until the cabbage is cooked through but still has some texture. Stir in the dissolved cornflour and stir the soup until it's slightly thickened.

Beat the eggs in a small bowl and slowly stir them into the simmering soup with a fork or a chopstick so that they form little strands. Add pepper, taste the soup, and add salt if necessary. Serve immediately in warm bowls and garnish with the coriander.

COMFORTING BROCCOLI SOUP

This is quick, nourishing and satisfying, a good soup to have in your repertoire for a fast meal. SERVES 4

   1 tablespoon olive oil
   1 lb kielbasa or smoked ham, in small chunks
   4 fat garlic cloves, chopped
   1 (14½-oz) can diced tomatoes, including juice
   1¼ pints hot chicken stock
   Salt and pepper to taste
   1 large bunch broccoli, about 1¼ lb, stems peeled
        and chopped finely, florets chopped
   1 teaspoon red pepper flakes, optional
   ½ oz chopped Italian parsley
   1 oz grated Parmesan cheese

Per Serving: Protein: 17 g   Fat: 24 g   Carbohydrate: 7.1 g

In a Dutch oven or a heavy soup pot, heat the olive oil over medium heat and add the meat chunks. Sauté until lightly golden. Add the garlic and cook for 1 minute. Add the tomatoes and chicken stock, cover, taste for seasoning and bring to the boil.

Add the broccoli pieces and return to the boil, then lower to a simmer and cook, uncovered, for 10 minutes or until the broccoli stems are tender. Ladle the soup into warm bowls and add a big pinch of hot pepper flakes if you like. Sprinkle parsley and Parmesan over each bowl and serve immediately.

Salads

〽

Whether they're first-course salads or main-dish hearty salads, you'll find yourself eating salads every day. It's easiest to just grab some expensive baby mesclun greens that are all washed and ready to go, but that gets boring after a while. The greens possibilities are almost endless: watercress, rocket, endive, cabbage ribbons, Asian greens like tat soi, parsley, endive and even – if you have a herb garden – all herbs, a particularly intriguing salad. You'll make a lot more salads with a lot less grief if the greens are cleaned and waiting in your crisper in the refrigerator, so it's worth being organized about it, at least some of the time.

A bed of greens makes the perfect foil for protein picked up at the market or leftovers in the refrigerator – everything from takeaway chicken cut into strips to smoked salmon or turkey, leftover steak, prawn and crab and lobster to plain old ham and cheese. A salad is also the perfect place to play with higher-carb foods that can be offered in small amounts, such as fruit: orange slices, pear or apple wedges, chunks of mango. Additional protein can come from hard-boiled eggs, cheese (salty cheeses like feta and ricotta salata are particularly good in salad) and bacon bits.

Dressings can be rich and creamy, light and zesty, whatever suits the ingredients. Herbs such as mint, tarragon, dill and basil are wonderful snipped into salads. Garnish salads with toasted nuts, cheese dice, strips of sweet pepper, pitted Greek olives, slivers of sun-dried tomato, a scattering of croutons, and Parmesan cheese. Something crisp – a frico (page 124) or the gouda crisps on page 126 or a few little fried pappadums – finishes the plate and adds a lot to a salad's appeal.

BASIC EARLY SUMMER CHOPPED VEGETABLE SALAD

Before the tomatoes arrive, there are other joys of summer to make salad out of. This one is classic. It's refreshing and almost instant. SERVES 4

    1 bunch radishes, chopped
    1 medium cucumber, chopped
    6 spring onions, chopped
    2 green sweet peppers, seeded and chopped
    4 fl oz sour cream
    Salt and pepper, lots of pepper, to taste
    1 tablespoon cider vinegar, optional
    1 tablespoon chopped dill, optional

Per Serving: Protein: .9 g   Fat: 6 g   Carbohydrate: 6.4 g

Put the vegetables in a salad bowl and mix the remaining ingredients together in a small bowl. Stir the dressing into the vegetables and mix well.

MUSHROOM, CHEESE AND PROSCIUTTO SALAD

This is really an appetizer salad, but it also works for a light lunch or supper. SERVES 4

½ lb cremini mushrooms, caps only
1 tablespoon fresh lemon juice
⅓ lb Swiss cheese, cut into matchsticks
3 tablespoons olive oil
Salt and lots of pepper to taste
4 thin slices prosciutto, cut into little squares
1 bunch rocket, heavy stems removed

Per Serving: Protein: 12.7 g   Fat: 21.5 g   Carbohydrate: 2.7 g

Wipe the mushroom caps clean with a slightly damp paper towel and cut into thin slices; put them in a serving bowl. Sprinkle the lemon juice over the mushroom slices. (You can do this half an hour ahead of serving.)

When ready to serve, add the cheese, oil, salt and pepper and prosciutto to the mushrooms and toss well. Serve on a bed of rocket on salad plates.

PARSLEY SALAD

Refreshing, unusual and so good you'll make it often.
You can use curly parsley or Italian flat-leaf, but remember that some people find curly parsley tends to stick in
their throats. SERVES 4

Plucked leaves from 2 bunches parsley
4 oil-packed sun-dried tomatoes, drained and
sliced thinly
½ oz grated Parmesan cheese

DRESSING
2 fl oz olive oil
2 tablespoons fresh lemon juice
2 garlic cloves, pressed
Salt and pepper to taste

Per Serving: Protein: 2.1 g　Fat: 16 g　Carbohydrate: 2.5 g

Be sure the parsley is completely dry, then put it in a
serving bowl. Add the sun-dried tomatoes and Parmesan
and toss together.

In a screw-top jar, shake the dressing ingredients together until well combined, then pour over the salad.
Toss thoroughly and serve immediately.

GREEK SALAD

This is such a mainstay of the low-carb life, and it's often so badly made, that it's worth having a recipe just to remind ourselves how to make it. SERVES 4

   1 lb tomatoes (3 medium), in quarters
   1 medium cucumber, peeled if necessary and
        sliced
   1 oz coarsely chopped flat-leaf parsley
   1 medium green sweet pepper, sliced thinly
   4 spring onions, including the firm green, sliced
        thinly
   2 fl oz extra virgin olive oil
   Salt and pepper to taste
   3 oz crumbled feta cheese
   12 kalamata olives, pitted
   Pinch of oregano

Per Serving: Protein: 1.5 g   Fat: 18 g   Carbohydrate: 7 g

Place the vegetables in a serving bowl. Pour the olive oil over and sprinkle with salt and pepper. Mix well. Crumble the feta cheese on top and dot with the olives. Sprinkle oregano over the dish and serve.

GREEK SALAD, NO TOMATOES

This is more like tossed salad than regular Greek salad, but it's equally good. SERVES 4

12 oz torn romaine leaves
3 spring onions, sliced, including the firm green
1 large cucumber, peeled if necessary, sliced thinly
4 oz feta cheese
2 fl oz olive oil
2 tablespoons red wine vinegar
Dash of cinnamon
Pepper to taste
8 kalamata olives, pitted

Per Serving: Protein: 1 g   Fat: 13 g   Carbohydrate: 2 g

Put the romaine, spring onions, and cucumber in a salad bowl and toss. Crumble the feta cheese on top. In a screw-top jar, mix the oil, vinegar, cinnamon and pepper and shake well. Pour the dressing over the salad and toss well to combine. Tuck in the olives and serve immediately.

POTATO SALAD

Just kidding. Actually this is cauliflower salad, but it tastes almost exactly like potato salad and the texture isn't wildly different. You'll probably have leftover dressing, depending on the size of the cauliflower. SERVES 6

1 cauliflower, cut into florets
2 oz sliced spring onions, including the firm green
3 celery sticks, chopped finely, including some
      inner leaves
½ green sweet pepper, chopped finely
½ oz chopped parsley
Salt and pepper to taste

DRESSING
2 teaspoons Colman's dry mustard
2 tablespoons cider vinegar
1 cup mayonnaise, Hellmann's

3 hard-boiled eggs, chopped
½ to 1 teaspoon celery seeds, to taste
Paprika for garnish

Per Serving: Protein: 3 g   Fat: 32.1 g   Carbohydrate: 4.8 g

Steam the cauliflower florets until tender but not soft. Set aside to cool.

Put the spring onions, celery, sweet pepper and parsley in a large salad bowl. Add salt and pepper.

Make the dressing: mix the mustard, vinegar and mayonnaise together in a small bowl until smooth.

When the cauliflower is cool, chop and add it to the vegetables and mix with enough dressing to just coat the vegetables. Stir in the eggs and celery seeds and mix well. Sprinkle paprika on top and cover with plastic wrap. Let sit in the refrigerator for at least 2 hours for flavours to develop.

MEXICAN CAULIFLOWER SALAD

This salad takes cauliflower in an unusual direction. If you have Mexican oregano, so much the better. SERVES 6

15 oz cooked cauliflower florets, page 120
3 fl oz vinaigrette, page 116
½ teaspoon oregano, preferably Mexican
1 avocado, cubed
3 oz ricotta salata or cream cheese, cubed

Per Serving: Protein: 1.7g Fat: 19g Carbohydrate: 2.8g

Mix the cauliflower with the vinaigrette and oregano. Toss lightly with the avocado and cheese and serve on a platter.

PEPPERY COLESLAW

This is *New York Times* food writer Suzanne Hamlin's famous coleslaw, which has been widely copied and attributed. That's because it's so delicious that everyone claims it as their own. You will too. The recipe makes a lot, but it just gets better as it ages, which is why you start a day ahead. SERVES 10

SLAW

2 lb green cabbage, cored and shredded

1 small turnip, peeled and shredded

2 carrots, peeled and shredded

4 radishes, chopped

3 oz finely chopped red onion

½ oz finely chopped Italian parsley

3 tablespoons minced fresh dill

DRESSING

8 oz mayonnaise

4 fl oz cider vinegar

1 teaspoon sugar

¼ teaspoon ground black pepper

⅛ teaspoon ground white pepper

¼ teaspoon hot red pepper flakes, optional

½ teaspoon salt

Per Serving: Protein: .7 g   Fat: 17.6 g   Carbohydrate: 5.2 g

In a large bowl, toss together the slaw ingredients. In a small bowl, whisk together the dressing ingredients. Add the dressing to the slaw and toss, mixing thoroughly. Taste for salt and toss again. Cover and refrigerate for 24 to 48 hours, stirring from time to time. Just before serving, taste for seasoning and stir thoroughly.

TEX-MEX COLESLAW

This is a mellow coleslaw but you can add fire in the form
of more spices, minced hot peppers or hot pepper sauce.
SERVES 6

  6 oz shredded cabbage
  4 oz sour cream
  1 tablespoon mayonnaise
  1 tablespoon cider vinegar
  Salt and pepper to taste
  ½ teaspoon chilli powder
  ½ teaspoon ground cumin
  1 teaspoon mango fat-free dressing(page 38),
        optional
  1 tablespoon chopped coriander

Per Serving: Protein: .6 g   Fat: 5.8 g   Carbohydrate: 2.6 g

Put the cabbage in a mixing bowl. In a small bowl,
combine all the remaining ingredients except the coriander. Mix the dressing into the cabbage thoroughly, then
stir in the coriander. Refrigerate for at least half an hour
to develop flavour.

Three Crispy Crunches

FRICO

This crisp little wafer of cheese hails from Friuli in Italy, where it's made with Montasio cheese – not usually available here, but you can use Parmesan. It may take a try or two to get this technique right, but you'll be very glad you did. These are delectable, with a wonderful crunch.
SERVES 3

½ lb coarsely grated Parmesan cheese
1 tablespoon melted butter or olive oil
Optional: 1 teaspoon cumin seed or caraway
            seed

Per Serving: Protein: 20 g   Fat: 18 g   Carbohydrate: 2 g

Measure out a third of the cheese. Brush a 7-inch non-stick frying pan with a teaspoon of the butter or oil. Add the cheese, spreading it out evenly. Add a third of the optional seeds, scattering them over the top of the frico. Cook over medium-low heat for 3 to 4 minutes or until the cheese melts and gets crusty (but don't let it brown). Press down on the top of the frico with a spatula and pour off any oil that accumulates. Turn and cook for 1 more minute, until the edges are crisp.

Remove the frico to a baking sheet covered with paper towels. Blot any extra oil and let cool to room temperature. Remove any crumbs in the pan and make the other 2 fricos in the same manner.

FRICO BOWL

To make a little frico bowl to serve a salad, drape the hot frico over an upside-down bowl and let it cool and dry in place.

CORN CRISPS

This is an old-time recipe that's truly delicious. You can instantly update it by adding lots of pepper and Parmesan or a small spoonful of cumin seeds just before it goes into the oven.

SERVES 12

4½ oz white or yellow stone-ground
    cornmeal
8 fl oz boiling water
½ teaspoon salt
3 tablespoons melted butter

Per Serving: Protein: .5 g   Fat: 3 g   Carbohydrate: 4.5 g

Preheat the oven to 400°F/200°C/Gas Mark 6. Stir the cornmeal and boiling water together in a large glass measuring cup. Add the salt and melted butter. Mix well and pour onto a baking tray. Using a spatula, spread the batter out as thinly as you possibly can—the thinner, the crispier.

Bake the cornmeal for half an hour or until crisp and golden brown. Break into 12 roughly even pieces.

GOUDA CRISPS

These have their origin in Patricia Wells's recipe for
Cheese Crisps in her <u>Patricia Wells at Home in Provence</u>
(Scribner) – she makes them with a local sheep cheese.
This version uses Gouda and spicy seeds, cumin or car-
away. The cumin has an exotic taste that goes with
Indian or Mexican flavours; the caraway is much more
familiar, and would be very good with a glass of vodka.
If you have a toaster oven, it's perfect for making these.

For each wafer:

SERVES 1

**1 tablespoon coarsely grated Gouda cheese
(chilled cheese is easier to grate)
Pinch of cumin seeds or caraway seeds**

Per Serving: Protein: 1 g   Fat: 2 g   Carbohydrate: 0 g

Using a nonstick baking sheet, make little mounds of the
cheese spaced at least 2 inches apart. Spread the cheese
out a bit in a free-form circle so it will melt evenly. The
mounds may stay round or they may spread into cheese
oysters. Sprinkle the seeds over the top.

Slide the baking sheet under a preheated grill, 3 or 4
inches below the heat. You'll have to turn the sheet
several times so that the wafers cook evenly; they're done
in just a couple of minutes, when they're bubbly and
golden brown at the edges. Remove the baking sheet from
the oven, let it sit for another minute or two, and remove
with a spatula to a cake rack to cool. Blot any oil with
paper towels. Let the baking sheet cool before making
another batch.

The wafers will keep for a week tightly covered.

ASIAN COLESLAW

You don't have to make this with napa cabbage, the most commonly available Chinese cabbage, but it makes a subtle difference in both flavour and texture that seems right with the Asian seasonings. Taste the dressing to be sure you need the sweetener. You may want a sweet taste and you may want some fire, in which case use the hot pepper flakes. SERVES 6

1 head napa cabbage
¼ cup minced spring onions, including some
    green
1 tablespoon minced fresh ginger

DRESSING

3 fl oz rice wine vinegar
1 tablespoon soy sauce
2 tablespoons dark sesame oil
2 tablespoons safflower oil
1 stick Canderel or 1 teaspoon sugar, optional
½ teaspoon hot red pepper flakes, optional

1 tablespoon minced coriander
1½ oz chopped roasted peanuts, optional

Per Serving: Protein: 3.3 g   Fat: 14 g   Carbohydrate: 2.7 g

Remove and discard the outer leaves of the cabbage and shred the rest of the head – you should have about 12 oz of shredded cabbage. Mix the cabbage with the spring onions and ginger in a bowl and set aside.

Make the dressing: just mix everything together, tasting to see if you need the sweetener or the pepper flakes.

Stir the dressing into the vegetables and toss well to mix. Serve in a salad bowl with the coriander and peanuts sprinkled over the top.

FENNEL AND ORANGE SALAD

This very refreshing salad gives you the exhilarating taste
of orange – but not a lot of it. SERVES 8

   1 head Boston lettuce, in bite-size pieces
   2 medium fennel bulbs, trimmed and sliced thinly
      crosswise
   Salt and pepper
   Extra virgin olive oil
   1 navel or Valencia orange, peel and white pith
      removed
   16 black olives, pitted

Per Serving: Protein: trace   Fat: 5.5 g   Carbohydrate: 3.5 g

Mix the lettuce with the fennel slices. Add salt and
pepper to taste and toss with just enough olive oil to
barely coat the greens. Mix well.

Slice the orange crosswise as thinly as possible, removing any seeds. Quarter the slices and lay them over
the top of the salad; trickle a little more olive oil on top.
Decorate the oranges with the olives; salt and pepper
lightly and serve immediately.

RED AND GREEN COLESLAW

You don't have to add the mango, of course, but it makes
an intriguing difference. If you leave it out, add ½ teaspoon more vinegar. SERVES 4

  4 oz finely shredded green cabbage
  2 oz finely shredded red cabbage
  2 spring onions, including the firm green, in thin
        rounds
  1½ teaspoons cider vinegar
  1 tablespoon mango fat-free dressing
  1 tablespoon Dijon mustard
  1 tablespoon mayonnaise
  2 oz sour cream
  Salt and pepper to taste
  2 teaspoons caraway seeds

Per Serving: Protein: .4 g   Fat: 5.2 g   Carbohydrate: 4.3 g

Mix the two cabbages and spring onions together in a
large bowl. Mix the remaining ingredients – except the
caraway seeds – together in a screwtop jar and shake well.
Pour over the cabbage and toss well to combine. Add the
caraway seeds and mix well. Taste for seasoning and let it
sit in the refrigerator for 30 minutes to develop flavour.

OLD-FASHIONED CUCUMBER SALAD

Good with fish, good on a buffet table, pretty good in general. And made in moments. You could make this more substantial by adding crumbled feta cheese.

SERVES 4

1½ lb cucumbers

2 oz sour cream

2 tablespoons white vinegar

¼ teaspoon salt

⅛ teaspoon white pepper

1 tablespoon snipped chives

1 tablespoon snipped fresh dill

Per Serving: Protein: .3 g   Fat: 2.5 g   Carbohydrate: 2.7 g

Peel the cucumbers and remove the seeds. Slice them thinly and put them in a bowl. In a mixing bowl, combine the remaining ingredients and pour over the cucumbers. Toss lightly and transfer to a serving bowl. Garnish the bowl with sprigs of fresh dill and serve within half an hour.

SPANISH CAULIFLOWER SALAD

This is a carnivore's variation on *Greens* author Deborah Madison's exuberant way with cauliflower. It has strong, lively tastes that take our familiar vegetables to a new level. The secret is to slice the cauliflower as thinly as possible. SERVES 4

> 1 small cauliflower
> 2 oz watercress
> 2 spring onions, sliced finely
> 4 oz diced celery heart and leaves
> 1 small green sweet pepper, sliced thinly
> 1 small cucumber, peeled, seeded and chopped
> 12 green Spanish pimiento-stuffed olives, halved
> 1 tablespoon capers, rinsed
> 8 oz smoked ham, diced
> 1 oz parsley leaves
> Sherry Vinaigrette, page 133

Per Serving: Protein: 10.4 g   Fat: 3.1 g   Carbohydrate: 7.5 g

Remove the green leaves from the cauliflower and cut off the heavy stem near the base. Separate the head into florets and peel the stalks. Lay each floret on a work surface and slice it lengthwise as thinly as you can. Slice the stalks the same way. Put the slices into a mixing bowl.

Remove the large stems from the watercress and roughly chop the rest. Put in the mixing bowl along with the remaining ingredients except the vinaigrette. Toss everything together, then add the vinaigrette and toss again.

SHERRY VINAIGRETTE

MAKES ABOUT 4 FL OZ, TO SERVE 4

2 garlic cloves, coarsely chopped
Salt to taste
1 hard-boiled egg
1½ tablespoons sherry vinegar or aged red wine
       vinegar
1 teaspoon Dijon mustard, optional
6 tablespoons extra-virgin olive oil
Pepper to taste

Per Serving: Protein: 1.5 g   Fat: 22.4 g   Carbohydrate: .9 g

Pound the garlic with ¼ teaspoon of salt in a mortar
until it breaks down into a purée, then add the egg yolk
and mash it in well. (Discard the white or dice it and add
to the salad.) Combine the garlic, vinegar and mustard in
a small bowl, then whisk in the oil and season with pepper. Taste and correct the balance; the dressing should
be a little on the tart side.

TABBOULEH

This Middle Eastern classic is such a favourite that it
seems a pity we can't have it. Well, we can't have the
gummy version jammed with cracked wheat, but there's
another tradition in the Middle East, where the tabbouleh
is often more of a parsley salad with just a little grain and
all the same zesty flavours. The amount of grain may seem
miserly, but it will swell once it soaks in water. This salad
keeps well, so you can make a lot and serve it for several
days. SERVES 4

> 1½ oz medium-grain bulgur (cracked wheat)
> ½ cucumber
> Salt
> 1 large bunch Italian flat-leaf parsley (1 ⅓ cups
>   chopped)
> 4 spring onions, including an inch of the greens
> 1 teaspoon coarse sea salt
> 2 tablespoons olive oil mixed with 1 drop pure
>   lemon oil, page 41
> 1 tablespoon fresh lemon juice
> ⅛ oz chopped mint leaves
> 4½ oz chopped tomato, no seeds
> Pinch of ground cumin

Per Serving: Protein: 1 g   Fat: 7.1 g   Carbohydrate: 10 g

Put the bulgur in a bowl and cover with water; let it
sit for 30 minutes. Peel the cucumber and cut it in half
lengthwise. Scoop out the seeds. Chop it into small dice,
toss with a sprinkle of salt, and set it to drain in a colander in the sink while the bulgur is soaking.

Meanwhile, wash and completely dry the parsley. You can use stems and all; chop the whole bunch. Chop the spring onions.

When the bulgur is finished soaking, drain it through a sieve into the sink, then roll it in a towel to dry – it should be as dry as possible. Put the bulgur in a bowl with the spring onions and sea salt; with your hands, work the spring onions and salt into the grains for several minutes.

Mix in the olive oil, lemon juice, mint and tomatoes. Dry the cucumber dice with a kitchen towel and add that too. Mix everything together well to combine, add the cumin, and taste for seasoning. Let it sit for at least half an hour to develop flavour.

MAUDE SALAD

This famous salad was invented at the much-missed
Chasen's restaurant in Beverly Hills and named after the
owner, Maude Chasen. It speaks of a happier era, when a
rich and delectable salad wasn't politically incorrect. Cut
the chilli sauce in half and you'll reduce the carbs to 6.2
per serving. SERVES 8

1½ lb shredded mixed lettuces – iceberg, romaine,
      chicory
1½ lb seeded diced tomatoes
4 hard-boiled eggs, chopped
2 bunches chopped chives (about ½ cup)
4 oz crumbled Roquefort cheese

Per Serving: Protein: 21 g   Fat: 78 g   Carbohydrate: 8.2 g

DRESSING
8 oz mayonnaise
6 oz sour cream
2 garlic cloves, minced
4 fl oz chilli sauce
2 fl oz red wine vinegar
Salt and pepper to taste
3 oz crumbled Roquefort cheese

Combine the lettuces, tomatoes, eggs and chives in a salad bowl. Toss and chill until ready to serve.

Make the dressing: blend everything but the salt and pepper and Roquefort in a bowl. Add salt and pepper to taste. Stir in the Roquefort and mix well.

When ready to serve, remove the salad from the refrigerator and toss with the dressing. Sprinkle the salad with the remaining cup of Roquefort.

SALMON AND GREEN BEAN SALAD
WITH DILL

This combination of tastes is simply winning – perfect
low-carb fare that everyone else will love too. SERVES 4

1½ lb salmon fillet
Olive oil for the salmon
Salt and pepper
1 lb steamed green beans
4 spring onions, chopped, including some of the
     firm green
1 tablespoon chopped fresh dill
2 tablespoons fresh lemon juice
2 fl oz extra-virgin olive oil
1 teaspoon lemon thyme leaves or 1 tablespoon
     chopped parsley

Per Serving: Protein: 34 g   Fat: 32 g   Carbohydrate: 7.4 g

Rub the salmon all over with olive oil and sprinkle
with salt and pepper. Set aside on a baking sheet to season for at least 5 minutes or up to half an hour.

Preheat the grill. Grill the salmon for 8 to 12 minutes,
or until it's done all the way through but still juicy.
Remove from the oven and let cool.

Put the beans in a large serving bowl. Add the spring
onions and dill; mix well. In a small screwtop jar, shake
up the lemon juice, oil and salt and pepper to taste. Pour
the dressing over the beans. Flake the salmon over the
beans and toss everything together well. Sprinkle the
herbs over the top and serve.

Tuna and Green Bean Salad with Dill

You can make the same dish with three 3½-oz cans of tuna in place of the cooked and cooled salmon, preferably Genova tuna imported from Italy. With the tuna, use a red wine vinaigrette.

WATERMELON SALAD WITH PECANS AND FETA

This wonderful salad sometimes appears on breakfast tables in the Middle East. For low-carb cooks, it's probably best considered a relish, since we can't eat a huge amount of it – but it's much too good to leave out of the repertoire. SERVES 4

    14 oz watermelon cubes, seeds removed
    3 oz feta cheese cubes
    8 toasted pecan halves, chopped
    8 slivered mint leaves
    1 tablespoon fresh lime juice
    Grinding of fresh pepper

Per Serving: Protein: 1.2 g   Fat: 2.7 g   Carbohydrate: 6.5 g

Mix everything together and toss well. Serve right away.

THAI-STYLE PRAWN SALAD

This quick salad depends on a couple of condiments: Thai spices and mango fat-free dressing. But you could also use cider vinegar with orange zest and a drop of vanilla for the dressing. SERVES 2

>   1 tablespoon Thai spices
>   2 garlic cloves, chopped
>   ¾ lb medium raw prawns
>   1 hard-boiled egg, chopped
>   1 celery stick plus some of the inner leaves,
>   chopped finely
>   2 spring onions, chopped, including the firm
>   greens
>   ½ medium cucumber, seeded and chopped
>   2 tablespoons chopped coriander

Per Serving: Protein: 45 g   Fat: 50.1 g   Carbohydrate: 9.1 g

DRESSING
2½ oz mayonnaise
1 tablespoon mango fat-free dressing
Salt and white pepper to taste

1¼ oz chopped roasted peanuts

In a large saucepan heat $1^{1}/_{3}$ pints of water with the Thai spices and garlic. When it's boiling, toss in the prawns and cook just until they turn pink and curl. Drain in a colander in the sink. Remove shells when the prawns are cool enough to handle and chop roughly.

Meanwhile, assemble everything else in a medium-size salad bowl and make the dressing by whisking together the mayonnaise, the dressing and salt and pepper to taste.

When the prawns are ready, mix everything together and top with a scattering of peanuts. Or serve the salad on a bed of greens and top with the peanuts.

COBB SALAD

If you have hard-boiled eggs hanging around – as you should – and you bring home a rotisserie chicken, you can have this classic Hollywood salad ready in about 10 minutes. SERVES 4

    1 head iceberg lettuce, chopped
    1 small head romaine, chopped
    1 bunch watercress, chopped
    4 inner celery sticks, sliced diagonally
    1 avocado, diced
    2 large tomatoes, chopped
    1 whole roast chicken breast, chopped, about
        7½ oz
    2 hard-boiled eggs, chopped
    ¼ lb blue cheese, crumbled
    8 bacon slices, fried crisp and crumbled
    3 fl oz olive oil
    2 tablespoons white wine vinegar
    Salt and pepper to taste
    1 garlic clove, crushed

Per Serving: Protein: 28.9 g   Fat: 65 g   Carbohydrate: 7.9 g

Mix the greens, avocado, tomatoes and chicken in a large salad bowl. Scatter the eggs, cheese and bacon over the top. In a screw-top jar, mix the remaining ingredients and shake well. Remove the garlic and drizzle the dressing over the salad. Toss at the table just before serving.

MIDDLE EASTERN LAMB SALAD

You can serve the salad without the lamb, of course, but it's a particularly delicious, zesty combination of flavours.
SERVES 4

½ leg of lamb, butterflied
1 tablespoon olive oil
Salt and pepper to taste
1 teaspoon ground cumin
2 garlic cloves, pressed

Per Serving: Protein: 65.9 g   Fat: 41.7 g   Carbohydrate: 4.4 g

SALAD
2 oz pecan pieces
4 oz feta cheese, crumbled
2 fl oz olive oil
1½ tablespoons fresh lemon juice
4 oz baby spinach leaves
½ oz mint leaves, chopped coarsely
Salt and pepper to taste

Rub the lamb all over with the oil and then with the salt and pepper, cumin and garlic. Grill the lamb, turning once, until it reaches an internal temperature of 135°F for medium-rare. This will take about 40 minutes on a charcoal or gas-fired grill.

While the lamb is cooking, make the salad. Toast the pecan pieces on a baking sheet in a 325°/170°C/Gas Mark 3 oven for about 10 minutes or until they smell toasty. Mix the remaining ingredients together in a salad bowl and toss well. Scatter the pecans over the top. Serve thin slices of the warm grilled lamb over the salad.

TUNISIAN ROASTED VEGETABLES
WITH TUNA

In Tunisia this traditional salad is grilled and served as an
appetizer. But it's easy to oven-roast the vegetables, and
the salad is so good that it's worth adding an extra can of
tuna and serving it as a main course.

SERVES 4 AS A MAIN COURSE

> 4 sweet peppers – red, green, yellow or a
>   combination
> 1 medium onion, unpeeled
> 4 medium tomatoes
> 1 small green chilli – jalapeño or serrano – seeded
>   and minced
> 3 tablespoons olive oil
> 1½ tablespoons fresh lemon juice
> Salt and pepper to taste
> 2 (3½-oz) cans light tuna packed in oil, drained
> 2 hard-boiled eggs, cut into wedges
> 6 anchovy fillets, page 38, optional

Per Serving: Protein: 14.7 g   Fat: 6.2 g   Carbohydrate: 10.3 g

Preheat the oven to 475°F/220°C/Gas Mark 7. Put
the peppers and onion on a baking sheet on the top shelf
of the oven for 30 minutes. Add the tomatoes for the last
5 minutes. The vegetables should be soft and very well
browned.

Peel and seed the peppers (page 297), then dice them.
Peel and dice the onion. Peel the tomatoes, take out as
many seeds as you can, and dice the flesh. Save any juices
for the salad.

Put the vegetables in a serving bowl and stir in the chilli. Whisk the oil and lemon juice together in a small bowl and add salt and pepper to taste. Pour the dressing over the vegetables and toss gently. Crumble the tuna over the top of the salad and arrange the egg slices over the tuna. Sprinkle the chopped anchovies over the salad and serve.

Sauces, Marinades and Salsas

꒰꒰꒰

A diet that allows butter, cream, olive oil, eggs, olives, nuts and cheese clearly offers the cook a cornucopia of ingredients to make food sing. Though we've tended to think of sauces as French, and therefore rich and expendable, in fact they're endlessly versatile and delicious, and not even necessarily rich.

If you can take a few extra minutes to make real mayonnaise – in a blender or a food processor or by hand – you'll be endlessly rewarded. All sorts of flavourings go into the real thing, from the classic garlicky aioli of Provence to smoky chipotle chillis from Mexico. You can add herbs and spices almost ad infinitum. But real mayonnaise is so good it stands alone – and good shop-bought mayonnaise isn't too far behind.

A butter sauce is almost instant: just melted butter and the pan juices plus a jolt of whatever seems missing (something hot, something spicy, something smoky, something tart, a particular herb or spice). It can be just butter and a little sherry vinegar or balsamic vinegar, or just butter and chopped toasted nuts. Or just ghee (page 45), heated into a nutty-tasting sauce.

Marinades are more familiar from the low-fat era. Here's a good place to use citrus, lots of garlic and other elements that are a little too high-carb to use in any quantity – you get the flavour in the marinade without the carbs.

Salsa is one of those crossover foods from the high-carb diets – fresh and delicious and wonderfully useful, it goes on almost everything. Make your own or find a good commercial product that doesn't use sweeteners.

The most important thing is to remember to use these great flavour enhancers. If you're not used to making something extra to serve with the main course, try to make it a habit. Plain grilled food, however delicious, can get boring, and these tasty elements hold the secret to making it new and fresh every time.

ROMESCO SAUCE

One of the classic sauces from Catalonia in Spain, this one is hot and addictive. It goes with meat, fish, shellfish, chicken, salad, almost anything you can think of.

MAKES 16 SERVINGS

> 2 oz blanched almonds
> 3 garlic cloves, unpeeled
> 2 medium tomatoes
> 1 dried hot chilli pepper
> 3 tablespoons red wine vinegar
> Salt to taste
> 4 fl oz olive oil

Per Serving: Protein: .5 g   Fat: 8.4 g   Carbohydrate: .9 g

Preheat the oven to 350°F/180°C/Gas Mark 4. Put the almonds, garlic, tomatoes and chilli pepper on a baking sheet and roast them for 10 to 15 minutes. The almonds should be lightly browned and the vegetables and garlic should be soft. Peel the tomatoes and remove the seeds. Slip the peel off the garlic.

Put the almonds, tomatoes, garlic and chilli pepper in a blender and grind thoroughly. Add the vinegar and salt, then gradually trickle in the oil until the sauce thickens. The sauce will keep for several days tightly covered in the refrigerator.

ANCHOVY BUTTER

Very good on rye or sesame crackers and with smoked fish or sardines. Just spread some on a cracker, add the fish, and top with a couple of sweet onion rings and a few watercress leaves. MAKES 12 TEASPOONS, 6 SERVINGS

> ½ teaspoon anchovy paste or ½ anchovy, soaked in
>   milk for 15 minutes and minced
> ½ teaspoon minced parsley
> Several drops of fresh lemon juice
> 4 tablespoons unsalted butter, at room
>   temperature

Per Serving: Protein: trace   Fat: 7.3 g   Carbohydrate: trace

With the back of a fork, mix the ingredients together until smoothly combined. Put the anchovy butter in a little crock to serve or store it in the refrigerator, tightly sealed.

TARATOR

There's a soup called tarator in Yugoslavia – made with cucumbers and yogurt – but there's also this sauce by that name in the Middle East. Tarator sauce is very good over steamed vegetables, especially beetroot and cauliflower. SERVES 8

2½ oz hazelnuts, walnuts or pine nuts, toasted
         (page 48)
2 garlic cloves, crushed
2 fl oz olive oil
3 tablespoons fresh lemon juice
4 fl oz yogurt
Chilli powder to taste
Salt to taste

Per Serving: Protein: 2.4 g   Fat: 11.9 g   Carbohydrate: 2.1 g

Put everything but the chilli powder and salt in the bowl of a food processor and blend smooth. Pour the sauce into a bowl and add the chilli powder, stirring it in well. Add salt to taste.

CHIMICHURRI SAUCE

Argentina is the homeland of this addictive sauce, which is served with the incomparable Argentine mixed grill – chicken, ribs and sausages. Just remember to make it a few hours ahead for best flavour. SERVES 12

4 fl oz olive oil
2 fl oz red wine vinegar
1 large onion, chopped
1 garlic clove, crushed
2 oz finely chopped parsley
2 oz finely chopped coriander
1 teaspoon dried oregano
¼ teaspoon ground red pepper (cayenne)
1½ teaspoons salt
1 teaspoon ground black pepper

Per Serving: Protein: 0 g   Fat: 9.3 g   Carbohydrate: .7 g

Whisk together the oil and vinegar, then add the other ingredients. Let stand for several hours to develop flavours.

TABLE SALSA

This fresh salsa adds zest to anything it touches —
everything from eggs to grilled meat to pork rinds to
carnitas. Don't make it more than half an hour before
you serve it or it will lose some of its sparkle. If you want
the salsa really hot, leave the chilli seeds in — extra fibre,
after all. MAKES ABOUT 18 TABLESPOONS

> 1 medium tomato, chopped
> 1 oz chopped spring onions
> 2 tablespoons roughly chopped coriander
> 2 serrano chillis or jalapeños, chopped finely
> ½ teaspoon salt
> 1 tablespoon fresh lime juice

Per Serving: Protein: 0 g   Fat: 0 g   Carbohydrate: .5 g

Mix everything together. After about 3 hours, the salsa
will begin to seriously deteriorate and lose flavour.

HORSERADISH CREAM

This could hardly be easier to make, and it's especially delicious with roast beef. Fresh horseradish is best but hard
to find; if you're using bottled horseradish, drain it well
and squeeze dry first. SERVES 8

> 8 fl oz double cream
> 1 tablespoon grated horseradish, or to taste

Per Serving: Protein: .6 g   Fat: 10 g   Carbohydrate: .9 g

Whip the cream until you have soft peaks. Stir in the
horseradish and serve at once.

ORANGE MAYONNAISE

Good for dipping and also for using as the base for a chicken salad. Add a little curry powder to take it in a different direction. Instead of the juice, you could use a couple of drops of citrus oil, page 39, and thin the mayonnaise with a little mild vinegar, such as champagne vinegar or rice vinegar. MAKES 8 SERVINGS

    8 oz mayonnaise
    2 teaspoons grated orange zest
    2 tablespoons fresh orange juice
    1 teaspoon mild curry powder, optional

Per Serving: Protein: trace   Fat: 22 g   Carbohydrate: .3 g

Mix everything together in a bowl and let sit for half an hour to develop flavour.

CHIPOTLE MAYONNAISE

Making this mayonnaise depends on having the chipotle paste, page 36. Once you've made this, though, you'll keep it on hand willingly. It seems created to eat with prawns, but it's also delicious with other fish, chicken and vegetables. MAKES 12 SERVINGS

2 garlic cloves, pressed
2 tablespoons chipotle paste, page 36, or 2 canned
      chipotle peppers in adobo, rinsed, seeded
      and minced
12 oz mayonnaise

Per Serving: Protein: trace   Fat: 22 g   Carbohydrate: .5 g

Mix everything together in a food processor and serve in a bowl to dip into.

CURRIED MAYONNAISE

This won't be a lot better if you make it from scratch, so you may as well use a good brand of prepared mayonnaise, like Hellmann's. A nice mild curry powder is the right thing here – if you can't find one you like, use garam masala, an Indian spice mix that's widely available. If you can't find the mango dressing, use apple cider vinegar.

MAKES 2 SERVINGS

2 oz mayonnaise
½ teaspoon mild curry powder
1 teaspoon mango fat-free dressing

Per Serving: Protein: 0 g   Fat: 11 g   Carbohydrate: trace

Mix everything together in a small bowl and keep refrigerated.

GARLIC MAYONNAISE

This is a useful item to have on hand, and it will keep for several days in the refrigerator. It's the essential element for the aioli platter on page 191 (see Two Great Feasts), but also good for dipping vegetables and spooning into certain soups. Try adding a teaspoon of Dijon mustard along with the egg. Leave out the garlic and you have regular mayonnaise. MAKES 8 SERVINGS

> 3 garlic cloves
> ½ teaspoon sea salt
> 1 egg yolk
> 1 whole egg
> 1 cup mild extra-virgin olive oil
> 1 teaspoon fresh lemon juice or more to taste

Per Serving: Protein: .5 g   Fat: 14 g   Carbohydrate: trace

Cut the garlic cloves lengthwise and then mince them. Using a mortar and pestle, work the salt into the garlic until you have a paste (or do this on a plate with the back of a fork if you have no mortar). Scrape the garlic paste into the bowl of a food processor. Add the egg yolk and whole egg and pulse briefly to blend. With the feed tube open and the machine running, pour the oil in a slow but steady stream into the bowl until it begins to come together to form the mayonnaise. Add the lemon juice. Serve immediately or refrigerate for several days, tightly sealed.

BASIL MAYONNAISE

Delicious with raw vegetables. MAKES 8 SERVINGS

8 oz mayonnaise: Hellmann's
¼ oz snipped fresh basil leaves
Several grinds of fresh pepper

Per Serving: Protein: trace   Fat: 22 g   Carbohydrate: trace

Mix everything together by hand in a small bowl. Keeps refrigerated, tightly covered, for a week.

CRÈME FRAÎCHE

This much milder form of sour cream is delicious with berries, or just about any place you'd use sour cream.
MAKES 16 FL OZ

8 fl oz double cream
8 fl oz sour cream

Per Serving: Protein: 12.2 g   Fat: 136 g   Carbohydrate: 16.4 g

Mix the two creams together well and let stand for 24 hours at room temperature. Place in a tightly sealed jar in the refrigerator. Keeps for 1 week.

BLUE CHEESE DRESSING

You can just throw everything but the chives together in the food processor to make this dressing, then stir in the chives – or if you'd like a little texture, you can make it by hand. MAKES 12 SERVINGS

> **4 oz blue cheese, such as Roquefort**
> **4 fl oz sour cream**
> **4 fl oz mayonnaise**
> **¼ teaspoon pepper**
> **Dash of hot pepper sauce**
> **½ oz minced chives**

Per Serving: Protein: 2.3 g   Fat: 11.9 g   Carbohydrate: .5 g

In a small bowl, break up the cheese with a fork and mash it lightly, leaving some small chunks. Add everything else but the chives and mix together thoroughly. Stir in the chives. Cover the bowl tightly and store in the refrigerator for up to 1 week.

PESTO

You may wish you had pasta for pesto, but that's no reason to forgo the pesto, which can go on fish, vegetables such as tomatoes and green beans, spaghetti squash and cheese – mozzarella and goat's cheese come to mind. The easiest way to make it is in a blender. **MAKES 12 SERVINGS**

> 8 fl oz olive oil
> 1 garlic clove, minced
> 2 oz basil leaves, preferably small
> 3 tablespoons pine nuts or walnuts
> 1 oz grated Parmesan cheese

Per Serving: Protein: 1.8 g   Fat: 20.7 g   Carbohydrate: .3 g

Put the olive oil in the blender and add everything but the cheese. Blend until smooth, scraping down the jar if necessary. Transfer the pesto to a bowl and stir in the cheese. It will keep for a couple of days in the refrigerator.

To Freeze Pesto

To freeze pesto, make it without the cheese and the garlic; add those when you defrost it.

TAPENADE

You can buy jars of tapenade in speciality markets, but this is so easy and so much more delicious that it's worth making just to have it around. It will keep, tightly covered in the refrigerator, for several weeks. You can also add little chunks of tuna to tapenade. **MAKES 8 SERVINGS**

6 oz imported black olives, such as kalamatas,
       pitted (see instructions page 162)
4 anchovy fillets
2 tablespoons drained capers
1 teaspoon Dijon mustard
1 tablespoon white wine vinegar
Optional: 2 or 3 drops pure orange oil, page 39

Per Serving: Protein: .8 g   Fat: 3.7 g   Carbohydrate: .8 g

Combine everything in the bowl of a food processor and blend briefly to combine.

OLIVADA (OLIVE PASTE)

You can of course buy this already prepared – for a price – but it's much more delicious if it's homemade. And it's so easy and so useful that it's worth doing.

What do you do with olivada once you've got it? It's terrific spread on salmon to be grilled (page 217), as the base for tapenade, spread on grilled aubergine or dolloped on devilled eggs. **MAKES 8 SERVINGS**

6 oz imported black olives, such as kalamatas

1 oz drained capers

2 small garlic cloves, minced

½ teaspoon dried thyme

1 or 2 tablespoons olive oil, as needed

1 or 2 drops pure lemon oil, page 39

Per Serving: Protein: .2 g   Fat: 5.2 g   Carbohydrate: 1.1 g

To pit the olives, put them on a cutting board and cover several at a time with the flat side of a large chef's knife or cleaver. With your fist, press down on the surface of the knife to open the olives. Once they're all open, just pull the stones out with your fingers.

Mix everything but the two oils together in the bowl of a food processor and process until you have a rough paste. Mix the olive oil with the lemon oil and add slowly with the motor running until you have a loose paste.

Cover the olivada tightly and store in the refrigerator, where it will keep for weeks.

Olivada With Tuna

Add a can of drained flaked tuna and mix well. Serve spread inside red pepper boats, page 297, as an hors d'oeuvre.

PEANUT BUTTER

Making your own can be as easy as dumping a can of roasted peanuts in the food processor and processing away. But the best peanut butter, like the best coffee, is freshly roasted, and it's a snap to make. Just find the freshest raw peanuts you can – you may have to mail-order them – and you're in business. You can make them without salt (not as good in my opinion) and without extra oil (it'll be more like peanut paste than peanut butter). You can leave the skins on if you like their slight bitterness. And of course you can roast them as much as you like, anywhere from lightly golden to dark gold – beyond that, they tend to taste a little bitter. Stop roasting a bit before you think the nuts are ready; peanuts cook from the inside out, so they continue to cook a bit after they come out of the oven. Like commercial peanut butter, a 2-tablespoon serving of homemade has 7.7g protein, 16g fat, and 4.8g carbs. MAKES ABOUT 8 OZ

1 lb raw peanuts, skinned
1 teaspoon salt
1 tablespoon peanut oil

Preheat the oven to 325°F/170°C/Gas Mark 3. Spread the peanuts out on a roasting pan or a baking sheet with shallow sides. Roast them for 20 minutes, stirring occasionally. You may want to roast them another 5 or 10 minutes; taste a peanut and see what you think. Once they're roasted, let the peanuts cool before proceeding.

Put half the peanuts and half the remaining ingredients in the bowl of a food processor. Process until creamy; remove the peanut butter to a storage jar and process the remaining batch.

Keep the peanut butter covered and in the refrigerator, where it will keep for at least 1 month.

Chunky Peanut Butter

Process a third of the peanuts first, just until they're roughly chopped. Set them aside and proceed with the rest of the peanuts. Mix the chopped peanuts into the finished peanut butter.

Nut Butters

Make almond, cashew and hazelnut butter the same way. Try mixing almonds and hazelnuts together.

CRANBERRY SAUCE

SERVES 12

1 lb cranberries
Zest of 1 orange, grated
Canderel to taste

Per Serving: Protein: .1 g   Fat: trace   Carbohydrate: 2 g

Put the cranberries in a heavy saucepan with 4 fl oz of water. Cook over medium heat until the cranberries pop and deflate into a sauce. Add the orange zest and the sweetener to taste. Cool to room temperature before serving.

Main Dishes

////

Main dishes are the easiest category of all to work with – protein, whether it's grilled, roasted, fried, sautéed, simmered or braised. Dinner may just be a burger and salad when you're rushed, but there are almost no limits on what you can improvise within the guidelines.

If you have a barbecue, summer turns out to be a series of great quick meals, punched up with sauces and salsas and served over salads, cooked greens or sliced tomatoes. To make life even easier, cook extras, both protein and vegetables, to make instant leftover dishes – steak salad, chicken salad, marinated roasted vegetables etc.

Cold-weather dishes such as stews and pot roasts are perfect for low-carb cooks, both for entertaining and home cooking. Favourite dishes like chilli and brisket turn up over and over on the list of what people would really like to eat. In traditional cooking, a lot of these dishes require potatoes or flour, but they're really not necessary – meat will brown perfectly well without flour as long as it's dry and you've salted it just before browning. For potatoes, try substituting turnips in a stew (old wrinkled ones will be bitter, so avoid those).

You may notice that contemporary recipes often use a lot of sugar for main dishes – a little sugar will most likely accomplish the same thing, and may be a good way to incorporate some sweetness into your meal without completely blowing it. A touch of brown sugar in a spice rub for meat, for instance, or a teaspoon of marmalade in a marinade may bring up new dimensions of flavour with minimal carb impact. But know your own limits: if a little sweetness will send you looking for more, just stick with the savoury dishes, which are entirely satisfying on their own.

CRISPY CHICKEN CUTLETS

A great way to cook boring chicken cutlets – this is a
lower-carb adaptation of the way Eileen Weinberg makes
them at her Times Square takeaway shop, Good & Plenty
To Go. Just remember to let the chicken sit for a couple
of hours before baking to develop flavour. SERVES 6

> **6 chicken cutlets**
> **Salt**
> **Pepper to taste**
> **8 oz mayonnaise**
> **½ teaspoon pure lemon oil, page 39, or 2 fl oz fresh
>   lemon juice**
> **2 garlic cloves, minced**
> **2 spring onions, chopped, including the firm
>   green**
> **Several sprigs fresh thyme, leaves only**

Per Serving: Protein: 14.6 g   Fat: 31.3 g   Carbohydrate: .6 g

Salt the cutlets lightly and rub the salt in on both sides.
In a small bowl mix together the remaining ingredients.
Spread the flavoured mayonnaise over the chicken, coat-
ing both sides, and let it marinate for 2 hours.

Preheat the oven to 350°F/180°C/Gas Mark 4. Put
the cutlets on a foil-lined baking sheet and bake for 20 to
30 minutes or until the outside is golden brown and
crispy. If they're not crispy, run them under the grill.

ONE-POT CHICKEN WITH RED PEPPERS

Make this dish when red sweet peppers are plentiful and cheap in the market, at the end of summer. You can use all chicken thighs – eight – if you'd rather. SERVES 4

3 tablespoons olive oil
4 chicken thighs
2 boneless chicken breasts, cut in half crosswise
Salt and pepper to taste
6 garlic cloves, chopped
1 medium onion, chopped
1 thick slice bacon, diced
2 red sweet peppers, seeded and chopped
1 bay leaf
1 teaspoon dried thyme
1 (14-oz) can diced tomatoes, including juice, or
    1 lb skinned, seeded and chopped tomatoes
Chopped parsley

Per Serving: Protein: 23.3 g   Fat: 24.3 g   Carbohydrate: 8.4 g

Heat the oil in a heavy pot, such as a Dutch oven. When it's hot, add half the chicken pieces and fry over medium heat until they begin to colour. Remove the cooked chicken and brown the remaining pieces. Add salt and pepper. Add the garlic and onion and cook until they begin to colour. Add the cooked chicken to the pot along with the bacon, peppers, bay leaf and thyme. Fry until the bacon begins to colour, then add the tomatoes and let it all bubble. Stir everything together, turn the heat down to low, cover and simmer for an hour or longer, until the juices are reduced to a sauce. If this hasn't happened after an hour and a half, remove the chicken and turn the heat up to thicken the sauce. Check the seasoning, remove the bay leaf and serve hot, sprinkled with parsley.

CHICKEN IN THE POT

This old French classic couldn't be easier or more comforting. Prep time is about five minutes, cooking time about an hour. You'll have lots of delicious chicken stock left over for making soup. This is basic; add mushrooms if you like. SERVES 4

> 1 (3½- to 4-lb) roasting chicken
> 1 (13½-oz) can chicken stock
> 1 chicken bouillon cube
> 1 fat leek, well washed and chopped
> 1 carrot, scraped and cut into large chunks
> 3 medium turnips, peeled and cut into large
>   chunks
> 2 celery sticks, chopped, plus a sprig of leaves
> Salt and pepper

Per Serving: Protein: 41.8 g   Fat: 20.8 g   Carbohydrate: 5.7 g

Rinse the chicken inside and out and put it in a Dutch oven or another heavy pot – about 10½ pints is the right size. Add the chicken stock, the bouillon cube, crumbled, and enough water to cover the chicken. Bring to a simmer and skim off the foam that rises to the surface.

Add the vegetables, tucking them in around the chicken. Cover the pot but leave the lid slightly askew. Cook at just below a simmer for 30 minutes, then turn the chicken so it will cook evenly. Cover again and cook for 30 more minutes.

Remove the chicken to a platter and keep warm under a loose covering of foil. Transfer the vegetables to a bowl. Skim the fat from the surface of the stock and strain the stock. Taste for seasoning.

Slice the chicken and place it in warm soup plates. Add salt and pepper to taste. Arrange the vegetables around the chicken and ladle about 4 fl oz of stock over the top.

The Bird

An unstuffed turkey can be cooked at a higher temperature (which makes for a juicier bird). Try this method, which is favoured by several prominent Manhattan restaurateurs. Cooking time will be 2½ to 3 hours.
SERVES 8

1 (12- to 14-lb) turkey, preferably fresh
1 lb sliced smoked bacon
1³/₄ pints turkey stock (made from giblets) or
        chicken stock
Salt and pepper to taste

Per Serving: Protein: 33.2 g   Fat: 5.6 g   Carbohydrate: 0 g

Rinse the turkey inside and out and place on a rack in a heavy roasting pan. Let the bird sit for several hours, covered with a kitchen towel, to come to room temperature.

Preheat the oven to 450°F/230°C/Gas Mark 8. Arrange the bacon slices over the turkey breast. Put the bird in the oven and roast for half an hour. Turn the heat down to 375°/190°C/Gas Mark 5 and remove the bacon to use for another purpose. Don't baste the turkey; just let it cook until done. (Use an instant-read thermometer to check: the inner fold of the thigh should be 165°.) If it begins to look perfectly brown too soon, cover the breast loosely with foil. When the turkey's done, remove it to a serving platter to rest for 10 minutes, tented with foil.

To make pan gravy, pour off all but 2 fl oz of the fat.

Add 1³/₄ pints of turkey or chicken stock to the pan and scrape up all the little bits. Put the roasting pan over medium heat and boil to reduce the juices by half, stirring frequently. Add salt and pepper to taste.

SAUSAGE STUFFING WITH NUTS

This stuffing seems more like a main course than a side dish. It harks back to the forcemeat stuffings of classic French cuisine that moistened the dry interiors of wild game birds. It's rich, dense and savoury – a little goes a long way, notes Suzanne Hamlin, who created it.

SERVES 4

2 oz pecan halves
2½ oz pine nuts
2 tablespoons olive oil
4 oz minced onion
8 oz bulk pork sausage
1 green sweet pepper, seeded and diced
½ oz minced parsley
2 tablespoons chopped fresh sage or thyme
        leaves, optional
¼ teaspoon freshly grated nutmeg
Ground black pepper to taste
2 large eggs

Per Serving: Protein: 14 g   Fat: 37 g   Carbohydrate: 7.6 g

Preheat the oven to 350°F/180°C/Gas Mark 4. Spread the pecans out on a baking sheet. Spread the pine nuts out on another baking sheet. Toast each batch of nuts for 5 to 8 minutes, until they begin to smell nutty and take on colour. Check the pine nuts frequently, since they can easily burn. Cool the nuts and break the pecans into large pieces.

In a large frying pan, heat the olive oil and add the onion. Cook for 2 minutes over medium heat. Add the sausage, breaking it up with the side of a spoon. Cook slowly until the sausage is browned.

Stir in the nuts and the remaining ingredients except the eggs. Whisk the eggs together lightly and combine with the sausage mixture. Transfer the stuffing to a greased 9-inch baking dish. Cover with foil and bake on the middle rack of the oven for 25 minutes.

What's Inside the Turkey?

Stuffing seems virtually synonymous with bread crumbs, so what's the alternative for the low-carb Christmas? Here are two options, all variations on real recipes that never had any bread in them to begin with. And they're both delicious.

SAUERKRAUT STUFFING

MAKES 8 SERVINGS, ENOUGH FOR A 12-LB TURKEY

4 bacon strips, diced
1 large onion, sliced thinly
1 lb sauerkraut, well rinsed and drained
1 teaspoon caraway seeds
1 tart apple, chopped
1 cup dry white wine
Pepper to taste

Per Serving: Protein: 1 g   Fat: 6.5 g   Carbohydrate: 13 g

In a large frying pan over medium heat, cook the diced bacon until it's golden. Add the onion and cook for 4 minutes longer. Add the sauerkraut, caraway and apple. Toss well and cook for 5 minutes. Add the wine and simmer for 5 more minutes. Season, drain off any extra liquid and stuff the turkey with the sauerkraut mixture. Roast as usual.

GINGERED WILD RICE STUFFING

Exotic and luxurious, this variation of a James Beard stuffing can be even more festive if you add ½ lb of chopped wild mushrooms, sautéed in butter until the liquid they release is reabsorbed.

MAKES ENOUGH FOR A 12-LB TURKEY; SERVES 9

10½ oz wild rice
1 rounded teaspoon salt
4 tablespoons butter
Turkey liver, chopped very finely
1 large onion, chopped very finely
3 oz very finely chopped celery and inner
      celery leaves
1 garlic clove, chopped very finely
1 oz chopped parsley
½ teaspoon dried thyme
½ teaspoon dried rosemary
½ teaspoon dried marjoram
Big pinch of ground ginger
Ground black pepper to taste
2 oz chopped walnuts

Per Serving: Protein: 1.6 g   Fat: 8.8 g   Carbohydrate: 12 g

Cook the wild rice: rinse the rice in a strainer in the sink. Pour 1¾ pints of cold water into a heavy saucepan, add the salt, cover and bring to a boil over medium heat.

Uncover and simmer for about 35 minutes or until the rice is just tender but still has lots of texture. Drain in a strainer over the sink and set aside.

Melt the butter in a wide frying pan and gently sauté the turkey liver until brown, about 4 minutes. Add the onion and celery and sauté for 4 more minutes, until the onion softens. Add the garlic, parsley, thyme, rosemary, marjoram and ginger. Stir well to combine.

In a mixing bowl, combine the rice and the seasonings. Mix in the nuts. Stuff the turkey just before roasting and close the cavity with a skewer.

GARLICKY BAKED CHICKEN

Throw this simple chicken dish together the night before
you plan to serve it, then just bring it to room temperature and tuck it in the oven when you're ready to eat.
You'll cut the carbs even lower if you use the lemon oil
instead of the fresh lemon juice. SERVES 4

> 1 tablespoon paprika
> Salt and pepper to taste
> 8 chicken thighs
> 3 garlic cloves, pressed
> 2 fl oz olive oil
> 3 tablespoons fresh lemon juice or ½ teaspoon
>   pure lemon oil
> Pinch of oregano

Per Serving: Protein: 31 g   Fat: 26.2 g   Carbohydrate: 1.7 g

Rub the paprika, salt and pepper well into the chicken
pieces. In a small bowl, mix together the garlic, oil and
lemon juice. Put the chicken in a glass or ceramic roasting pan and pour the marinade over it. Turn the chicken
with tongs to coat it completely, then cover and refrigerate overnight.

Bring to room temperature before baking. Preheat the
oven to 400°F/200°C/Gas Mark 6. Sprinkle the chicken
with oregano. Put the uncovered roasting pan with the
chicken in the oven and roast for 40 minutes, turning the
pieces once. Serve on a bed of watercress.

FRIED CHICKEN

There are several options here: you can use regular flour to dredge the chicken before it goes in the pot (which will cost you about 5 carbs per serving, not bad), you can use nut flour (about 3 carbs per serving, and a little expensive), or you can use ... pork cracklings! This sounds bizarre, but it's delicious – the chicken is incredibly crispy and you'll probably find everyone begging you for the recipe.

To make the pork cracklings stick, the secret is dipping the chicken first in a formula developed by San Francisco restaurateur Nancy Oakes: egg white and cream – another bizarre idea, but it works perfectly. SERVES 4

8 chicken thighs

1 tablespoon paprika

Salt and pepper to taste

Peanut oil or lard for frying, about 1¼ pints

3 large egg whites

3 fl oz double cream

1 teaspoon red hot sauce

1½ cups crumbled pork cracklings, page 43

Per Serving: Protein: 38.9 g   Fat: 33.6 g   Carbohydrate: .8 g

Several hours before you want to cook the chicken, rinse it well, trim off any odd bits, pat it dry and rub it with the paprika, salt and pepper. Set aside to season for 2 hours or refrigerate if it will be longer.

Heat the oil in a Dutch oven over medium heat. Meanwhile, whisk the egg whites in a bowl with the cream and the hot sauce. Put the crumbled pork cracklings in a soup plate. Using tongs, dip the chicken pieces first in the egg white mixture, then in the pork cracklings, coating well. When the oil reaches 370°F/190°C, it's ready for the chicken.

Fry the chicken pieces in two batches, cooking them 10 minutes on each side or turning them frequently, as you prefer. Don't let the temperature go over 375°/ 190°C. When the chicken pieces are done, remove them to a platter lined with paper towels and immediately salt and pepper them. Cook the second batch of chicken. Filter the oil through a coffee filter and refrigerate to use a second time.

ROAST CHICKEN WITH EGG STUFFING

This mother-and-child reunion dish is certainly unusual, but before you pass it by, try it; the stuffing is amazingly good, and you can play with the ingredients almost endlessly. Basically it's glorified egg salad, using one hard-boiled egg per pound of roast chicken. The recipe is Suzanne Hamlin's inspired response to the challenge of no-bread stuffing.

You can make the stuffing several hours ahead; just cover and refrigerate it until you're ready to cook the bird. For a 6-pound roasting chicken (cut recipe in half for a 3-pounder): SERVES 6

> 6 large hard-boiled eggs, chopped
> 1 cup finely chopped fennel or celery, plus a few
>   minced leaves
> 3 spring onions, including the firm green, in thin
>   rounds
> 2 oz mayonnaise
> Salt and lots of pepper to taste
> Optional: the chicken liver, cut in small pieces
>
> 1 6-lb roasting chicken
> 1 tablespoon extra-virgin olive oil

Per Serving: Protein: 35.3 g   Fat: 23.8 g   Carbohydrate: 1.5 g

In a mixing bowl, combine the eggs, fennel, minced leaves and spring onions. Stir in the mayonnaise and combine. Add salt and pepper and the optional liver and stir again to blend.

Stuff the chicken just before roasting. Rinse out the cavity and dry it well. Spoon in the stuffing and secure the opening to the cavity with a skewer.

Preheat the oven to 450°F/230°C/Gas Mark 8. Put the stuffed bird in a heavy roasting pan, breast up, and rub all over with olive oil. Slide the pan into the oven on the middle rack. After 10 minutes, run a spatula under the chicken and move it around a little so it doesn't stick. Roast until the leg wiggles easily and the juices run clear when you poke a cooking fork into the breast where it meets the leg. A 6-pound chicken will be done in about 70 minutes; a 3-pound bird takes 35 to 40 minutes. Let the cooked chicken rest for 10 minutes on a serving platter before slicing. To serve, spoon the stuffing onto plates and moisten with some of the cooking juices.

ASIAN ROAST DUCK

Duck always seems like a hassle, but this one is simplicity itself. Just remember to let it sit with its seasonings in the refrigerator for a couple of days so it will be crispy.
SERVES 2

> 1 (5-lb) duckling, neck and giblets removed
> Coarse salt and pepper to taste
> 3 garlic cloves, pressed
> 1 tablespoon 5-spice powder
> 1 orange, quartered
> 2 spring onions
> 2 tablespoons sherry
> Garnish: chopped spring onions

Per Serving: Protein: 21.5 g   Fat: 32.1 g   Carbohydrate: .5 g

Wash and dry the duck two days before you plan to cook it. Sprinkle the duck with salt and pepper, and rub it with garlic and 5-spice powder, all over and inside. Leave the duck unwrapped on a refrigerator shelf to dry out and season – this will make the skin crispy. Let it come to room temperature before cooking.

Preheat the oven to 375°F/190°C/Gas Mark 5. Prick the duck all over with a wire brush – but just the fat; don't pierce the flesh. Put the quartered orange and spring onions (bent) in the cavity. Put the duck on a rack in a shallow roasting pan and roast for 1 hour and 15 minutes. About halfway through the cooking, pierce the skin at the joint where the leg and breast meet on each side. Let the duck rest under tented foil for 20 minutes before carving.

Pour off almost all of the fat from the drippings and add 2 tablespoons of sherry to the drippings in the pan.

Scrape them up over medium heat until you have a little sauce; season to taste. Quarter the duck and serve with the pan sauce, with spring onions scattered over.

JERK TOFU

Keep jerk tofu around for a snack (let it marinate overnight) or serve it hot for dinner over a bed of stewed greens or stir-fried collard greens. This zesty tofu is based on an idea of soya queen Dana Jacobi.

SERVES 8 AS A SNACK, 4 AS A MEAL

> **1 lb extra-firm tofu, frozen, defrosted, sliced
>   lengthwise in quarters, and squeezed dry
>   (page 187)**
> **2 teaspoons jerk seasoning**
> **Olive oil for the frying pan**

Per main-course serving: Protein: 12.1 g   Fat: 1 g
Carbohydrate: 2.6 g

In a glass dish large enough to hold the tofu slices, smear half the jerk seasoning over the bottom. Add the tofu slices and cover them with the remaining jerk seasoning. Cover with plastic wrap and set aside to marinate overnight.

When you're ready to cook, scrape off the paste. Heat a heavy frying pan and add a spoonful of olive oil. When it's hot, drop in the seasoned tofu slices and cook them for 4 minutes on each side. Serve over greens or refrigerate to use as a snack.

Tofu Tips

This best of all the vegetable protein sources is a useful item to have on hand, even if you're not fond of tofu.

- To bring out its best, use extra-firm tofu and freeze it first, right in the packet, for at least 24 hours. Defrost, drain off the liquid, and either slice and squeeze out as much liquid as you can or crumble and squeeze. This extra step will give it a better texture and make it easier to work with. It will also save you the extra work of the elaborate pressing routine you'd need to use otherwise.

- Tofu can be added to soups and stews but it's much better if you sauté it in a little oil to crisp it first.

- Fried tofu is especially delicious – it gives the best texture and has a lovely golden colour. Take this additional step before you add tofu to a stir-fry.

The Stir-Fry

If you can manage to live without the rice, stir-fries offer the low-carb cook convenience, great taste and a chance to play in the kitchen. There are only a few rules. You don't even need a wok; you can use a large frying pan and just add a little more oil because the surface is wider.

Many stir-fry recipes use relatively high-carb ingredients – cornflour, sugar, oyster sauce, hoisin sauce. Skip the cornflour but go ahead and use a pinch of sugar; use just a little of the high-carb sauces. Use snow peas sparingly (pick up a few from the salad bar). Here are the basic points:

1. Cut the ingredients roughly the same size – diced, shredded, or sliced – and make sure they're dry.

2. Have everything ready at the edge of the stove. Stir-frying goes like lightning, so have your cooking shovel in hand, ready to stir and scoop.

3. Use the highest possible heat.

4. Heat the wok for ½ minute before adding peanut oil.

5. Add the oil in a circle around the edge of the wok.

6. The oil is ready when tiny bubbles form, wisps of smoke rise, and a piece of spring onion floats and sizzles when dropped in.

7. Add the meat, chicken or seafood and cook while stirring for a minute or two.

8. Add the vegetables and minced garlic, ginger and spring onions. Cook and stir for several more minutes – fewer for delicate things like asparagus, more for broccoli (steam it briefly in the microwave to speed things along, but be sure it's dry before you add it to the wok).

9. Add the seasonings: low-carb stir-fry sauce, or soy sauce and chilli oil, or five-spice powder, hot pepper flakes, mushroom soy sauce, rice wine vinegar, oyster sauce, hoisin sauce, pinch of sugar, etc. Mix well and cook for another minute.

10. Nuts should be crisped in the hot oil first, before you add any of the other ingredients, then set aside. Fold them into the stir-fry just before serving.

Using these basic ideas, play with ingredients you have on hand. It's almost impossible to come up with a combination that doesn't taste pretty good.

CURRIED TOFU

This light, zesty curry can be made in just a few minutes if you have the tofu ready – i.e. frozen, defrosted, drained and pressed (see instructions on page 187). It's another good reason to keep tofu in the freezer. SERVES 2

½ lb firm tofu, in 1-inch cubes
1 tablespoon peanut oil
1 small onion, sliced thinly
1 small green sweet pepper, sliced thinly
2 serrano chillis, seeded and minced
2 teaspoons curry powder
4 fl oz canned coconut milk
4 fl oz chicken stock
Salt to taste
1 oz chopped coriander leaves
3 tablespoons chopped roasted peanuts

Per Serving: Protein: 15.9 g   Fat: 26.5 g   Carbohydrate: 6.5 g

Press the tofu dry on paper towels. Heat the peanut oil in a large frying pan, and when it's hot add the tofu cubes. Sauté, turning frequently, until the tofu is golden brown. Add the onion and pepper and cook until they've wilted a little. Add the curry powder, the coconut milk and the chicken stock. Stir well to combine and add salt to taste.

Bring to a simmer and let the tofu cook for several minutes, until the sauce begins to thicken. Serve in soup plates garnished with the coriander and peanuts.

Two Great Feasts

Here are two informal but delectable meals to set out on great platters. They're both based on the traditional French grand <u>aioli monstre</u> of Provence – which features salt cod and a bevy of steamed vegetables to be consumed with generous amounts of intensely garlicky mayonnaise. Here, poached cod or snapper substitutes for the salt cod in the French version. There's also a Mexican version based on prawns, with a smoky chipotle pepper mayonnaise that's also very garlicky. Both versions can be served hot or at room temperature. Serve something refreshing – grapes, melon – for dessert.

THE FRENCH VERSION

Choose any or all of the vegetables listed below as well as some hard-boiled eggs. Steam the vegetables (except for the cherry tomatoes and peppers) earlier in the day and serve them at room temperature – or, if you prefer, reheat them for half a minute in simmering water.

Young turnips, peeled and quartered
Asparagus stalks, tough ends snapped off
Green beans, tailed
Cauliflower, cut into florets
Cherry tomatoes
Small courgettes, cut in half lengthwise
Red sweet peppers, thickly sliced
Small fennel bulbs, trimmed and quartered
The Garlic Mayonnaise, page 157

THE FISH

Have one fillet per person of cod or red snapper. Bring 1¾ pints of water to a boil with 1 garlic clove, a bay leaf and ¼ teaspoon salt. Reduce the heat to a simmer and add the fish. Turn off the heat and cover the pot; let it stand for 10 minutes or until the fish flakes. Remove fish from the pot with a slotted spoon and place on a platter. Surround with the vegetables and eggs and serve with a big bowl of aioli.

THE MEXICAN VERSION

Use the same vegetables as above, but instead of the white fish, use prawns. Add to the cooking stock a few peppercorns and some mustard seeds. Cook the shelled prawns just until they turn pink and begin to curl. Drain and set aside.

CHIPOTLE MAYONNAISE

2 garlic cloves, pressed
2 canned *chipotle chillis en adobo*, rinsed,
        seeded and minced, or 2 tablespoons
        chipotle purée, page 36
12 oz mayonnaise

Mix everything together in the food processor and serve in a bowl with the prawns, vegetables and eggs.

A LOT LIKE PIZZA

Next to pasta and bread, pizza is probably the most missed food on the low-carb diet. This ersatz pizza is built on a raft of tofu, which doesn't sound very appetizing, but actually you could get to love it. Vegetarians will obviously want to skip the pepperoni. SERVES 5

1 lb extra-firm tofu, frozen and thawed, page 187
Olive oil
Oregano
Salt and pepper
Pizza sauce (recipe follows)
Fresh basil leaves, optional
6 oz shredded mozzarella, or more to taste
Pepperoni slices, optional

Per Serving: Protein: 18.2 g Fat: 18 g Carbohydrate: 3 g

Carefully slice the tofu lengthwise into 5 slices. Place the slices on a double layer of paper towels and cover with another double layer. Gently press down on the tofu with your palms, trying to press out as much liquid as you can without breaking or crumbling the tofu.

Heat a tablespoon or two of olive oil in a nonstick frying pan over medium-high heat. Add the tofu slices and sauté for several minutes on each side until crisp. Remove the tofu to a baking sheet with a rim, spaced well apart. Sprinkle with oregano and salt and pepper to taste. Spread a couple of tablespoons of pizza sauce over the slices, add the basil leaves if using, and top with the cheese and pepperoni.

Run the tofu pizza under the grill just until the cheese is melted and golden.

Note that leftover pizza slices make a good snack —
reheat them in a toaster oven.

PIZZA SAUCE

SERVES 8

1 tablespoon olive oil
1 (14½-oz) can diced tomatoes
2 garlic cloves, pressed
Sprinkle of oregano
Sprinkle of ground red pepper (cayenne)
Salt and pepper to taste
Squirt of tomato concentrate from a tube (or 1 to 2
        tablespoons tomato purée)

Per ¼ cup Serving: Protein: .8 g   Fat: 3.5 g   Carbohydrate: 3.6 g

Heat the oil in a small frying pan over medium heat.
Add the tomatoes and garlic, sautéing until the tomatoes
begin to lose a little of their liquid. Add the remaining
ingredients and let the sauce cook down until almost
all the liquid is gone and the mixture is thick, about 5
minutes. If it's chunkier than you'd like, purée it in the
food processor.

The sauce will keep for several days in the refrigerator. To use after storing, drain off any liquid that's accumulated and heat briefly in the microwave.

AUBERGINE PIZZA

This dish lies somewhere between aubergine parmigiana and pizza. It's a layer of golden brown aubergine crust topped with pizza sauce and little bits of topping, so that every bite is a little different. You can get fancy and use bits of goat's cheese, drizzled with a little pesto, or just use cheese all by itself. SERVES 4

1 lb aubergine, peeled and cut into ⅓-inch slices
2 tablespoons olive oil
Oregano
Pepper
Salt to taste
2 oz pizza or pasta sauce, page 194
4 slices Genoa salami, quartered, or 8 slices
      pepperoni
1 thick slice fresh mozzarella, diced
2 pieces oil-packed sun-dried tomato, in bits
2 tablespoons grated Parmesan cheese

Per Serving: Protein: 2.8 g   Fat: 10 g   Carbohydrate: 6.1 g

Preheat the oven to 425°F/220°C/Gas Mark 7. Brush the aubergine slices lightly with olive oil on both sides and place them on a baking sheet in the oven. Bake for 10 minutes, turn and bake for 15 more minutes. The slices should be golden brown on both sides – if they're not, turn the lighter side down and bake for a few more minutes.

Fit the aubergine slices into a 10-inch pie plate with shallow sides. Cut extra pieces to fill in the blanks. Sprinkle the aubergine with oregano, pepper and a little salt, then spread the sauce thinly over the top. Scatter the salami, cheese and tomato bits evenly over the top and finish with a drift of the Parmesan cheese.

Grill the pie until the cheese is bubbly and beginning to brown.

FIVE-MINUTE CLAM STEW

This homey recipe is the invention of the late gastronome Roy Andries de Groot, who claimed to serve it several times a month. And why not? It's fast, it's made from staples and it's delicious. The canned baby clams from Thailand are particularly good. SERVES 4

8 tablespoons butter
3 (10-oz) cans minced clams
1 teaspoon thyme
4 drops hot pepper sauce
Dash of Worcestershire sauce
Salt to taste
2 pints light or single cream
½ lemon
Paprika
Finely snipped fresh dill
Finely snipped watercress leaves

Per Serving: Protein: 24.7 g   Fat: 49.8 g   Carbohydrate: 20 g

In a 3½-pint saucepan, melt all but 2 tablespoons of the butter over medium heat, but don't let it brown. Strain the clams through a sieve and reserve the clam broth. When the butter is melted, stir in the thyme, hot sauce, Worcestershire and salt. Cook for a minute, then add the clam broth and turn the heat to high, stirring occasionally until the mixture reaches a boil. Lower the heat and add the cream, stirring — be careful not to let the cream boil. When the cream is hot, add the clams, stir again, and cook for 2 minutes.

Ladle the stew into 4 heated bowls. Squeeze a little lemon juice into each bowl. Divide the remaining butter in quarters and drop a piece in the centre of each portion. Sprinkle a ring of paprika around the butter and add an outer ring of the snipped greens. Serve immediately.

Plain Green Wrapper

LETTUCE PACKAGES

Sometimes you just want something a little like a sandwich that's not just stuck on a cracker. It could be a tortilla, or it could be a leaf wrapper. If you remember the great little lettuce packages they serve in Vietnamese restaurants, it may not seem so strange to do just that: tuck your salad or sandwich filling into a lettuce leaf. This can be anything from tomato, mayonnaise and bits of bacon (BLT) to curried egg salad to chicken shreds with an Asian sauce. This idea comes from Martin and Sally Stone, who fill their leaves with bean concoctions – not on our diet, alas.

Here's how:

SERVES 1

**Large romaine leaves, iceberg lettuce leaves
or Savoy cabbage**

Per Serving: Protein: 0 g   Fat: 0 g   Carbohydrate: trace

Fill a large pan with water and bring it to a boil. Have a bowl of ice water ready to dunk the leaves as soon as they come out of the pan, with paper towels nearby to dry them. Drop a few leaves at a time into the pan and let them cook for just half a minute, then pull them out with tongs and send them to the ice water. Leave them there for a minute and then dry them well.

Have your filling ready. Put the leaf rib side down on a work surface and press down gently with your hand –

but you don't want the leaves to break. Put a mound of
the filling on the bottom half of the leaf and fold in the
two sides of the leaf. Roll up the leaf into a little package and put it on a plate seam side down. Repeat with remaining leaves and filling.

VINE LEAVES

These are now available in jars in most supermarkets.
You don't have to be traditional and stuff vine leaves
with a rice mixture. You can just give them a good rinse,
pull off the stems and tuck something interesting inside,
such as a finger of feta cheese. Add a little pepper and a
couple of drops of olive oil and wrap up the package.
You can either grill these or sauté them in a little olive
oil in a frying pan until the cheese starts to melt.

SALMON IN VINE LEAVES

This is New York chef Rozanne Gold's idea for baking
salmon fillets – delicious, and even better with a little
tapenade spread over the salmon before it's wrapped.
For each serving, use a 6-ounce salmon fillet and spread
it with 1 tablespoon of tapenade. Set aside to season for
2 hours. Wrap the fish in 2 rinsed and stemmed vine
leaves, tucking in the ends to make a tidy package. Preheat the oven to 450°F/230°C/Gas Mark 8. Put the
salmon packages in a baking dish filmed with olive oil.
Paint the tops of the vine leaves with a little more oil and
send them to the oven for 8 minutes.

TUNA WITH MINT, GARLIC AND SOY

Easy, unusual and versatile — you can either grill this tuna or barbecue it. The key thing is to salt it first for half an hour to bring out the flavour. SERVES 2

2 tuna steaks, 1 inch thick
Salt
Olive oil
1 garlic clove, minced
1 tablespoon soy sauce
1 tablespoon chopped mint
Lemon wedges

Per Serving: Protein: 34 g   Fat: 1.4 g   Carbohydrate: trace

Half an hour before cooking, rub the tuna steaks lightly with salt and olive oil and let stand. Mix together the garlic, soy and mint. Just before cooking, rub the seasoning into the steaks and either grill or barbecue for 2 minutes per side — the tuna should be rare. Serve immediately with lemon wedges.

OYSTER STEW WITH MUSHROOMS

You can buy the oysters already shelled; be sure to save
the liquid that comes with them. If they don't feel
smooth, they may still have some sand on them, so give
them a quick rinse.

If you have wild mushrooms, so much the better –
chanterelles, morels, they'd all be delicious with the oysters. And a big pinch of saffron added with the cream
will make the dish even better. SERVES 4

1 lb brown or white market mushrooms

3 tablespoons butter

1 shallot, minced

3 dozen shelled oysters, with their liquid

8 fl oz double cream

Salt and pepper

Chopped parsley to garnish

Per Serving: Protein: 10 g   Fat: 33 g   Carbohydrate: 9.7 g

Wipe the mushrooms clean with slightly damp paper
towels and chop them coarsely. Warm the butter in a
wide frying pan and when it's starting to sizzle, add the
shallot and mushrooms. Cook them over medium-low
heat, stirring several times, until the mushrooms begin to
reabsorb their juices, about 10 minutes. Set aside.

In a large saucepan, warm the oysters and their liquid
over medium heat uncovered for about 3 minutes or until
they just begin to curl – the edges will look like they're
starting to grin. Take out the oysters and set aside; let the
liquid continue to cook down until it's just a few table-
spoonfuls. Add the cream and cook for 5 minutes more,
then add the mushrooms and oysters. Heat for 2 more

minutes, add salt and pepper to taste, and serve immediately in soup plates with parsley scattered over.

BAKED SEA BASS

Start the sea bass a couple of hours before you plan to
cook it. It works equally well as a hot or a cold dish,
served with one of the seasoned mayonnaises in the
Sauces chapter (pages 147-165). SERVES 4

1 whole sea bass, about 4 lb

MARINADE
1 garlic clove, minced
½ teaspoon salt
Pepper to taste
2 tablespoons fresh lemon juice
4 fl oz olive oil
2 teaspoons dried oregano

Per Serving: Protein: 26.8 g   Fat: 9.9 g   Carbohydrate: 1.3 g

Put the fish on a piece of foil large enough to wrap
around it.

Make the marinade: in a small bowl, mash the garlic
with the salt and pepper. Add the lemon juice and whisk
in the olive oil and oregano.

Pour half the marinade over the fish and rub it in on
both sides. Wrap the foil closely around the fish and put
in the refrigerator to season for a couple of hours.

Preheat the oven to 350°F/180°C/Gas Mark 4. Open
the foil, pour the remaining marinade over the fish, and
seal the package again.

Set the fish package on a baking sheet and bake for 40 to 50 minutes, or until the flesh is opaque when tested with the point of a knife.

Remove the foil and serve the fish on a platter, hot or cold, or at room temperature, with a seasoned mayonnaise sauce.

NUT-CRUSTED SWORDFISH

You can use almost any kind of nuts here: almonds, walnuts, pecans or macadamia nuts. SERVES 4

4 (6-oz) skinless, boneless swordfish pieces
Olive oil
Salt and pepper
3 oz chopped nuts, with their skins
½ teaspoon dried thyme
5⅓ tablespoons butter, melted

Per Serving: Protein: 32.6 g　Fat: 29.6 g　Carbohydrate: 1.1 g

Preheat the oven to 450°F/230°C/Gas Mark 8.

Rub the fish all over with olive oil and sprinkle with salt and pepper. Set aside for 5 minutes to season.

Mix the nuts with the thyme and put on a plate. Put the melted butter on another plate. Dip the fish in the butter and then in the nut mixture, patting to be sure it sticks.

Put the crusted fish on a baking sheet and roast for about 6 minutes or until done.

Bringing up Flavour

When you're making very simple grilled or roasted meats and poultry and fish, it helps to bring out the natural flavours as much as you can. The best way to do this is with good old sea salt and its frequent companion, olive oil. Time is the secret ingredient.

- Fish steaks and fillets: rub fish all over with olive oil and sprinkle with salt. Let sit for at least 5 minutes to develop flavour.

- Steaks: Mediterranean cook Paula Wolfert films steak with olive oil, sprinkles it with coarse salt and refrigerates it uncovered overnight.

- Meat in general: presalting and letting the meat sit to develop flavour doesn't, as some cookbooks warn, make it less juicy – it just makes it more flavoursome.

- Pork: today's extra-lean pork often leaves a lot to be desired in the taste and juiciness department. Brining is San Francisco restaurateur Nancy Oakes's way around that problem. This is her formula: dissolve ½ cup of salt in 9 cups of hot water. Let the brine cool in the refrigerator and then add the pork, weighing it down so it stays submerged. Eight hours will do it. You can add flavouring ingredients like garlic, thyme, bay leaf, chillies, citrus zest, mustard, etc. Some pork comes already brined; check the label to be sure.

ROASTED SWORDFISH WITH HERBS

The fish roasts in the grill on a bed of herbs: rosemary,
sage, thyme – just one or all three if you have them.
SERVES 4

    4 (6-oz) pieces boneless, skinless swordfish
    Olive oil
    Salt and pepper
    4 sprigs rosemary
    4 sprigs sage
    4 sprigs thyme
    4 sprigs lemon thyme

Per Serving: Protein: 28.8 g   Fat:9.3 g   Carbohydrate: 0 g

Rub the fish all over with olive oil and sprinkle with
salt and pepper; set aside for 5 minutes to season.

Make 4 little beds of herbs for the fish on a baking
sheet, saving the lemon thyme to put on top. Arrange the
fish on top of the herbs and preheat the grill. Strip the
leaves of lemon thyme from the branches and distribute
the leaves equally over the swordfish pieces. Set under the
grill and roast until the fish is cooked; about 6 minutes.
It should be opaque when you test it with the point of a
knife.

NEW ORLEANS SPICY PRAWNS

These delectable prawns, served at Upperline restaurant in New Orleans, work as a first course or a small meal on its own. You can leave out the white pepper if you don't have any – or buy some; it has a distinct taste all of its own that works together with, not instead of, black pepper.

SERVES 2 AS A MAIN DISH, 4 AS A FIRST COURSE

1 lb medium prawns, shelled and deveined

MARINADE:
2 fl oz olive oil
1 teaspoon ground red pepper (cayenne)
1 teaspoon chilli powder
1 teaspoon ground cumin
½ teaspoon ground white pepper
Several grinds of black pepper

SPICY MAYONNAISE
8 oz Hellmann's mayonnaise
2 teaspoons chilli powder
1 garlic clove, minced

2 tablespoons butter
½ red onion, sliced
Salt to taste
Romaine lettuce to make a bed for the prawns

Per Serving: Protein: 46 g   Fat: 110 g   Carbohydrate: 3.9 g

Mix the prawns with the marinade ingredients in a bowl and let it sit for ½ hour. Meanwhile, stir the spicy mayonnaise ingredients together.

In a frying pan large enough to hold the prawns, melt the butter over high heat. When it's sizzling, toss in the prawns and the onion. Shake the pan and toss the prawns; they're ready when they're pink and they start to curl, in just a couple of minutes. Salt them and remove from the heat.

Arrange romaine leaves on individual plates and divide the prawns among them on top of the greens. Serve the mayonnaise on the side.

HOT PEEL-IT-YOURSELF
PRAWNS TWO WAYS

One of these recipes is genteel, the other gutsy – but both are to be eaten outdoors, on tables spread with newspaper or oilcloth. It's a good idea to serve small hot towels too (wring them out in hot water and steam them in the microwave).

PRAWNS WITH DILL BUTTER
SERVES 1

1 chopped garlic clove per person
Several peppercorns per person
⅓ lb medium prawns per person
2 oz butter per person
1 teaspoon minced fresh dill per person
½ teaspoon fresh lemon juice per person

Per Serving: Protein: 30.6 g   Fat: 46.6 g   Carbohydrate: 2 g

Bring a pot of water to the boil and add the garlic and peppercorns. Drop in the prawns and cook them just until they turn pink and curl. Remove immediately and drain.

Melt the butter and add the dill and lemon juice. Give each person a plate with prawns and a small bowl for the dill butter and let them peel their own.

NEW ORLEANS PRAWNS
SERVES 1

**2 teaspoons shrimp boil or seafood seasoning per
person
¼ lemon per person
⅓ lb medium prawns per person
Hot pepper sauce**

Per Serving: Protein: 30.6 g   Fat: 2.6 g   Carbohydrate: 2.2 g

Heat a pot of water to the boil and add the spices and
the lemon. Add the prawns and cook just until they turn
pink and curl. Remove immediately and drain. Serve with
more lemon wedges and pass a bottle of hot pepper
sauce.

MARGARITA PRAWNS

This has all those great margarita flavours, plus prawns and avocado and coriander. It takes almost no time to make; shelling the prawns is the only real work here.
SERVES 4

1 lb large prawns, shelled and deveined
2 tablespoons fresh lime juice
2 tablespoons butter
1 jalapeño pepper, seeded and minced
3 garlic cloves, chopped
1 teaspoon ground red pepper (cayenne), optional
Salt and ground black pepper
2 fl oz tequila
12 oz romaine lettuce sliced in ribbons
1 avocado, pitted, peeled and diced
2 tablespoons chopped coriander leaves

Per Serving: Protein: 23.9 g   Fat: 15 g   Carbohydrate: 5.5 g

Put the prawns in a bowl and pour the lime juice over; mix well. In a wide nonstick frying pan, melt the butter. When it's foaming, add the minced pepper and garlic and cook for 2 minutes over medium heat. Add the prawns and lime juice and the cayenne and cook for about 4 more minutes, or until the prawns are pink and start to curl. Add salt and pepper to taste, then pour in the tequila. Cook for 3 minutes more or until the liquid is reduced to a little sauce.

Serve the prawns on a bed of romaine ribbons, decorated with the avocado and sprinkled with coriander.

Crusty Coating for Roast Beef, Lamb or Pork

This extremely simple, extremely flavoursome crust from
Sally and Martin Stone has – amazingly – no bread
crumbs. First rubbing the meat with salt and dry mustard
dramatically improves the flavour.

SERVES 6

Beef, lamb or pork roast
Salt
2 teaspoons Colman's dry mustard

CRUST

2 oz Dijon mustard
2 garlic cloves, crushed
1 tablespoon soy sauce
1 tablespoon olive oil
1 tablespoon crumbled dried rosemary (for
        pork or lamb) or thyme (beef)

Per Serving: Protein: 0 g   Fat: 2.2 g   Carbohydrate: .3 g

Salt the roast all over and rub with the dry mustard.

Mix the crust ingredients together and cover the
roast with it. Let it stand for 2 hours to develop flavour.

Cook the roast on a rack in a roasting pan as explained below.

BEEF AND LAMB

SERVES 6

For a 3-pound roast of top sirloin or a 4-pound half leg of lamb, preheat the oven to 500°F/250°C/Gas Mark 10. Roast the meat for 15 minutes, then lower the heat to 350°/180°C/Gas Mark 4 and roast for 45 minutes more, or until the internal temperature is 130° for medium rare. Let the meat rest on a serving platter for 20 minutes under tented foil before carving.

PORK

Per Serving: Protein: 104 g   Fat: 49.5 g   Carbohydrate: 0 g

For a 5-pound boneless pork loin, preheat the oven to 400°F/200°C/Gas Mark 6. Roast the pork for 15 minutes, then lower the heat to 350°/180°C/Gas Mark 4 and cook for about 1 hour or until the internal temperature is 300°F/145°C. Let roast rest on a serving platter for 20 minutes under tented foil before carving.

LIME SCALLOPS

Simplicity itself – and you can either grill or barbecue these zesty skewered scallops. Be sure to let them marinate for at least a couple of hours to develop flavour. The recipe comes from Eileen Weinberg of Good and Plenty to Go in Manhattan. SERVES 6

> 2 lb sea scallops
> 4 fl oz fresh lime juice
> 3 tablespoons olive oil
> Dash of salt and pepper to taste
> 2 limes, in wedges, for skewering
> Garnish: 2 tablespoons chopped coriander

Per Serving: Protein: 25.3 g   Fat: 8.2 g   Carbohydrate: 4.2 g

Mix the scallops, lime juice, oil and seasonings together in a glass bowl and let marinate for at least 2 hours. When you're ready to cook, thread the lime wedges and scallops on skewers – 1 lime wedge, then 3 scallops, etc. Cook under the grill or over a charcoal barbecue for 5 or 6 minutes, turning once. Serve the skewers sprinkled with the coriander.

WHOLE POACHED SALMON

For a summer dinner party, there are few dishes so elegant as the whole salmon – and you make it completely ahead. The only catch is that you need a fish poacher, bought or borrowed. The classic accompaniment is green mayonnaise (add 1 oz each finely chopped parsley, watercress and spinach to a cup of mayonnaise. Snip in a few chives and add lemon juice and zest to taste.) Serve the salmon on a bed of greens, simply decorated with lemon slices and sprigs of dill – or make a dramatic presentation by layering unpeeled cucumber slices like scales (or tiles) over the fish. SERVES 10

1 whole salmon, about 10 lb, gutted
3 celery sticks, cut up
3 carrots, cut up
1 medium onion, cut up
2 tablespoons salt
1 teaspoon pepper
½ oz chopped parsley
15 fl oz dry white wine
Garnishes: lemon slices, dill sprigs, cucumber
    slices

Per Serving: Protein: 45.2 g   Fat: 24.6 g   Carbohydrate: trace

Place the salmon on the rack in the fish poacher. Arrange the vegetables around it, add salt and pepper and parsley, and pour over the wine. Add cold water to cover the fish. Put the lid on the poacher and set it over 2 burners on medium heat. Once the liquid comes to a boil, turn the heat down to a gentle simmer. Set the timer for 25 minutes.

Check the fish with a fork next to the backbone; probably it won't be done for another 15 minutes or more, but you want to catch it when it comes away from the bone and is an opaque pink, not red. Remove it from the poacher while still on the rack. Once it's cool, remove the skin on the top side – or you can cover and refrigerate it, then remove the skin before serving, even the next day. Garnish as desired (see above) and serve with green mayonnaise.

The One and Only Tortilla

One of the frustrations of low-carb eating is all the great Mexican food you can have – guacamole, salsa, carnitas – without being able to eat the high-carb tortillas that make it so satisfying. But the La Tortilla Company has come to our rescue with a whole-wheat, oat-fibre tortilla that costs just 3 carbs. It's a little chewy, especially if you fry it, but this tortilla works for everything from chips to wrap-up sandwiches to quesadillas (just slice some cheese and put it between two of these tortillas, grill on both sides in a dry frying pan, and you've got a terrific snack). A few leaves of coriander strewn over the cheese will taste even better.

I like this tortilla so much I use it for breakfast toast as well – I just throw it over a gas burner until it begins to puff up, then turn it briefly so it has a few toasty marks. You can also heat the tortillas in a microwave or a frying pan.

These tortillas are available from the Low Carb Megastore (page 390). You can order in bulk and freeze them. Be sure you get the Fat-Free tortillas; there are several others with higher carb counts.

CITRUSY SALMON PAVED WITH
POPPY SEEDS

Oven-roasting fillets of salmon is a deliciously quick way
to deal with them. You can ask the fishmonger to remove
the skin from the fillet if you like. Give each fillet a quick
feel before you begin the recipe to be sure there are no
lurking tiny bones. SERVES 4

> 4 salmon fillets, about 6 oz each
> Juice of ½ Valencia orange
> Juice of ½ lemon
> Salt and pepper to taste
> 3 tablespoons melted butter
> 1½ teaspoons poppy seeds

Per Serving: Protein: 33.8 g   Fat: 26.8 g   Carbohydrate: 4 g

In a shallow glass dish large enough to hold the fillets
in one layer, mix the juices and the salt and pepper. Lay
the salmon over the mixture, then turn to coat both sides.
Let the fillets season for 20 minutes at room temperature,
turning once.

Line a shallow baking dish with aluminium foil and
brush it with 1 tablespoon of the butter.

Preheat the oven to 425°F/220°C/Gas Mark 7.
Arrange the fillets in the foil-lined dish, then press the
poppy seeds into the top sides. Roast the salmon for 8 to
12 minutes, depending on thickness. When it's done, heat
the remaining butter and drizzle over the fish.

SALMON WITH GARLIC CREAMED SPINACH AND CHANTERELLES

This is a variation of a very simple but very delicious meal that appears on the spring menu at Gramercy Tavern in New York City. It's the perfect solution to the entertaining problem – both elegant and easy, and no one would ever guess that it's diet food. If you can't find chanterelles, other wild mushrooms work well here.

SERVES 4

4 salmon steaks, about 1 inch thick
Olive oil for grilling the salmon
Salt and pepper to taste

GARLIC CREAMED SPINACH
3 lb fresh spinach, cleaned and stemmed
2 fl oz double cream
1 garlic clove, chopped
2 tablespoons butter
Salt and pepper to taste

½ lb chanterelles or other wild mushrooms,
     trimmed and cleaned
2 tablespoons butter

Per Serving: Protein: 34 g   Fat: 29.4 g   Carbohydrate: 5 g

Rub the salmon all over with olive oil and salt and pepper it generously. Set aside to season on a grill pan.

Make the spinach: in a large pot over medium heat, wilt the spinach in just the water that clings to it after rinsing. Meanwhile, put the cream and garlic in a small saucepan and heat gently for a few minutes, then turn off the heat and let the garlic steep in the cream. When the spinach is done, still bright green but entirely wilted, drain it well in a colander and squeeze the moisture out of it.

Now cook the chanterelles: melt the butter in a frying pan over medium heat and add the mushrooms when it's sizzling. Cook the mushrooms until they have a golden brown edge, about 5 minutes.

Meantime, slide the salmon about 4 inches under the grill – turn the steaks after 5 minutes; they will be done in about 5 more minutes. Test with the point of a knife. Heat the spinach and add the butter, salt and pepper. Just before serving, heat the cream and add it to the spinach, mixing in well until it almost disappears. Reheat the mushrooms and serve at once.

BOWL OF RED

Yes, chilli is on this regimen, as long as you don't toss in beans or a lot of tomatoes. That means Texas-style chilli, which is probably the best anyway. You can add chopped canned chilli peppers to the brew or toss in cubes of plain old green sweet pepper. But here's the basic chilli.

SERVES 8

2 tablespoons olive oil (or lard, if you have it)

1 large onion, chopped

3 garlic cloves, crushed

4 lb boneless chuck steak, in dice or ground for chilli

4 oz ground mild red chilli, preferably New Mexican

2 tablespoons ground cumin

2 teaspoons dried oregano

1 tablespoon sweet paprika

1 teaspoon cider vinegar

4 fl oz strong brewed coffee or 1 tablespoon instant coffee powder

1⅓ cups water as needed

1 tablespoon salt

½ teaspoon ground red pepper (cayenne), optional

2 tablespoons cornmeal

Optional garnishes: sour cream, chopped coriander, grated cheese

---

Per Serving: Protein: 38.6 g   Fat: 64.5 g   Carbohydrate: 6.6 g

In a large Dutch oven, heat the oil and cook the onion over medium heat until it's soft. Add the garlic and cook until it's transparent. Add the meat in several batches along with the chilli, cumin, oregano and paprika. Remove each batch to a large bowl as it's cooked. Stir and cook until the meat is browned, then put all the meat back in the pot and add the vinegar, coffee and enough water just to cover the meat. Add the salt and cayenne and stir well.

Cover the pot and cook over low heat for 2 hours, stirring from time to time. Remove the lid and simmer for a final hour. Skim off any fat on the surface. Add the cornmeal and stir in well. Cook for 15 more minutes and serve hot in deep bowls. Garnish with sour cream, chopped coriander and grated cheese.

MEAT LOAF

This is more or less Mom's meat loaf, with a couple of twists. To save carbs on ketchup, you can spread a little salsa over the meat loaf before you add the bacon strips. Drain it in a strainer first to get rid of extra liquid.

SERVES 6

 2 sesame rye crackers, crushed in a food processor
 3 fl oz milk
 3 lb meat loaf mix (veal, pork and beef), at room
        temperature
 2 tablespoons butter
 1 large green sweet pepper, minced
 2 oz chopped onion
 6 large garlic cloves, pressed
 1 teaspoon dried thyme
 2 large eggs, lightly beaten
 1 tablespoon Worcestershire sauce
 1 teaspoon paprika
 1 teaspoon salt
 1 teaspoon ground black pepper
 2 tablespoons ketchup or strained salsa
 4 bacon strips

Per Serving: Protein: 41.8 g   Fat: 74.7 g   Carbohydrate: 5.9 g

Preheat the oven to 350°F/180°C/Gas Mark 4. Put the cracker crumbs in a small bowl and pour the milk over them. Set aside.

Put the meat in a large bowl. Melt the butter in a frying pan and add the green pepper and onion. Cook gently for about 3 minutes or until soft, stirring often. Add the sautéed pepper and everything else but the ketchup and bacon to the meat and mix it lightly with your hands.

Put the meat loaf into a glass loaf pan and spread the ketchup over the top. Lay the bacon over the ketchup and bake the loaf for 1 hour and 15 minutes. Remove from the oven and let it rest for 10 minutes before slicing.

ITALIAN MEAT LOAF

No Italian would recognize this version of meat loaf, but it's a good choice for a dinner party, since it's sort of festive – for meat loaf. You could make one long skinny meat loaf, but you risk having the centre undercooked, so it's safer to form two loaves and bake them in a roasting pan. SERVES 10

1 tablespoon olive oil
1 medium onion, chopped
3 lb meat loaf mix – pork, beef and veal
1 teaspoon salt
½ green sweet pepper, chopped finely
½ red sweet pepper, chopped finely
4 oz crushed garlic croutons
2 teaspoons Italian mixed herbs (oregano, basil,
        rosemary, thyme)
½ teaspoon ground black pepper
½ teaspoon paprika
2 large eggs, lightly beaten
4 fl oz single cream
3 oz prosciutto, diced

6 oz diced fresh mozzarella
4 oz grated Swiss cheese
½ oz grated Parmesan cheese

Per Serving: Protein: 34.7 g   Fat: 39 g   Carbohydrate: 4.2 g

Preheat the oven to 350°F/180°C/Gas Mark 4. In a small frying pan over medium heat, warm the olive oil and add the onion. Sauté the onion until it's soft.

In a large mixing bowl, mix all the remaining ingredients (saving out a handful of the cheeses) together with your hands, including the onions. Mould the mixture into two loaves and place them in a roasting pan or another pan large enough to hold them with no crowding – there should be a couple of inches between the meat loaves and the edge of the pan so that they'll brown all over.

Bake the meat loaves for 45 minutes, then scatter the remaining cheese over the tops. Return to the oven until an instant-read thermometer registers 310°F/155°C at the centre of the loaves, anywhere from 15 to 45 minutes more. Let the meat loaves rest for 10 minutes before serving.

Meat Loaf With Tomato Sauce

You can serve the meat loaves with a fresh tomato sauce like the one on page 194.

BEEF STROGANOFF

This dish is so seldom served anymore that it's hard to re-member how delicious it is. Instead of the classic noodles, serve the stroganoff on a nest of cauliflower purée, page 302. SERVES 4

1½ lb boneless sirloin or fillet of beef

Salt and pepper

4 tablespoons butter

1 tablespoon safflower oil

1 medium onion, sliced thinly

½ lb portobello mushrooms, sliced

1 tablespoon instant flour to thicken

8 fl oz beef stock

2 tablespoons Dijon mustard

8 oz sour cream

Garnish: 1 tablespoon each chopped dill and chives

Per Serving: Protein: 80.8 g   Fat: 73.3 g   Carbohydrate: 7.7 g

Slice the meat across the grain into thin (⅓-inch) strips. Season the meat with salt and pepper and let it stand for 2 hours to develop flavour.

In a wide nonstick frying pan, melt 2 tablespoons of the butter and the oil together; when they stop foaming, sear the beef over high heat, a few strips at a time, till browned on both sides but still rare. Remove the meat to a platter as it browns. Add the onion and sauté over medium heat until browned, about 5 minutes. Add the mushrooms and sauté until the liquid they give off disappears. Transfer all the vegetables to the platter with the meat.

In the same pan, melt the remaining 2 tablespoons of butter over medium heat. When it starts to bubble, add the flour, stirring it with a wooden spoon until it foams. Keep stirring for a minute or two, then add the stock and keep stirring until the sauce thickens. Add the mustard and stir until smooth.

Return the meat and vegetables to the pan, toss well and simmer in the sauce for several minutes to heat through. Add the sour cream and heat it but don't let it boil. Serve the stroganoff with fresh dill and chives scattered over the top.

THAI-STYLE BEEF CURRY

This spicy dish is Thai convenience food — all you need is
a little 4-ounce can of red curry paste (at Asian food
stores) and canned coconut milk, and you're set. Especially good served over a bed of buttered spinach. If the
beef cubes are larger than 1 inch, the cooking time will
be much longer. SERVES 6

> 2 tablespoons peanut or olive oil
> 3 tablespoons Thai red curry paste, see page 39
> 1 pint canned coconut milk
> 2½ lb beef chuck steak, cut into 1-inch cubes
> Salt and pepper to taste
> Garnish: ½ oz chopped coriander

Per Serving: Protein: 61 g   Fat: 35 g   Carbohydrate: 3 g

In a Dutch oven, warm the oil over low heat and add
the curry paste. Stir and cook over low heat for about 5
minutes, then add the coconut milk. Cook and stir for another 3 minutes. Add the beef, bring to a boil and lower
the heat to a gentle simmer. Cook covered for 1½ to 2
hours, stirring from time to time. By now the meat
should be soft; if it's not, continue cooking until it is.
Raise the heat and cook uncovered for another 10 minutes or until the sauce is thick. Taste for seasoning and
serve garnished with the coriander.

OVEN BARBECUED BRISKET

This is one of the few non-sweet barbecue sauces in the world, teamed with brisket to make a no-mess, deeply flavoursome dish to feed a crowd. Although this is a cinch to make, it's better if you start a day ahead. The deckle, or front-cut brisket, is especially delicious. SERVES 12

SAUCE

½ (10-oz) bottle Worcestershire sauce

1 fl oz hot pepper sauce

4 tablespoons butter

7 fl oz cider vinegar

½ tablespoon ground black pepper

1 teaspoon salt

1 teaspoon red pepper flakes, optional

4 garlic cloves, pressed

1 large beef brisket, about 4 lb

Per Serving: Protein: 45 g   Fat: 19.3 g   Carbohydrate: 4.7 g

Combine all the sauce ingredients in a saucepan over medium heat and bring to a boil. Stir well, lower the heat and simmer for 10 minutes, stirring frequently. Let cool and refrigerate until ready to use – the sauce will keep for several days.

The day before you plan to serve the brisket, rub it with additional salt and the garlic paste, put it in a foil-lined roasting pan, and cover it generously with sauce. Pull the foil up over the meat to make a tightly sealed package. Let it sit overnight in the refrigerator to develop flavour.

In the morning, let the brisket come to room temperature, about 2 hours. Preheat the oven to 325°F/170°C/ Gas Mark 3. Roast the brisket, still in its package, for 5 hours, then remove it from the oven. Pull the foil down around the meat and return it to the oven to brown. It should absorb most of the sauce and be perfectly done in another half hour.

BEEF BURGOYNE

This American version of Boeuf Bourgogne is a good oven stew that requires minimal effort. You may need more wine and consommé, so have them ready in case the stew begins to dry out. It will take about 3 hours altogether.
SERVES 6

> 2½ lb round steak or London broil, in 2-inch
>   cubes
> 2 tablespoons olive oil
> 3 garlic cloves, chopped
> ½ teaspoon dried thyme
> 3 bay leaves
> Salt and pepper to taste
> 4 fl oz canned consommé, or more as needed
> 4 fl oz Burgundy, or more as needed
> 6 whole shallots, peeled
> 1 lb market mushrooms, trimmed and quartered
> 1 tablespoon instant flour to thicken, if needed

Per Serving: Protein: 61 g   Fat: 22.7 g   Carbohydrate: 5.6 g

Preheat the oven to 350°/180°C/Gas Mark 4. Trim off any extra fat and pat the meat dry with paper towels. Heat the oil in a Dutch oven and, when it's hot, brown the meat all over. Add the garlic, thyme and bay leaves. Add salt and pepper, the liquids and the shallots. Bring to a boil on top of the stove, cover the stew and bake in the oven for 1 hour.

Check for moisture; if the stew seems to be getting dry, add another 4 fl oz of each of the liquids. Add the shallots. Bake for another 1½ hours.

Half an hour before serving, add the mushrooms and stir in well. If, when the stew is ready, the sauce seems thin, remove the solids and sprinkle 1 tablespoon of instant flour over the sauce. Cook the sauce down a bit over high heat and add the meat and shallots back in to reheat before serving.

A DIFFERENT HAM

Instead of the usual overly sweet ham glazed with more sugar, try this winey, orangey one. It's hard to say how much of the marinade penetrates the meat, but even if all of it did, you wouldn't have a lot of carbs here.

A partially cooked ham will be tastiest, if you can find one. Remember to start the ham 4 days ahead. SERVES 25

> 1 large ham, about 12 lb
> 1 bottle Sauterne
> 2 large Valencia oranges, quartered
> 6 dried hot red chilli peppers
> 20 peppercorns
> ½ oz chopped celery leaves
> 1 oz chopped parsley
> Cloves to decorate the ham

Per Serving: Protein: 40 g   Fat: 76 g   Carbohydrate: 4 g

Four days ahead, marinate the ham: stab it all over many times with the tines of a cooking fork or a skewer, then put it in a large plastic bag. Add the wine, which should completely cover the ham when the bag is closed; if it doesn't, add water to the right level. Squeeze the juice from the oranges over the ham and add in the orange skins. Add everything else except the cloves. Seal the bag tightly with a rubber band and refrigerate until ready to bake.

Four days later, remove the ham from the bag and place it on a rack in a roasting pan. Let it come to room temperature, about 4 hours. Preheat the oven to 300°F/150°C/Gas Mark 2. Strain the marinade to use for basting the ham. Score the ham and decorate with the cloves. Put the ham in the oven and bake until it reaches a temperature of 300°F/150°C for an uncooked ham, 260°F/130°C for precooked, basting frequently with the wine sauce.

CARNITAS

This is a wonderful idea for a casual dinner party. If you haven't had these succulent little morsels of pork tucked into tortillas with guacamole, pickled onions, salsa, sour cream, etc., you'll find them addictive. In Mexico they're cooked in giant cauldrons of lard. Here there are two ways of cooking them: California gardener/cook Sylvia Thompson's oven-roasted carnitas are juicy and delicately flavoured; Chicago restaurateur Rick Bayless fries his in lard, which is truer to the Mexican style, and ends up with a crunchy exterior. Either recipe can be made with pork shoulder or country-style ribs, which are actually butterflied chops from the blade end of the pork loin. For a crowd, use the oven-roasted ones.

If you're dieting, you may want to tuck your carnitas into large romaine leaves instead of tortillas. Or slice some ribbons of romaine as a bed for a carnitas salad, add the other elements and toss them together lightly with your fork.

However you cook them, serve the carnitas with bowls of:

Guacamole, page 59
Table salsa, page 153
Chunks of tomato
Pickled onions, page 240
Sprigs of coriander
Tortillas and/or large romaine leaves
Lime wedges to squeeze over the meat

FRIED CARNITAS
This pork-fried-in-lard is still politically incorrect, but it's certainly delicious and it's definitely low-carb.

Ideally you'll use a good brand of lard or render it yourself – but in the real world all we can usually get is the
supermarket standard, and it will be fine. You can filter
the used lard through a coffee filter and save it to use
several times again. SERVES 4

> **2 lb pork shoulder or country-style ribs**
> **1 lb lard**
> **2 fl oz water**
> **Salt to taste**

Per Serving: Protein: 62 g   Fat: 30 g   Carbohydrate: 0 g

Cut the meat into ½-inch-thick strips, 4 inches long
and 2 inches wide. In a Dutch oven or kettle, melt the
lard over a low flame. Add the pork and the water. Simmer the meat gently, uncovered, for about 40 minutes,
until it's tender, turning from time to time. Raise the
heat to medium-high and fry the pork for about 10 minutes, until it's golden brown and crunchy all over. Drain
on paper towels and salt well; serve immediately.

OVEN-ROASTED CARNITAS

This slow-cooking recipe takes about 5 hours to cook, although it's simplicity itself. Just be sure to start early.

SERVES 8

> **4 lb bone-in pork shoulder or country-style ribs**
> **Beef stock and water, mixed half and half, to**
> **   barely cover meat (about 7 fl oz stock)**
> **1 tablespoon peppercorns**
> **1 bay leaf**
> **1 teaspoon thyme**
> **1 teaspoon oregano, preferably Mexican oregano**
> **3 garlic cloves, chopped**

Per Serving: Protein: 63 g   Fat: 30 g   Carbohydrate: 4 g

Preheat the oven to 350°F/180°C/Gas Mark 4. In a Dutch oven (or a Mexican cazuela, if you have one), cover the meat with the mixed stock and water and add the other ingredients. Roast the meat uncovered for 2½ hours, adding more liquid if necessary. Drain off the stock and reserve.

Lower the heat to 275°F/140°C/Gas Mark 1 and cook for another 2 hours or more, moistening with stock from time to time. The meat is done when it's just about falling off the bone. When ready to serve, chop the meat roughly and reserve the rib bones for some private nibbling – just reheat them in a 350°F/180°C/Gas Mark 4 oven.

PICKLED ONIONS

Start these at least half an hour before you plan to use
them. SERVES 8

> **2 red onions, thinly sliced**
> **2 fl oz mild vinegar**
> **1 bay leaf**
> **Several peppercorns**
> **½ teaspoon oregano, preferably Mexican**

Per Serving: Protein: .4 g   Fat: trace   Carbohydrate: 2.4 g

Place the onion rings in a colander in the sink. Heat a
kettle of water to a boil and pour it over the onions. Put
the onions in a glass bowl and add cold water just to cover
them. Add the remaining ingredients and stir gently to
mix. Cover and refrigerate until ready to serve.

ROAST LEG OF PORK WITH SAGE AND GARLIC

This is a great alternative to smoked ham for a party and it's one of the simplest things in the world to cook. Meat guys Bruce Aidells and Denis Kelly came up with the sage-wrapped garlic clove idea. If you like the crispy pork skin – cracklings right on the meat – get the leg a day or two ahead and let the skin dry out while the pork rests uncovered in the refrigerator. If you don't want the skin, just strip it off and rub the pork all over with mashed garlic, sage, salt and pepper. Whole legs of pork (also called fresh hams) aren't always available, so you may have to order yours ahead. The roast will be easier to slice if you have the butcher remove all but the shank bone and tie the roast. Plan on about 5 hours cooking time.

SERVES 12

> **1 whole leg of pork (10 to 14 lb), boned and tied**
> **12 garlic cloves**
> **36 fresh sage leaves, optional**
> **Salt and pepper to taste**

Per Serving: Protein: 112 g   Fat: 94 g   Carbohydrate: 1 g

Preheat the oven to 450°F/230°C/Gas Mark 8.

If you're cooking the pork with the skin on, puncture it lightly all over with the tines of a cooking fork. Make 36 slashes in the skin all over the leg. Cut the garlic cloves lengthwise in thirds. Tuck a sage leaf around each sliver and push the slivers into the slashes in the pork.

If you're cooking the pork without the skin, remove it and rub the roast with a paste made from the garlic, sage and salt and pepper.

Place the pork on a rack in a roasting pan in the lower third of the oven and roast for 20 minutes. Lower the heat to 325°/170°C/Gas Mark 3 and roast for 3 more hours, turning the pork from time to time so that it roasts evenly – don't baste it. Check the temperature with an instant-read thermometer. The pork will be ready when it reaches 300°F/145°C, which will probably take another hour or so. If the skin isn't crispy, roast it at 450°F/230°C/Gas Mark 8 for another 10 to 20 minutes. Let the pork rest loosely covered with foil for 20 minutes before serving. To serve, cut off the skin, for serving in small pieces, then slice the pork.

SOUTHERN-STYLE SMOTHERED PORK CHOPS

This is the sort of good home cooking that got lost in the low-fat era. But it's still delicious, a wonderful way to cook today's extra-lean pork, which otherwise isn't too flavoursome. Collard greens are just right with the chops.

Look for chops that have some fat around the edges; cut it off, dice it and sauté over medium heat in a heavy frying pan for about 20 minutes or until the fat has cooked off and you have just the cracklings left. Drain them well, salt them, and you have a great cook's treat.

SERVES 4

    2 tablespoons flour
    Salt to taste
    ½ teaspoon pepper
    4 shoulder-cut or loin pork chops with bone,
        about 6 oz each
    2 tablespoons vegetable oil or rendered pork fat,
        see above
    1 medium onion, sliced thinly
    8 fl oz hot chicken stock

Per Serving: Protein: 25 g   Fat: 23.7 g   Carbohydrate: 5.3 g

Preheat the oven to 350°F/180°C/Gas Mark 4. On a plate, mix 1 tablespoon of the flour, the salt and the pepper. Dredge the chops in it on both sides. In a heavy frying pan over medium-high heat, brown the chops in the oil or fat until they're golden brown. Put them in a baking dish to fit snugly.

In the same pan, sauté the onion slices over medium heat, stirring frequently, until they're soft and golden.

Add the remaining tablespoon of flour and stir in thoroughly. Continue stirring and add the hot stock slowly. Cook for about 3 minutes more or until the sauce begins to thicken. Pour the sauce over the chops, cover tightly with foil and bake for 20 minutes.

Remove the foil and bake for another 20 minutes.

RUBBED RIBS

These are incredibly easy and incredibly good. Of course it's even easier to cook the ribs rubbed with just salt and pepper – good, too. The recipe calls for a few spice-rack items you may not have, but it's worth getting them to make these ribs often. Baby back ribs seem like a nice idea, but they don't have as much flavour as the big guys.
SERVES 4

THE RUB
1 tablespoon paprika
½ teaspoon chilli powder
½ teaspoon ground black pepper
1 teaspoon celery salt
1 teaspoon lemon pepper seasoning
¼ teaspoon garlic powder
¼ teaspoon onion powder
¼ teaspoon ground red pepper (cayenne)
½ teaspoon salt

THE RIBS
1 tablespoon dark brown sugar
2 racks meaty spareribs
Olive oil

Per Serving: Protein: 51.4 g   Fat: 53.6 g   Carbohydrate: 3 g

To make the rub, mix everything together in a bowl and store in a screw-top jar. Makes almost 3 tablespoons, enough for 2 racks of ribs.

Make the ribs: mix the sugar into the spices. Rub the ribs with olive oil, then rub them all over with the spice rub. Preheat the oven to 325°F/170°C/Gas Mark 3. Put the ribs in a baking dish and cover loosely with foil. Bake for 2 hours, then remove the foil and continue baking until the meat is just ready to pull away from the bone, about another half hour.

LAMB SHANKS

This is one of those comfort foods that need to be served on a bed of cauliflower purée. SERVES 4

> **3 tablespoons olive oil**
> **4 lamb shanks**
> **6 garlic cloves, sliced**
> **1 teaspoon dried rosemary**
> **Salt and pepper to taste**
> **1 tablespoon balsamic vinegar**
> **4 leeks, including some of the green, sliced thickly**
> **8 fl oz dry red wine**

Per Serving: Protein: 30 g   Fat: 24.5 g   Carbohydrate: 7 g

Preheat the oven to 350°F/180°C/Gas Mark 4. Heat the olive oil in a Dutch oven over medium-high heat until hot. Add the lamb shanks and brown thoroughly all over – you may have to do this in batches. Add the remaining ingredients and stir to combine, then cover the pot and put it in the oven for 2 hours or until the meat is almost falling off the bone.

LAMB YOU CAN EAT WITH A SPOON

This old French recipe produces incredibly succulent, velvety lamb pieces that literally fall off the bone. It's a wonderful dinner-party dish – by the time your guests arrive, the entire house will be perfumed with amazing fragrance. Because it takes up to seven hours to cook, all the work is done ahead.

For your carb-eating guests, you can include lots more carrots and onions and toss in some potatoes, as Suzanne Hamlin does in her version of this dish. SERVES 8

    1 (7-to-9-lb) leg of lamb
    Salt and pepper
    2 medium onions, quartered, or 4 fat shallots,
            peeled
    2 carrots, cut in large pieces
    1 whole head of garlic, cloves peeled and halved
    6 bay leaves
    1 bunch fresh thyme or 1 tablespoon dried thyme
    2 bottles red wine – rioja or Chianti
    4 turnips, peeled and quartered
    Optional: 4 medium potatoes, peeled and
            quartered

Per Serving: Protein: 60 g   Fat: 37.2 g   Carbohydrate: 5.4 g

Measure your pan before you buy the lamb; it should be a large heavy-lidded casserole, 14 × 11 inches, or a large roasting pan with a cover. If the lamb won't fit in the pan, have the butcher crack the shin bone and just tuck it up along the side of the lamb.

Preheat the oven to 425°F/220°C/Gas Mark 7 and put the rack at the lowest level.

With a sharp knife, cut away most of the fat on the lamb. Sprinkle the lamb with salt and pepper and rub it into the meat.

On the bottom of the pan, make a nest of the onions, half the carrots, half the garlic, half the bay leaves and half the thyme. Put the lamb on top. Put the pan in the oven and roast uncovered for 20 minutes, then lower the heat to 300°/150°C/Gas Mark 2. Remove the roasting pan from the oven, pour the wine over the lamb, and add the rest of the ingredients except the turnips and optional potatoes.

On the stovetop, bring the ingredients to a boil, then cover and return to the oven. Cook for 2 hours, then turn the lamb over and add the turnips. (Add potatoes at this point if you're using them.) Cook for another 2 hours, checking from time to time to see that the vegetables are cooking evenly – move them around with a spoon.

Check to see how the lamb is cooking – when it's done, it will fall off the bone when you pierce it with a fork. A large leg may take 6 hours or more, however. If the lamb is done and it's nowhere near serving time, just leave it on top of the stove and reheat gently when you're ready for it.

Using two large serving spoons, remove the lamb and vegetables to a serving platter and cover with foil to keep warm. Skim the fat from the cooking liquid. Pour all the liquid into a saucepan and boil it down over medium-high heat for about 20 minutes, until the sauce is thick. Serve the sauce on the side with the lamb and vegetables.

LEG OF LAMB WITH A TAPENADE CRUST

You can make this Provençal-style roast with its heady aromas using either a half leg of lamb – the shank end will be the meatiest – or a whole leg. The tapenade recipe makes enough for a whole leg. Let the lamb come to room temperature for several hours before roasting. The longer it sits under the crust, the more flavoursome it will be.

There are two versions of the tapenade: a classic one with real anchovy fillets and pitted olives, and a no-fuss version with olive paste and anchovy paste.

SERVES 10 (WHOLE LEG)

TAPENADE:

3 oz pitted imported black olives or olive paste

1 large garlic clove, pressed

2 teaspoons drained and rinsed capers

2 anchovies or 2 teaspoons anchovy paste

¼ teaspoon dried rosemary, crushed

1 tablespoon fresh lemon juice

½ teaspoon Dijon mustard

Olive oil as needed (for the pitted olives)

Lots of freshly ground pepper

THE LAMB

1 whole leg of lamb or 1 shank half leg, at room
     temperature

Salt

Per Serving: Protein: 61 g   Fat: 38.7 g   Carbohydrate: .7 g

For pitted olives and anchovy fillets: in the food processor, blend the olives, garlic, capers, anchovies and rosemary until almost smooth. Add the lemon juice, mustard and a little oil to moisten. Season with lots of pepper.

For olive paste and anchovy paste: blend all the ingredients together in a small bowl with a fork.

Trim the fat from the lamb. Rub the lamb with salt and cover it with the tapenade paste; place it on a rack in a roasting pan to season for 2 hours.

Preheat the oven to 350°F/180°C/Gas Mark 4. Roast the lamb for 20 minutes to the pound, or until it reaches an internal temperature of 260°F/130°C for medium rare. Remove from the oven and let sit under a tent of foil to reabsorb the juices for 20 minutes before carving.

MIDDLE EASTERN AUBERGINE BAKE

The minced lamb at the supermarket is often very cheap
– and loaded with fat. This is a good way to use it, since
you can cook the lamb and drain off almost all the fat before adding it to the dish. It's worth making extra oven-
roasted aubergine so you can toss this dish together for a
week-night meal. Leftovers are delicious. SERVES 4

1 medium aubergine, oven-roasted (page 275)
1 tablespoon olive oil
2 oz diced onion
2 garlic cloves, pressed
¾ lb minced lamb
1 teaspoon ground cumin
¼ teaspoon cinnamon
1 teaspoon sweet paprika
¼ teaspoon chilli powder
Salt and pepper to taste
1 (14½-oz) can diced tomatoes, including juice
1 oz crumbled feta cheese
½ oz grated Parmesan cheese

Per Serving: Protein: 18.7 g   Fat: 27.8 g   Carbohydrate: 9.7 g

Prepare the aubergine and set aside. Preheat the oven
to 375°F/190°C/Gas Mark 5. In a large frying pan, heat
the olive oil and when it's hot, add the onion. Sauté the
onion until it's soft, then add the garlic and sauté for
another minute. Remove the onion mixture to a bowl
and return the pan to the heat.

Crumble the lamb into the hot pan and sauté until it's
beginning to brown. Pour off any fat that's accumulated
and add the spices and salt and pepper. Stir well and sauté

until the lamb is completely brown. Return the onion mixture to the pan and add the tomatoes. Let simmer until most of the juices have evaporated.

In a large gratin dish, make a layer of aubergine slices. Cover with half the lamb mixture and crumble feta cheese on top. Add another layer of aubergine slices and the remaining lamb mixture. Sprinkle the top with the Parmesan.

Bake for 30 minutes, or until the cheese is melted and golden brown.

BASIC QUICHE

This is about as simple as it gets. All you need is an 8-inch quiche pan and you're in business. SERVES 6

Butter for the quiche pan
6 large eggs
8 fl oz double cream
Salt and pepper to taste
4 oz grated cheese – Swiss, Gruyère, Cheddar etc.

Per Serving: Protein: 12.9 g   Fat: 16.3 g   Carbohydrate: 2.4 g

Preheat the oven to 350°F/180°C/Gas Mark 4. Have ready a buttered quiche pan.

Beat the eggs in a bowl with the cream and salt and pepper. Add the cheese, mix well and pour into the quiche pan. Bake for 40 minutes or until golden brown on top. Serve hot or warm or at room temperature.

Bacon or Ham Quiche: add 4 oz of crisp bacon bits or diced ham.

Spinach Quiche: add 8 oz of cooked, squeezed-dry chopped spinach with a little freshly grated nutmeg.

FRIED EGGS WITH CHEESE

This is instant dinner for four. Use another serious hard cheese if you don't have pecorino or pepato, a delicious peppered sheep's cheese. SERVES 4

> **2 tablespoons butter**
> **4 thick slices pecorino or pepato cheese**
> **4 large eggs**
> **½ teaspoon salt mixed with ½ teaspoon ground cumin or chilli pepper or a combination**

Per Serving: Protein: 10.3 g   Fat: 15.7 g   Carbohydrate: .6 g

Heat the butter in a wide nonstick frying pan over medium heat. When it's melted, add the cheese slices and cook them until they begin to bubble, in just a few minutes.

Crack an egg on top of each cheese slice, lower the heat and partially cover the pan. Cook gently until the whites are set and the yolks are opaque. Carefully lift out the cheese slices with a spatula and dust the tops with the spicy salt.

MIDDLE EASTERN EGGS

These are delicious scrambled eggs with a cumin-chilli-coriander combination which can go either way.

SERVES 4

> 2 tablespoons butter
> 2 spring onions, including the firm green, sliced
> 1 green chilli, seeded and minced
> 1 teaspoon ground cumin
> 8 large eggs, beaten with salt and pepper to taste
> 2 tomatoes, seeded and cut into small cubes
> 1 tablespoon chopped coriander
> Hot pepper sauce, optional

Per Serving: Protein: 12.2 g   Fat: 16.7 g   Carbohydrate: 4.2 g

Melt the butter in a large frying pan over medium-high heat, and when it's foaming add the spring onions, chilli and cumin. Sauté until the spring onions are soft. Add the eggs and tomato pieces and scramble together with the onions and chilli. Just before serving, stir in the coriander and add the hot pepper sauce. Decorate the platter with more sprigs of coriander.

GREEN CHILLI SOUFFLÉ

A delectable casserole – but you don't have to peel any
peppers and it goes together in just a few minutes. If you
want this dish hotter, add a minced seeded jalapeño in
with the cheese. It's easier to arrange the chillis if the
sides of the dish slope a bit – a Mexican cazuela is perfect.

SERVES 6

> 2 tablespoons butter for the dish
> 4 (4-oz) cans whole peeled chillis
> 8 oz Muenster or jack cheese or a mixture,
>   shredded
> ½ lb ham, diced
> 8 large eggs
> 1 pint double cream
> 1 teaspoon salt
> 1 teaspoon ground black pepper

Per Serving: Protein: 27.2 g   Fat: 59 g   Carbohydrate: 4.6 g

Preheat the oven to 350°F/180°C/Gas Mark 4 and
butter a casserole with sloping sides or a soufflé dish.
Line the dish, bottom and sides, with the chillis (these
will form a crust when the soufflé is cooked). Make a
layer of the cheese and then of the ham. Beat the eggs well
in a bowl and add the cream, salt and pepper. Mix well,
then pour into the dish.

Bake the soufflé for 40 minutes or until the top is
golden brown and the centre is cooked. Serve immediately.

THE FRITTATA

If you've ever struggled with flipping an omelette or served one that looked hilarious, the frittata's for you. Some people flip frittatas too, but there's an easier way: just cook the eggs in the frying pan on top of the stove until they're set on the bottom, then run them under the grill to cook the top.

You can make a little sauce for the frittata by sizzling some sherry vinegar with butter in a small frying pan; you can treat it like pizza and add everything you've been missing in pizza, you can slice a wedge in half horizontally and make a frittata sandwich, or you can just have a frittata snack with leftovers. Frittatas work for breakfast, lunch and dinner, and they're ready in minutes. You can crumble up tofu and add it, you can make them with Egg Beaters if you're a cholesterol-phobe – they're just about perfect.

All you need is a 10-inch nonstick ovenproof frying pan and some vegetable to tuck into the frittata – let's say it's chopped mushrooms. It could also be courgettes (3 small) with some torn basil leaves tossed in. You can also make a larger frittata with 6 eggs. SERVES 4

> 4 extra-large eggs
> Salt and pepper to taste
> 2 tablespoons olive oil or butter
> 9 oz chopped mushrooms
> 1 oz grated Parmesan

Per Serving: Protein: 10.3 g   Fat: 15.6 g   Carbohydrate: 3 g

Using a fork, mix the eggs in a bowl with the salt and pepper. Heat the oil or butter in a 10-inch ovenproof frying pan and add the mushrooms. Cook until the mushrooms are soft. Pour the eggs over the mushrooms.

Cook the frittata over medium heat until the bottom is set. Sprinkle the cheese over the top, then run it under the grill until golden brown. Serve hot, warm or at room temperature.

Pizza Frittata

Just before the frittata goes under the grill, add 2 fl oz pizza sauce over the top, pepperoni slices, 3 oz shredded mozzarella and a sprinkle of oregano

---

Per Serving: Protein: 8 g   Fat: 12.8 g   Carbohydrate: 1.4 g

---

Broccoli Frittata

Dice 3 oz of cooked broccoli and 2 oz of roasted red peppers (from a jar) and scatter them over the eggs in the frying pan. Crumble 2 oz feta cheese on top.

Per Serving: Protein: 8.3 g   Fat: 13.5 g   Carbohydrate: 3.4 g

---

Side Dishes

In ordinary cookbooks, the side dishes are often heavy on the starch — potatoes, rice and other grains, beans — but here they're mostly vegetables. Some of the dishes feature ingredients from the hero-vegetable category in the next section, but they're highlighted here because they're so useful. Others are moving in the direction of the starchy dishes — spaghetti squash, for instance, and the turnip gratin, which so closely mimics a luscious potato dish. And there's one lone grain — or rather, grass: wild rice, which has so much fibre that it sneaks in under the wire here.

Dishes from other sections can come in under the side-dish umbrella, too; some first courses can turn into side dishes, and even some main courses can too, such as a skinny sliver of quiche. If you're serving guests, the easiest way to make it a feast is to increase the number of side dishes. This is a perfect way to include beetroot, for instance, a relatively low-carb vegetable that not everyone loves (see the recipe on page 294).

Remember that purées of cauliflower and broccoli will go a long way towards reminding you of mashed potatoes, and potato skins will make up for almost everything you're missing about potatoes. And take another look at turnips — sweet-young-thing turnips with purple shoulders are just delectable, cooked and mashed with cream and interesting seasonings like ginger and mace. Turnips need a little sweetness, and the sweet spices fill that role.

Finally, don't be afraid to mix vegetables – broccoli and cauliflower seem made for each other, but try spinach with courgettes, green beans with red peppers, cauliflower with everything. For more ideas, get some great vegetable books: Bert Greene's *Greene on Greens* is a good place to start, as is Marian Morash's *The Victory Garden Cookbook* and, for exotica, Elizabeth Schneider's *Uncommon Fruits and Vegetables*. The happier you are with the vegetables you're eating, the easier it will be to stay on the low-carb regimen long-term.

ASPARAGUS WITH ZESTY HERBS

The intensely green herb sauce in this recipe seems to intensify the fresh spring quality of asparagus. You can make the asparagus ahead and just put the sauce together at the last minute. SERVES 6

3 lb asparagus

ZESTY HERB SAUCE
10 basil leaves
4 watercress sprigs plus more for garnish
5 large mint leaves
Small handful of parsley
1 tablespoon chopped chives
½ teaspoon coarse salt
¼ teaspoon pepper
2 tablespoons fresh lemon juice
3 fl oz extra-virgin olive oil

Per Serving: Protein: 0 g   Fat: 12.3 g   Carbohydrate: 4.4 g

Snap the ends off the asparagus spears at the point where they break naturally. Rinse them and tie them together loosely in bundles; cook in a saucepan full of boiling salted water with the tips standing above the pot. Test for doneness after 6 minutes; they should be al dente. Have ready a bowl of cold water in the sink and plunge the spears into it to keep their colour and stop the cooking. Drain on paper towels and set aside on a serving platter to come to room temperature.

Put the herbs in a blender, then add the salt and pepper. Blend for a second, then add the lemon juice. Pour in the oil in a trickle while the blender is running on low speed. Shortly before serving, pour the sauce over the platter of asparagus and garnish with watercress sprigs.

WILD RICE

Wild rice is expensive, both in money and carbs — 3 oz will cost you 15 grams of carbohydrates. But as grains go, that's almost nothing, and for a dinner party wild rice is a perfect choice, festive and delicious.

You can take the carbs down even further by mixing in 6 oz of chopped mushrooms sautéed with 2 slices of bacon, diced, plus 1 minced garlic clove, 1 teaspoon of Worcestershire sauce, salt and pepper and ½ teaspoon of grated lemon zest. Stir into the rice just before serving. Wild mushrooms would of course be even better.

For a sweeter take on wild rice, sauté 2 oz of chopped pecans in a tablespoon of melted butter. Remove the nuts when they're golden and add another tablespoon of butter. When the butter foams, add 4 sliced spring onions, including the firm green, and sauté until just beginning to wilt. Fold the nuts and spring onions into the hot cooked rice along with a teaspoon of minced orange zest. SERVES 6

7 oz wild rice

1⅓ pints water

1 teaspoon salt

½ teaspoon fresh lemon juice

2 tablespoons melted butter

Per Serving: Protein: trace   Fat: 3.6 g   Carbohydrate: 5.1 g

Put the wild rice in a strainer and rinse well under cold running water. Meanwhile, heat the water in a saucepan until it boils. Add the salt, the lemon juice and — slowly, in a steady stream — the wild rice. Let the rice boil gently over moderate heat for 35 to 40 minutes, until it's just tender; test a grain or two to see. When it's done, drain it in a sieve and return it to the hot pan. Cover and let sit for 5 minutes, stirring once or twice, to dry thoroughly. Add the melted butter and serve right away.

Roasted Vegetables

The Italians have always loved roasting vegetables, but it took Barbara Kafka, author of <u>Roasting: A Simple Art</u> (Morrow, 1995), to show us the full range of possibilities, from cabbage to – of all things – cucumbers. Kafka roasts almost all vegetables at 500°/250°C/Gas Mark 10 on the upper rack of the oven. She slicks them with fat – olive oil is the obvious choice – and puts them in a close-fitting pan. Add a pinch of dried herbs to the oil and perhaps a minced clove of garlic. Halfway through the cooking turn the vegetables so they'll cook evenly. When they're browned and done, add salt and pepper and perhaps a splash of balsamic vinegar.

Mixed roasted vegetables is an even better idea. Cut the vegetables in roughly 2-inch pieces and cook them according to the times listed below. To serve 6, use 3–4lbs of vegetables and put them in one layer in a medium-sized roasting pan with 3 tablespoons of herbed olive oil. Toss well and send to the oven, adding the more tender vegetables later according to the time chart.

30 MINUTES
Leeks, cut in 1-inch lengths

20 MINUTES
Courgettes, cut in 1-inch lengths
Medium-sized shallots
Small aubergines, quartered

15 MINUTES
Portobello mushrooms
Sweet peppers, cut in 2-inch chunks
Broccoli florets, including a piece of the peeled stem
Cherry tomatoes

COURGETTE PASTA

A dish similar to this has been on the menu at New York's Union Square Café for years – people love it, and not because they're avoiding pasta. Try the same technique and top the courgettes with pesto sauce. SERVES 2

    4 small courgettes
    2 tablespoons olive oil
    1 large garlic clove, pressed
    1 (14½-oz) can diced tomatoes
    1 teaspoon oregano
    Salt and pepper
    ½ lb cooked Italian sausage links, cut up
    Several leaves of fresh basil, torn
    1 oz grated Parmesan cheese

Per Serving: Protein: 20.7 g   Fat: 36.8 g   Carbohydrate: 11 g

Slice the unpeeled courgettes into ribbons, using a vegetable peeler and turning the squash as you go. Put 1 tablespoon of the olive oil in a saucepan over medium heat; when it's warm, add the pressed garlic. Sauté briefly, then add the tomatoes and oregano. Let the sauce simmer uncovered for a few minutes.

Meanwhile, heat the remaining tablespoon of oil in a wide frying pan; when it's hot, add the courgettes. Stir for several minutes until the courgettes are soft and the edges are clear. Add salt and pepper to taste, then mix in the sauce. Add the sausage and stir well. Stir in the basil and transfer to a serving dish. Scatter the Parmesan over the top.

COURGETTE PANCAKES

These delicious morsels should always be served immediately. SERVES 4

> **6 oz grated (on the largest hole) courgette**
> **Salt**
>
> BATTER
> **1 large egg, lightly beaten**
> **1 teaspoon water**
> **2 tablespoons grated Parmesan cheese**
> **1 tablespoon flour**
> **Lots of pepper**
> **4 basil leaves, snipped, optional**
>
> **1 tablespoon butter**
> **1 tablespoon olive oil**

Per Serving: Protein: 2.5 g   Fat: 8.4 g   Carbohydrate: 2.5 g

Put the shredded courgette in a colander in the sink and salt it lightly. Mix in the salt with your hands and leave the courgette to drain for 30 minutes. Squeeze out all the juices and blot the squash dry with paper towels.

In a large bowl, combine the batter ingredients and whisk until smooth. Mix in the courgette.

In a nonstick frying pan (or use a griddle), melt the butter and oil together over medium heat until foaming. Drop the batter by tablespoons into the pan and cook over medium-high heat until brown. Turn and brown the other side. Pile the pancakes on a platter, salt lightly and serve.

CUMIN AND COURGETTE PANCAKES WITH SALSA

These make a great little side dish. If you can't find masa harina (which you should keep in the freezer) you can use cornflour (made with ground, dried corn), which isn't much easier to find. If you can only find cornmeal, use that and add a beaten egg to the mixture. SERVES 4

2 medium courgettes, shredded
¼ cup masa harina, cornflour or cornmeal
⅛ teaspoon salt
⅛ teaspoon ground cumin
2 tablespoons olive oil
4 oz salsa

Per Serving: Protein: .5 g   Fat: 7.2 g   Carbohydrate: 7.2 g

In a bowl, mix the courgettes with the masa, salt and cumin – use your hands.

Heat the olive oil in a nonstick frying pan over medium-high heat. Meanwhile, make 12 little pancakes with the courgette mixture. When the oil is hot, add the little cakes, just a few at a time, and sauté them until they're golden on both sides. Repeat with the remaining pancakes, and keep the cooked ones warm on a platter under foil.

Serve the pancakes with the salsa.

SPAGHETTI SQUASH WITH
ROASTED PECANS

The point of this squash isn't its wonderful flavour – it has
hardly any – it's the crisp texture and the novelty of having squash turn into pasta right before your eyes. This
recipe is for a celebration dish, but spaghetti squash is
also good treated like pasta: just add a lot of butter, cheese
and salt and pepper. SERVES 6

> 1 spaghetti squash
> 6 tablespoons butter
> 1 teaspoon dark brown sugar
> 2 oz roasted pecans, chopped (page 48)
> ½ teaspoon cinnamon
> Salt and pepper to taste

Per Serving: Protein: .7 g   Fat: 20.6 g   Carbohydrate: 9 g

Preheat the oven to 350°F/180°C/Gas Mark 4. Prick
the squash in several places so it won't explode and set it
on a baking sheet in the oven for 1 hour. Remove it and
let it cool enough to handle.

Cut the squash in half lengthwise and remove the seeds
and stringy bits. Using a fork, gently pull the strands of
squash apart and lift them out of their shell. You can pile
them into a bowl and refrigerate until ready to assemble
the dish.

In a large frying pan, melt the butter and add the
brown sugar and the squash. Cook until heated through,
stirring gently. Add the remaining ingredients and stir
well. Serve immediately.

SUMMER SQUASH

This simple green and yellow dish tastes best when little
garden squash are in the market and basil is plentiful. But
you can also make it in other seasons and use other seasonings, such as oregano and parsley. SERVES 3

>   1 tablespoon butter
>   1 tablespoon olive oil
>   3 small squash, courgette and crookneck, grated
>   About 8 basil leaves, snipped
>   Salt and pepper to taste

Per Serving: Protein: 0 g   Fat: 8.3 g   Carbohydrate: 2.6 g

Melt the butter with the oil in a wide nonstick frying
pan. When it's foaming, add the squash and cook slowly,
while stirring frequently, over medium heat for about 8
minutes, or until just softened. Stir in the basil and salt
and pepper. Serve immediately.

FRIED PEPPERS

These succulent strips of red pepper don't need peeling and they store well in the refrigerator. Put them on an antipasto platter, serve them with a lunch buffet, or team them with grilled sausages. SERVES 4

1½ lb red sweet peppers
3 fl oz olive oil
Salt to taste

Per Serving: Protein: 0 g   Fat: 18.5 g   Carbohydrate: 7.6 g

Cut the peppers in half, seed them, and cut them in long ½-inch strips. Warm the oil in a large heavy frying pan over medium heat and add the peppers, skin side down. Cook without stirring for 7 minutes, then turn the pepper strips and cook them until they're soft. Remove from the pan with a slotted spoon and sprinkle with salt to taste. Serve hot or at room temperature, or store in a bowl covered with the oil from frying. Seal tightly and refrigerate. Bring to room temperature before serving.

CAPONATA

This pungent vegetable mélange can become addictive.
It's good with grilled chicken or meat and makes a great
lunch along with celery, cheese and hard-boiled eggs. It
also keeps for a week in the refrigerator. The recipe
comes from Roman cook Jo Bettoja. SERVES 6

2 medium aubergines, unpeeled

Coarse salt

2 canned Italian plum tomatoes, drained and seeded

2 large sweet peppers, 1 red and 1 yellow

2 medium courgettes

2 medium white onions

1 tablespoon rinsed capers, dried

3 oz pitted green olives

1 bay leaf

Pepper to taste

2 fl oz white wine vinegar

1 teaspoon sugar

4 fl oz plus 1 tablespoon extra-virgin olive oil

Per Serving: Protein: .1 g   Fat: 23.3 g   Carbohydrate: 9 g

Cut the aubergines into 1-inch cubes and place them
in a colander. Sprinkle with salt and toss. Weight the
aubergines with a heavy can on top of a plate and let drain
for 1 hour. Rinse and dry thoroughly with paper towels.

Purée the tomatoes and set aside.

Preheat the oven to 350°F/180°C/Gas Mark 4. Oil a
small roasting pan.

Halve the peppers, remove the seeds, and cut the peppers into 1-inch squares. Cut the courgettes into ¼-inch
rounds. Slice the onions thinly.

Put all the vegetables in the roasting pan along with the capers, olives and bay leaf. Sprinkle with salt and pepper.

Combine the vinegar and sugar in a saucepan; heat until the sugar dissolves. Pour the vinegar over the vegetables, then add the oil and mix thoroughly. Bake uncovered for 1½ hours, turning every 30 minutes. Serve at room temperature.

BAKED AUBERGINE

This recipe from Roman cook Jo Bettoja is a delicious way to cook garden-fresh aubergine, which doesn't require salting. If all you have is big-old supermarket aubergine, peel it and salt the slices (leaving them to drip in a colander in the sink) for half an hour before patting dry and baking. Leftovers are equally good – just store them in the refrigerator and bring to room temperature before using. SERVES 6

> **4 fl oz extra-virgin olive oil**
> **2 lb aubergine, in ½-inch slices**
> **Salt to taste**
> **2 tablespoons fresh lemon juice**
> **1 teaspoon oregano**
> **Pepper to taste**

Per Serving: Protein: 0 g   Fat: 18.6 g   Carbohydrate: 6 g

Preheat the oven to 425°F/220°C/Gas Mark 7. To make the first batch of aubergine: pour half the oil into a 15 × 12-inch roasting pan and spread it around the bottom. Dip half the aubergine slices in the oil to coat both sides and arrange them in the pan in one layer. Bake for 10 minutes. Turn the slices and bake for another 10 minutes, or until the aubergine is golden brown. Remove the aubergine to a serving platter and sprinkle with half the lemon juice. Crumble half the oregano on top and add pepper to taste.

Repeat the procedure with the remaining aubergine slices. The aubergine tastes best at room temperature; if it's been refrigerated, let it come to room temperature before serving. The flavour just improves from day to day, up to about 3 days.

CHOUCROUTE

Choucroute is French for sauerkraut – which you may think you don't like, but try it this way; it's sweet and mild and just right for a winter's evening. It's served surrounded by as many different kinds of grilled sausages as you can get your hands on, and a pot of mustard and one of horseradish at the table. The sauerkraut is even better made a day ahead, so it's a good company dish. SERVES 6

2 lb fresh sauerkraut (in the dairy case)

2 tablespoons butter

1 medium onion, sliced thinly

1 bay leaf

Lots of pepper

8 fl oz dry white wine

2 fl oz gin

1⅓ pints low-sodium beef stock

Per Serving: Protein: .3 g   Fat: 8.6 g   Carbohydrate: 2.2 g

Rinse the sauerkraut in a colander under running water, then leave it to soak in cold water for half an hour, changing the water twice, to sweeten it. Drain the sauerkraut and fluff it up a bit.

Preheat the oven to 325°F/170°C/Gas Mark 3. In a Dutch oven, melt the butter and add the onion. Cook the onion over medium-low heat for about 10 minutes, or until it's soft, stirring from time to time. Add the sauerkraut, bay leaf and pepper. Cover and cook for 10 minutes. Add the liquids and stir well.

Bake the sauerkraut covered for 5 hours, or until the liquid is absorbed. Remove the bay leaf and taste for seasoning; you may need to add salt.

FRIZZLED CABBAGE

This recipe breaks all the rules for cooking cabbage, yet brings out an amazing sweetness in the vegetable. It won't even be clear that this is cabbage you're eating. ... It makes a good nest for meatballs and a fast side dish. You can add seasonings to taste a few minutes before serving: nutmeg, paprika, cumin, dill, hot pepper sauce, whatever seems appropriate. But try it first plain. SERVES 2

  ¼ medium head of cabbage
  2 tablespoons butter
  Salt and pepper to taste

Per Serving: Protein: 0 g   Fat: 11 g   Carbohydrate: 2.7 g

Cut out the core of the cabbage and slice the remaining wedge in skinny slivers. Melt the butter in a wide frying pan and when it's foaming add the cabbage — you should have about 4 oz. Cook the cabbage over medium heat, turning frequently, until it begins to wilt, about 10 minutes. Lower the heat a little and continue to cook until the cabbage starts to brown and caramelize a bit, another 10 minutes or so — but don't let it burn. Season and serve immediately.

GREEN BEAN PACKAGES

Vegetables that come to the table wrapped as presents are always particularly appealing, and that's definitely the case here. SERVES 1

For each serving:
8 skinny green beans, stemmed
1 teaspoon melted butter
Salt and pepper
1 slice smoked bacon

Per Serving: Protein: 2 g   Fat: 16 g   Carbohydrate: 3 g

Preheat the oven to 400°F/200°C/Gas Mark 6.

Steam the beans for 4 minutes, or drop them into boiling water for the same period of time. Drain them, dry them and roll them in the butter. Add salt and pepper to taste.

Place the bacon slice on a baking sheet lined with foil and arrange the beans in the middle of it. Fold the ends around the beans — or make a spiral of bacon running around the bunch of beans. Bake for 20 minutes and serve hot.

TURNIP GRATIN WITH BLUE CHEESE

This delectable dish of Los Angeles chef Michael Roberts is luxurious enough for a major celebration meal — and everyone will think they're eating potatoes. SERVES 4

- **4 medium white turnips, sliced paper thin**
- **1 yellow onion, sliced thinly**
- **4 tablespoons unsalted butter, melted**
- **4 fl oz double cream**
- **4 anchovy fillets, chopped finely**
- **¼ teaspoon freshly grated nutmeg**
- **¼ teaspoon pepper**
- **2 oz crumbled Roquefort or other blue cheese**

Per Serving: Protein: 6.1 g   Fat: 27.4 g   Carbohydrate: 5.7 g

Preheat the oven to 375°F/190°C/Gas Mark 5. Toss together the turnips and onion with the butter in a 9-inch round baking dish. Cover tightly with foil and bake for 30 minutes.

In a small saucepan over medium heat, bring to a boil the cream, anchovies, nutmeg and pepper and cook for 1 minute. Remove the turnips from the oven and take off the foil. Pour the cream sauce over, toss well and sprinkle the blue cheese over the top. Return the turnips to the oven for an hour, uncovered. The gratin should be golden brown; if it isn't, run it under the grill for 3 minutes or until it colours.

GREEN BEAN PIE

The original version of this humble recipe hails from Liguria, on the Italian coast — where they would not be adding any walnuts to it. I learned this dish from Colman Andrews, who I hope won't mind my messing around with it. SERVES 8

> **Olive oil for the dish**
> **2 lb green beans, trimmed**
> **Salt**
> **½ onion, chopped finely**
> **1 garlic clove, minced**
> **1 tablespoon extra-virgin olive oil**
> **4 sprigs Italian parsley, chopped**
> **½ teaspoon dried oregano**
> **1 oz grated Parmesan cheese**
> **4 extra-large eggs, lightly beaten**
> **2 oz ricotta cheese**
> **Black pepper**
> **1½ oz chopped walnuts**

Per Serving: Protein: 7.4 g   Fat: 10.2 g   Carbohydrate: 7.5 g

Preheat the oven to 300°F/150°C/Gas Mark 2. Grease a 9-inch quiche dish with olive oil. Cook the beans for 10 minutes in a large pot of boiling salted water. Meanwhile, cook the onion and garlic in the olive oil in a nonstick frying pan for about the same amount of time. Drain the beans in a colander in the sink and let them cool under cold water. Set aside. Add the parsley and oregano to the onions and cook for 10 more minutes.

Cut the beans into 1-inch lengths. Remove the pan from the heat and stir the beans in with the onions, along with half the Parmesan and the eggs mixed with the ricotta. Transfer the mixture to the prepared quiche dish. Add the walnuts to the remaining Parmesan and scatter over the top.

Bake the pie for 45 minutes or until golden brown on top.

PAN-COOKED WATERCRESS

Good as watercress is raw, it's also delicious cooked — a little pricey, but very interesting. SERVES 6

> 3 tablespoons butter
> 1 garlic clove, crushed
> 4 bunches watercress, tough stems removed
> Salt and pepper to taste

Per Serving: Protein: 1 g   Fat: 5.5 g   Carbohydrate: .6 g

Melt the butter in a large frying pan and add the garlic. Cook over medium-high heat until the butter is foaming, then remove the garlic clove and add the watercress. Stir and toss the watercress until it's wilted, just a few minutes. Add salt and pepper to taste and serve hot.

PAN-COOKED RADISHES

Cooked radishes are delicious — and these also look pretty. SERVES 4

> 2 bunches red radishes, washed and trimmed
> 3 tablespoons butter
> 1 teaspoon salt
> Pepper to taste

Per Serving: Protein: 0 g   Fat: 8.2 g   Carbohydrate: trace

In a nonstick frying pan, melt the butter and add the radishes. Cook over medium heat until tender, about 4 to 6 minutes. Season with the salt and pepper and serve hot.

COUNTRY-STYLE GREENS

Some greens are higher in carbs than others – collards, for instance – but they're all so good for you that it's worth the extra couple of grams. Old Southern cooks add just a little flour to the greens to give them a creamy quality – more carbs again, but not enough to think about. It's up to you. SERVES 6

4 lb strongly flavoured greens – kale, collards,
      mustard greens, turnip greens or a mixture
1 lb pork shoulder butt, slashed to the bone in
      3 places
Salt and pepper to taste
1 tablespoon flour, optional
Pepper vinegar or cider vinegar

Per Serving: Protein: 10.4 g   Fat: 4.6 g   Carbohydrate: 3.9 g

Remove the stems from the greens and clean them thoroughly. Put them in a large pot – enamelled cast iron is perfect – with just enough water to cover. Add the pork butt. Bring the water to a boil, lower the heat and simmer, partially covered, for 2 hours or until the greens are soft and the meat is falling apart. Add salt and pepper to taste, then the optional flour, mixing well. Serve in soup plates with some of the meat mixed in and pass the pepper vinegar on the side.

SPINACH WITH A WHIFF OF GARLIC

A quick way to cook spinach for a dinner party.
SERVES 6

  2 lb spinach, stems removed
  2 garlic cloves, crushed
  2 tablespoons butter or olive oil
  Salt and pepper to taste

Per Serving: Protein: 0 g   Fat: 3.6 g   Carbohydrate: 1.6 g

Be sure the spinach is clean; then put it in a large
saucepan with just the water that clings to it. Cover and
cook over medium heat, stirring frequently. When the
spinach begins to crumple, drain it in a colander in the
sink, pressing it to extract as much water as possible,
then return it to the pot. Spear the garlic cloves on the
tines of a cooking fork and stir them thoroughly through
the spinach. Add the butter or olive oil. Season to taste
with salt and pepper and serve hot.

SPINACH CHEESE PIE

This is more or less what's inside the traditional Greek
spanikopita, minus the filo pastry layers. It's best made
with fresh spinach that's been plunged briefly into boiling
water – but frozen spinach works perfectly well too, so
that's what the recipe calls for. SERVES 8

2 (10-oz) packets frozen whole-leaf spinach,
    defrosted
2 tablespoons butter
1 bunch spring onions, including the firm green,
    chopped (about 3 oz)
½ medium onion, chopped
Salt and pepper to taste
6 eggs, beaten well
1 (15-oz) container whole-milk ricotta
½ lb feta cheese, crumbled
1 tablespoon chopped dill
½ oz chopped parsley
Pinch of grated nutmeg
Olive oil for the pan

Per Serving: Protein: 9 g   Fat: 16.9 g   Carbohydrate: 5 g

Preheat the oven to 350°F/180°C/Gas Mark 4.

Let the spinach drain in a colander in the sink. The easiest way to get all the excess moisture out of it is to line
your hand with a double thickness of paper towels and
squeeze handfuls of spinach dry. Then chop it and set
aside.

Melt the butter in a large frying pan; when it's foaming, add the spring onions and chopped onion. Cook
them over medium heat until they're soft, then add the

spinach and a sprinkle of salt and pepper, and cook for 3 minutes, stirring from time to time.

Beat the eggs in a large mixing bowl and whisk in the ricotta. Stir in the remaining ingredients, then oil a 13 × 9-inch baking dish well, including the sides. Mix the spinach with the egg-cheese mixture, taste for seasoning and pour into the pan.

Bake the pie for 30 to 40 minutes, until the moisture disappears and the top has dappled golden spots. Remove from the oven and let sit for 5 minutes before serving.

CREAMED SPINACH WITH PARMESAN

This is the way they make the unusually good spinach at
Bruno's Pen and Pencil restaurant in Manhattan.

SERVES 2

> 1 tablespoon olive oil
> 1 lb cleaned and stemmed spinach
> 3 fl oz double cream
> 1 teaspoon butter
> 1 teaspoon grated Parmesan cheese
> Freshly grated nutmeg to taste

Per Serving: Protein: 1 g   Fat: 23.4 g   Carbohydrate: 2.1 g

Heat the olive oil in a large frying pan over medium-
high heat. When it's hot, add the spinach and flip it in the
oil, using tongs, for 2 minutes. Remove the spinach to a
nest of paper towels and squeeze it dry. Chop it.

Add to the pan the remaining ingredients and cook
them down over high heat for a minute or two, until you
have a little sauce. Add the chopped spinach and mix it
well with the sauce. Serve immediately.

SPINACH WITH A TON OF BUTTER

This famous old recipe is so politically incorrect that
we're probably the only people who'd even consider eating it. But it's amazing; try it and astound your friends.
Just remember that it will be four days before they're as-
tounded; it takes spinach a long time to accommodate so
much butter. And who would have guessed our old diet
friend spinach could get so greedy?

The recipe is French, but there's also a Russian version
in which you sprinkle a teaspoon of vodka over the
spinach every day, and 2 teaspoons on the last day. You can
add lemon juice and a little grated nutmeg, too.

SERVES 4

2 lb spinach, heavy stems removed
1 lb unsalted butter
Salt and pepper to taste

Per Serving: Protein: 0g   Fat: 88g   Carbohydrate: 4g

Heat a big pot of salted water to the boil and add the
spinach. Turn off the heat and let it stand for 2 minutes,
then drain and rinse under cold water. Squeeze it gently
and chop it roughly.

Melt a quarter of the butter in a heavy saucepan over
low heat. Add the spinach and cook it gently, stirring constantly, until all the butter disappears into the spinach. Put
the spinach in a bowl and cover; chill until the next day.

Repeat the process with the next quarter of butter
and the same spinach for three days running. When you're
ready to serve the spinach, warm it through and add salt
and pepper to taste. Drain it of any liquid butter.

BROCCOLI WITH TOASTED PINE NUTS

This is a delicious combination that also works with cauliflower – or use half broccoli and half cauliflower.

SERVES 4

2½ oz pine nuts
1 head broccoli, florets only
2 fl oz olive oil
2 tablespoons fresh lemon juice
Salt and pepper

Per Serving: Protein: 4.8 g   Fat: 24.2 g   Carbohydrate: 7.4 g

Warm a small heavy frying pan and toast the pine nuts over a medium flame, stirring frequently to make sure the nuts don't burn. Take them out of the pan the minute they're golden.

Steam the broccoli florets (or cook in the microwave) until tender. Drain on paper towels.

Warm the olive oil in a large frying pan and when it's hot, add the broccoli. Cook just until the broccoli begins to turn golden in places, then add the lemon juice and salt and pepper. Add the pine nuts, stir well, and serve immediately.

BAKED CHARD WITH CHILLIS

In the same way that spinach is delicious with chillis, so is chard. In this dish they go together with melting cheese, sour cream and eggs – all you need is protein and salad to round out the meal. I know this recipe comes from a cookbook, but I've lost the source. SERVES 6

> 3 tablespoons olive oil
> 1 large bunch Swiss chard, washed, chopped and
>   spun dry in a salad spinner
> 2 oz chopped leeks
> 2 garlic cloves, pressed
> 2 jalapeño peppers, seeds and veins removed,
>   sliced thinly
> 4 large eggs
> 4 or 5 drops hot pepper sauce
> 4 oz sour cream
> 2 oz grated Monterey Jack cheese
> 1 teaspoon salt
> Freshly ground black pepper to taste
> 1 oz grated Parmesan cheese

Per Serving: Protein: 9.6 g   Fat: 19 g   Carbohydrate: 5 g

Preheat the oven to 350°F/180°C/Gas Mark 4. Grease a 9-inch-square baking pan with a little of the oil.

In a large frying pan or wok, heat the remaining oil over medium heat and cook down the chard while stirring until it starts to wilt. Add the leeks, garlic and peppers, and continue to cook for about 5 minutes or until all the vegetables are soft.

In a large bowl, beat the eggs and add the pepper sauce, sour cream, Jack cheese, salt and pepper. Stir in the chard. Mix well and spoon into the baking dish. Sprinkle the Parmesan over the top and bake uncovered for 25 minutes. Let cool for 5 minutes before serving.

POTATO SKINS

This is the only potato recipe I can think of that we can all eat — and it's so delicious that it will probably become one of your favourites. If you haven't eaten carbs for a while, you'll be amazed at the sweetness of the potato flesh.

It's up to you how much white to leave inside the skin — if you want to, you can scrape it all out without much trouble. If you leave, say, ¼ inch, you'll feel as if you ate a whole baked potato, but it will probably be only about 10 to 15 carbs. With steak and salad, that works even for restricted diets. And remember that the skins are full of nutrients.

A nice, big, flattish potato will give you the biggest ratio of skin to flesh. And it's worth going to the trouble of getting organic russet potatoes — farmers who want to clear their fields of pesticides plant potatoes because they absorb the poisons so readily.

You can serve the potatoes plain, with just butter and salt and pepper, or with those things plus paprika, or with cheese — any kind that's good with potatoes, such as Swiss, Gruyère, Parmesan, etc. But my favourite is peppercorn cheddar. SERVES 2

2 large baking potatoes
3 tablespoons butter, melted
Salt and pepper
Cheese, optional
Paprika, optional

Per Serving: Protein: 0 g   Fat: 17 g   Carbohydrate: 10 g

Preheat the oven to 400°F/200°C/Gas Mark 6. Scrub the potatoes and prick them in a couple of places with a cooking fork so they won't explode. Put them directly on a rack in the hot oven for 1 hour, or until the insides are tender and the skins are crisp. Remove from the oven and let cool slightly.

When the potatoes are cool enough to handle, cut them in half lengthwise. Scoop out the flesh with a big spoon – remove all of it or leave a little, as you like. Put the shells on a baking sheet with a rim. Using a pastry brush, paint the shells generously with the melted butter, add salt, pepper and either slices of cheese or grated Parmesan – 1 tablespoon is about right. You can also omit the cheese and just shake on a little paprika.

Put the baking sheet with the shells back into the oven for 10 to 15 minutes, or until the cheese is melted and the potatoes are golden and crispy.

No one's stopping you from serving these with the traditional sour cream and chives.

SAUTÉED BEETROOT

Beetroots are wonderfully earthy and sweet, and this simple way of cooking them gives them a bright new face.
SERVES 4

1 lb beetroots, trimmed
2 tablespoons butter
2 tablespoons fresh orange juice
Salt and pepper to taste

Per Serving: Protein: 1.4 g　Fat: 5.5 g　Carbohydrate: 8 g

Peel the beetroots and grate them coarsely. Melt the butter in a sauté pan, stir in the beetroots and cook, covered, for about 15 minutes. Just before serving, add the orange juice, salt and pepper, and reheat.

Your New Best Friends: The Vegetable Heroes

In the low-carb world, vegetables are king — some vegetables, anyway. These are the ones loaded with vitamins, minerals and fibre that are naturally low in carbohydrate — though often they taste quite sweet. It's hard to imagine that a sweet red pepper fits this profile but it does, and you'll find yourself turning to these powerhouses again and again for everyday meals.

Asparagus

Asparagus is almost the definition of spring, though of course it's available all year long now, imported from the ends of the earth without too much success. Try to buy asparagus out of the bundle and choose stalks the same size, whether they're thin or thick. Store it as if it were a bunch of flowers: pour an inch of cold water in a jar and add the asparagus — keep it refrigerated. Asparagus is a good source of potassium and folic acid, and also has some vitamins A, B and C. You can eat really fresh asparagus raw — try it — but you can also boil, roast or grill it. Snap off the ends at the point where they snap easily and you'll have the tender part. Six asparagus spears are 2.4 carb grams.

Boiled or Steamed Asparagus

FOR BOILED: Snap off tough ends where they break naturally. Rinse the spears. Lay the spears in a wide pan of salted water. Bring to a boil, then lower heat to a simmer. Test the asparagus after 4 minutes. When barely done, drain and dry on kitchen towels.

FOR STEAMED: Lay the spears in a steamer basket set over ½ inch or so of boiling water. Cover tightly and steam for 3 to 5 minutes or until almost tender; it will continue to cook a little as it cools. Remove the steamer basket from the pan and spread the asparagus out on a towel to cool.

Sauce the asparagus with orange mayonnaise, page 154.

Roasted Asparagus

Put the asparagus spears in a shallow ovenproof dish and toss with a little olive oil and salt and pepper. Roast at 400°F/200°C/Gas Mark 6 until tender, about 15 minutes. Scatter some grated Parmesan cheese over the top for the last 5 minutes or until the cheese is golden brown.

Sweet Peppers

Red, green, yellow, purple – whatever colour, they're all loaded with vitamin C and also have some vitamin A and some minerals. Look for firm peppers; farmers' markets will have thin-walled peppers, which are especially delicious. Red sweet peppers are cheapest in late summer and autumn when they're in season – a good time to make a lot of fried peppers. Two ounces of chopped sweet pepper are 2.4 carbs.

Roasted Peppers

Cut off the stem end of the peppers and pull out the seeds. Either slice them or cut them in half for roasting and put them on a baking sheet lined with foil. Roast skin side up for 20 minutes at 400°F/200°C/Gas Mark 6, then take them out of the oven and fold the foil up around them so they steam for 10 minutes. Remove the foil and pull off the blistered skin.

Pepper Hors d'oeuvres

For a snack, spread raw pepper slices with seasoned cream cheese (chives, smoked salmon, mixed herbs, etc.). For another hors d'oeuvre, spread red pepper slices with a little tapenade, page 161.

Garlic Pepper Strips

Grill some peppers over the dying coals after you've finished barbecuing dinner. Refrigerate them and cut them into strips the next day. Drizzle with olive oil; add a clove of minced garlic and salt and pepper. Let stand for 1 hour to develop flavour.

Cheese-stuffed Roasted Peppers

Take two roasted pepper halves and put a fat slice of smoked mozzarella on each one. Crumble a little oregano over the top and run under the grill until the cheese is bubbling.

Tunisian Pepper Salad

Make two peppers of different colours the heart of a
Tunisian-style salad: cut them in very small dice, then
add a small cucumber cut the same way, some spring
onions, a few chopped mint and parsley leaves, some
olive oil and lemon juice. Add salt and ground black
pepper to taste and a pinch of cumin. Let the salad sit for
half an hour to develop flavour.

Broccoli

The champion cruciferous vegetable, broccoli is thought
to have strong anti-cancer compounds. Broccoli is also
strong in vitamins A and C, as well as calcium, phosphorus, potassium and zinc. Choose broccoli with tightly
closed buds, the greener the better. You can eat the stems
as well as the florets; peel them and cut them into ½-
inch pieces, then cook them for about 3 minutes before
you add the florets – 4 or 5 minutes more and they should
be done, firm but tender. Broccoli is also a champion in
the carb department: you can have 2–3 ounces of it for a
mere 2.2 carbs.

Broccoli Purées

Cook the broccoli stems in boiling salted water for 5
minutes, then add the florets and cook for another 5 minutes or until tender. Drain and purée the broccoli in a
food processor or in a food mill; add enough cream to
make a thick purée. Add salt and pepper to taste.

- Finish with a little butter and grated nutmeg.
- Or finish with a little butter, some grated Parmesan cheese and a touch of roasted garlic purée.

Leftover Broccoli

Make extra broccoli and cook the chopped leftovers in a generous tablespoonful of olive oil to which you've added a crushed clove of garlic. Add salt and pepper to taste and toss in a few red pepper flakes, to taste. Remove the garlic before serving.

Broccoli With Sun-dried Tomatoes

Microwave chopped broccoli florets and toss them with grated Parmesan and some slivered sun-dried tomatoes.

Broccoli and Cauliflower With Lemon Butter

Cook broccoli with cauliflower. Boil or microwave — don't steam it or it will turn a terrible colour — and sauce it simply with butter, lots of lemon juice, salt and pepper.

Savoury Sautéed Broccoli

Try broccoli sautéed in olive oil and garlic with a little anchovy paste tossed in. A few black olives would be good with this.

Sautéed Broccoli Rabe

Broccoli rabe (also known as rape, broccoli raab or rapini) is a different creature, but also very good for you. It requires a brief dunk in boiling water before sautéing with olive oil, garlic and red pepper flakes.

Cabbage

Another anti-cancer vegetable hero, cabbage has vitamins A and C, phosphorus and folic acid. It comes in plain green, in red, and in the elegant savoy and Chinese cabbages. All of them are high fibre and delicious. Look for firm heads that feel heavy. They'll keep for about a week in the refrigerator. The rule for cabbage is to cook it either briefly or for a long time – or just have it raw, as in coleslaw. You can have 3–4 ounces of cabbage for 4.5 grams of carb.

Coleslaw

Coleslaw is the easiest, fastest, tastiest way to go. It tastes better if it has a half hour to develop flavour, but even fresh-made coleslaw is very good. If you're used to sweet coleslaw, you may need to add some Canderel for a while, but soon that will taste too sweet. Add snipped dill, celery seed, slivers of green pepper, spring onion rounds, even hunks of cheese and ham to make a main course.

Sautéed Red Cabbage

Sauté sliced red cabbage in olive oil in a wide frying pan. When it begins to wilt, add a couple of drops of pure orange oil (page 39) in a big spoonful of champagne vinegar. If you have any orange zest, add some too. Add a spoonful of drained capers and taste for seasoning.

Curried Cabbage

Add some mild curry powder to butter before sautéing sliced cabbage in it. Cover and cook for several minutes or until tender and add salt and pepper to taste.

Steamed Cabbage

Steam wedges of cabbage in a steamer basket over 2 inches of boiling water for a few minutes. Be careful not to overcook. Serve with melted butter into which you've stirred some paprika. Add salt and pepper.

Roasted Cabbage Strips

The Queen of Roasting, Barbara Kafka, likes to roast cabbage strips, which are delicious. She slices a 1-pound head in ½-inch strips, tosses the strips with a couple of spoonfuls of melted butter, puts them on a large baking sheet, and roasts them at 500°F/250°C/Gas Mark 10 for half an hour, turning to expose all the cabbage halfway through. Add a spoonful of caraway or cumin seeds to this mix, and add salt and pepper when it's finished.

Sautéed Cabbage

Sliced cabbage simply sautéed in butter is delicious finished with a little cream and snipped dill.

Cauliflower

Almost everything you can do with broccoli you can also do with cauliflower, yet they're completely different in character. Broccoli could never masquerade as potatoes, for instance, as cauliflower can. Cauliflower has a lot of vitamin C and some iron. Look for creamy white firm heads with no yellowing or bruises. You can eat cauliflower raw as a crudité. Four to five ounces of cauliflower florets are just 2.6 carbs – a long way from potatoes.

Cauliflower Purée

(This is a lot like mashed potatoes.) Steam cauliflower florets or microwave them until soft. Purée in a food processor or food mill and add butter and cream to taste. Season with salt and pepper and warm briefly in a saucepan.

Cauliflower Gratin

Make the purée above, spread it in a shallow baking dish and cover it with grated Parmesan cheese. Run under the grill until the cheese is golden brown.

Sautéed Cauliflower

Steam florets and then sauté them in olive oil with garlic and red pepper dice.

◆ Or sauté steamed florets in a little sizzling butter, then add sour cream and snipped dill.

Giant Cauliflower Pancake

Steam florets until soft. Melt butter in a frying pan; when it's warm, add a minced garlic clove. Add the cauliflower and mash it down with a potato masher until it sticks together in a pancake about half an inch thick. Sprinkle grated nutmeg over the top and add salt and pepper. Turn up the heat and fry the pancake on both sides until golden. Drain on paper towels and salt again; serve immediately.

Celery

Crisp is mostly what celery is — there are a few nutrients, but none of much note. The sweet inner ribs are a very different thing from the tougher outer ones; save the inner ones for eating raw if you're cooking the celery. Don't worry about strings; just cut the celery on the diagonal and they'll go away. The leaves are delicious in salad, but in a simple soup, such as chicken soup, a lot of celery leaves can turn bitter. A celery rib is less than 1 carb gram.

Celery Salad

Chop the ribs and some leaves and add some crumbled blue cheese and a few toasted cashew nuts. Toss with a red wine vinaigrette.

Celery as Hors d'oeuvres

Dip the inner celery ribs in olive oil, then in salt and pepper for a very informal hors d'oeuvre.

- Mix blue cheese with butter and fill inner celery ribs with it. Chopped toasted walnuts would be good with this, too.
- Serve a bouquet of celery ribs — the sweet inner ones — with your cheese course.

Celery Braised in Butter

Cut celery into ¼-inch pieces, toss in melted butter and cook over low heat in a covered saucepan for 20 minutes or until tender. Salt and pepper to taste.

Aubergine

Some people shy away from aubergine because they don't want to deal with the salting and draining to draw out the bitter juices. You don't have to worry about that with truly fresh aubergine from the farmers' market – otherwise you can use Japanese aubergine, the skinny Easter-egg-coloured ones that don't need salting. Aubergine isn't a nutritional powerhouse, though it does have some potassium and folic acid. Look for firm, shiny, light-in-the-hand aubergines and use them right away – it's old, stored aubergine that gets bitter. One-half cup of diced aubergine is 3.2 grams of carb.

Grilled Aubergine Slices

Just brush aubergine slices with olive oil, add salt and pepper and grill on both sides until they take on a golden brown colour in spots.

Aubergine Cannelloni

Slice an aubergine lengthwise ¼-inch thick and grill it. Mix up a little ricotta cheese with herbs – parsley, oregano – and roll the grilled aubergine around it. Put the aubergine rolls in an oiled baking dish and sprinkle a little grated Parmesan on top. Run the rolls under the grill until the cheese melts and serve them with a simple tomato sauce, page 194.

Grilled Aubergine Salad

Prepare aubergine slices for the grill, then make up a batch of garlicky red wine vinaigrette. Cover the aubergine slices with a few spoonfuls before grilling. When the slices are grilled, toss them with more vinaigrette and let cool to room temperature.

Grilled Japanese Aubergine

Prick whole Japanese aubergines in several places so they won't burst. Grill them on all sides until tender and the skin is charred. Split and serve with butter, salt and pepper and a little lemon juice.

Aubergine Mozzarella Sandwiches

Make the roasted aubergine slices on page 275 and cover each slice with a thin slice of mozzarella. Sprinkle a little oregano on top. Run under the grill until the cheese melts.

Sautéed Aubergine

Cut an aubergine into 1-inch cubes and salt it; leave it to drain in a colander for 30 minutes to 1 hour. Dry the cubes with paper towels. Heat olive oil with a crushed garlic clove in a wide nonstick frying pan; when it's hot, remove garlic and add the aubergine. Sauté until golden brown and tender, about 8 minutes. Add salt and pepper to taste and serve immediately.

Green Beans

Although they have some vitamin A and C, green beans and their ilk — wax beans, Italian beans, yard-long beans, etc. — aren't big on nutrients. But they're delicious and lend themselves to interesting preparations. Look for crisp but flexible beans. They're not called string beans anymore because the strings have been bred out of them, so all you have to do is snap off their tops and either steam them or cook them briefly in a lot of boiling salted water. Run them under cold water in the sink and dry well before proceeding with the recipe. One to two ounces of green beans is a little less than 4 carbs.

Green Beans With Nuts

Serve hot cooked green beans with a sauce of sizzling butter with chopped toasted hazelnuts. Or use pecans or walnuts.

+ Try steamed green beans served hot with pesto and chopped toasted walnuts.

Roasted Green Beans

Make a dressing of olive oil with lots of crushed garlic and some thyme and let it sit for a few hours to develop flavour. Remove the garlic before tossing the beans in the flavoured oil. Add salt and pepper, and roast in a single layer on a baking sheet at 450°F/230°C/Gas Mark 8 for 15 minutes, stirring every now and then.

Asian Roasted Green Beans

Proceed as for roasted green beans above, but use light sesame oil and a little soy sauce for the flavoured oil. Toss the cooked beans with toasted sesame seeds before serving.

Leftover Green Beans

These can be used for salad or heated up in olive oil or butter and served with lemon juice. Don't add the lemon juice or any other acid until just before serving or the beans will discolour.

- If you have leftover beans and cauliflower, toss them together with some fresh slivered mint and a lemony vinaigrette.

- Lightly steamed beans that still have a little crunch are delicious on the crudité platter.

Greens

These are everything from beet greens to collard greens – they're inherently delicious and endlessly good for you, so they're one of the backbones of the low-carb diet. They work as side dishes, as salads or as a bed for the main dish in place of noodles or potatoes or some other starch. Spinach (just over ½ gram of carb for 2 ounces, which means you can eat endless amounts) may be the all-time favourite, but rocket (less than ½ gram for 1 ounce) and mustard greens (4 grams for 2 ounces) and bok choy (under 1 gram per 2 ounces) aren't far behind. Kale and collard greens and chard are just under 4 grams for 1 ounce. Try mixing cooked greens together.

Frozen greens are obviously a big convenience, but fresh ones are incomparable. Once you get used to washing spinach – two or three rinses in warmish water in a big bowl – it seems like no work at all for such taste and nutritional dividends. Strip off the heavy stems of collards, kale and spinach. It's worth keeping frozen greens around for emergencies – you never want to be caught without vegetables.

Almost all greens are improved by an element of acid: vinegar or lemon juice. They also flourish with butter or olive oil or peanut oil or light sesame oil. Hot peppers are great with greens and so is a smoky taste – from bacon, liquid smoke or chipotle peppers (page 42).

Spinach Salad

Use only small young spinach leaves, flat or crinkled. For a main-dish salad, add smoked turkey or ham or both, cubes of Swiss cheese, chopped hard-boiled eggs and spring onions sliced in rounds. Make a creamy lemon dressing with Dijon mustard – just add a little mayonnaise with Dijon to a lemon dressing, page 116.

Spinach or Chard With Garlic and Lemon

Cut off the heavy spinach stems or the white chard stems (cook the chard stems separately, and longer). Chop the greens and put them in a big pot with just the water that still clings to them. Cook them down over medium heat until they begin to wilt into a clump. Drain in a colander and, when they're cool enough, squeeze dry with your hands. In a wide frying pan, heat several sliced garlic cloves with olive oil until they just turn golden. Add the greens and cook, stirring, for a couple of minutes. Add a splash of red wine vinegar or balsamic vinegar and salt and pepper to taste. Red pepper flakes would be a good idea here, too.

Simple Spinach Gratin

Rub a large gratin dish with olive oil. Chop 2 pounds of clean dried spinach, toss it with salt and pepper and put it in the gratin dish. Drizzle with 2 fl oz of olive oil and bake uncovered at 375°F/190°C/Gas Mark 5 for 40 minutes. Add a layer of grated Parmesan and ¼ cup of crumbled croutons; bake for 10 more minutes.

Baby Bok Choy

This is vegetarian cook Deborah Madison's wonderful way with these little bundles of green. Cut the bok choy in half lengthwise and soak them in a bowl of water for 15 minutes. Rinse carefully, especially at the base. Set them cut side down in a pan of simmering salted water for 4 minutes, or until tender. Remove to a platter with a pair of tongs. Season with a little salt and drizzle with a few teaspoons of peanut oil.

Southern Collard Greens

Put a ham hock on to simmer in a big pot of water for half an hour. Meanwhile, cut out the big ribs on the collard greens and slice the greens in big pieces. Add them to the pot along with a dried red pepper if you like. Cook the greens slowly, uncovered, for a couple of hours or until completely tender. Drain and serve with hot pepper vinegar.

Instant Collard Greens

Cut the washed leaves into skinny ribbons and dry them in a salad spinner. Heat some olive oil in a wok and, when it's hot, add the collards. Stir-fry over high heat for just a minute, until the greens are wilted. Add salt and pepper and hot pepper vinegar.

Leftover Greens

These can go into an omelette or frittata, be served at room temperature with a simple olive oil and lemon juice dressing, or jump into a frying pan with some olive oil, roasted peanuts and hot pepper flakes.

Mushrooms

These are among the biggest carb bargains at just a little over 2 grams for 3 ounces of chopped mushrooms – 2 shiitakes add up to 5 grams. They have a little niacin but not much else in the way of nutrients. Cremini (baby shiitake) mushrooms are tastier than button mushrooms, but ordinary market mushrooms have their place too. If the mushrooms seem dirty, wipe them with a damp paper towel; otherwise just brush them off and pull off the stems. Slice them raw into salads. Sauté them in a little butter with salt and pepper over medium-high heat for just 2 or 3 minutes, until they begin to brown. To grill them, paint the caps with melted butter and put them 4 inches below the heat for 2 minutes. Turn them over, paint the interior with more melted butter, and grill them for another 2 or 3 minutes, until golden brown. Try stuffing the mushrooms with cooked sausage or cheese – Gorgonzola on shiitakes is particularly good. All mushroom leftovers are delicious in omelettes or meat loaf.

Spaghetti Squash

This weird vegetable has a lot to offer the low-carb cook. For starters, ½ cup is only 5 carbs, not bad for a pasta pretender. It's a good source of folic acid and also has some potassium. Every time I cut into a spaghetti squash and pull away the layers of pasta-like strands, I'm amazed all over again. Still, spaghetti squash doesn't really taste like pasta (or like much of anything, for that matter), so don't set your expectations too high, and you won't be disappointed. When you're dying for pasta with pesto, though, you can be considerably cheered by spaghetti squash with pesto. I particularly like spaghetti squash baked into a gratin with a pasta sauce and grated Parmesan on top. You can also use it for cold 'noodle' salads: just soak it in ice water for 15 minutes to crisp it once it's cooked, then drain and dry the strands and proceed with a favourite Asian noodle recipe.

You'll most likely find a 2- to 2½-pound squash, which will give you about 4 cups of squash spaghetti. The easiest way to cook it is to bake it for an hour at 350°/180°/Gas Mark 4 – be sure to puncture it a few times with a cooking fork so it won't explode. Cut it open right away when it's cooked and take out the seeds and their darker yellow strings. The seeds tend to hide, so feel around for them. Pull away the layers of strands one at a time, or they'll be too thick. If you're not using the squash right away, store it in the refrigerator, where it will keep well for several days.

Tomatoes

The absolute joy of summer tomatoes leaves us feeling bereft the rest of the year. But there are some other possibilities: towards the end of the year some wonderful little Italian tomatoes still on their stems find their way into some markets – they're expensive, but a great treat. Cherry tomatoes are often better than any others out of season, especially the ones that come from Baja California. Israeli tomatoes are good, with thick skins. Plum tomatoes are good for baking, as are not-so-ripe supermarket tomatoes – just punch them up with balsamic vinegar and salt before you proceed. Tomatoes have a lot of vitamin C and some A and B, as well as potassium and other minerals. A medium tomato has only 4.3 carbohydrate grams; count on 1 gram for a cherry tomato.

Slow-baked Tomatoes

Slice tomatoes in half horizontally and put them on an oiled baking sheet, cut side up. Drizzle with olive oil and sprinkle with salt and pepper. Bake at 325°F/170°C/Gas Mark 3 for 2 to 3 hours or until the tomatoes collapse and begin to caramelize. Sprinkle with snipped basil and serve warm or at room temperature.

♦   Variation: Sprinkle the tomatoes with oregano when you add the salt and pepper; then add crumbled feta cheese on top when you serve.

Tomato and Mozzarella Salad

This classic is to be made only with vine-ripened tomatoes and really good mozzarella. You can either alternate slices of cheese and tomato on a platter and insert leaves of basil so they look perky – or serve everyone their own tomato, sliced almost all the way through, with cheese slices tucked into the tomato and basil added. Either way, drizzle with best-quality olive oil and sprinkle salt and pepper on top. The whole thing can be served on a bed of arugula, if you like.

Baked Tomatoes With Cheese

Put sliced tomatoes in a buttered shallow baking dish and sprinkle with sherry vinegar. Bake at 300°F/150°C/Gas Mark 2 for half an hour. Add a layer of snipped basil, sprinkle with a little cream and top with a thatch of grated cheddar. Bake for 15 minutes longer or until the cheese is melted and golden brown.

Pan-fried Tomatoes With Cheese

Cut tomatoes in half horizontally and put them in an ovenproof frying pan with a little olive oil on the bottom. Sprinkle with salt, pepper and oregano or basil. Cook over low heat for 10 minutes, moving the tomatoes around so they don't stick. Sprinkle the tops of the tomatoes with grated mozzarella and run the pan under the grill until the cheese melts.

Courgette

This humble vegetable is low in both flavour and nutrients, except potassium. To bring out the flavour, slice courgette or dice it and sprinkle with salt. Leave it to drain in a colander for at least half an hour, preferably an hour. Dry it off and proceed with the recipe. Little courgettes are by far the best; look for shiny firm ones without any blemishes. You can eat courgettes raw, but it's not much more than a novelty. Four to five ounces of courgette is 4 grams of carb.

Oven-roasted Courgette With Parmesan

Trim off the stem end of small courgettes and slice them in half lengthwise. Put a little olive oil in a baking dish just large enough to hold the squash in one layer and add them, turning to coat the courgettes with the oil. Start the courgettes cut side down and salt and pepper the tops. Roast at 500°F/250°C/Gas Mark 10 for 15 minutes. Turn the courgettes cut side up, add salt and pepper, and top with a scattering of grated Parmesan. Return to the oven for 10 more minutes.

Pan-roasted Courgettes

For this you use whole baby courgettes and coat them with olive oil in a frying pan the same way you would oven-roasted courgettes. Cook them slowly, uncovered, for 25 minutes or half an hour, until browned all over and tender, turning so they cook evenly. Sprinkle with snipped basil.

Sautéed Courgettes

Salt very thin slices of courgettes for 30 minutes to an hour; drain and pat them dry. Sauté in melted butter over high heat for about 4 minutes or until crisp-tender. Add some thin slices of pepperoni and some chopped parsley along with salt and pepper. You can also turn this into a shallow baking dish and top it with grated cheese, then run it under the grill.

Fried Courgette Salad With Mint

Cut the courgettes in half lengthwise and then into 2-inch pieces. Salt and drain as above. Rinse and pat dry with paper towels. Fry in a pan with olive oil and sliced garlic until tender and browned, about 15 minutes. Put the courgettes in a shallow serving bowl and pour a little red wine vinegar over them. Add salt and pepper and lots of chopped mint. Let sit for several hours to develop flavour.

Desserts

〽️

Life without dessert seems unthinkable, and yet it's
dessert that gets us into the most trouble. In the old low-
fat-diet school, fruit was the right answer, and it's still a
very delicious answer, but only some fruits — the low-
carb ones like berries, melons, peaches, coconut, grapes
(a few), oranges (limited) and of course rhubarb. If you're
serving plain fruit, or slightly sweetened fruit, add a plate
of low-carb biscuits — your own, or shop-bought ones
such as amarettini, pizzelle or almond thins.

Dessert (and rhubarb in particular) brings up the trou-
bling sweetener question (even vanilla is sweetened, but
unsweetened versions are available). See page 33 for
more on this subject. The recipes in this section use aspartame in the form of Canderel sticks and Canderel
Spoonful — but if you're serving dessert at a party, you
should either make the same dish using sugar as well as
the diet version or warn your guests that aspartame has
been used and offer an alternative, since some people are
allergic to it.

You can minimize both the artificial sweeteners and
the addiction to dessert (in case you're one of those people who react to any kind of sweet sensation adversely —
i.e. by gaining weight and losing control) by serving good
cheese with crackers for the guests and just a few slightly
sweet titbits: chocolate-covered coffee beans, spiced nuts,

chocolate-covered almonds, little nut meringues, chunks of Australian candied ginger.

However you work this out day to day, I'm a firm believer in having the birthday blowout once a year, which includes a favourite dessert for both lunch *and* dinner, along with pasta, bread and whatever else your heart most desires. Meantime, enjoy these alternatives, which will keep you where you need to be.

RICOTTA PUFFS

California cook Susan Costner makes a savoury version of
this dish that's also very good – just add lots of chopped
fresh herbs to the ricotta and drizzle a little olive oil on
top. (Leave out the lemon zest and Canderel, obviously.)
This wonderfully airy dish goes with almost everything.
SERVES 6

> **Butter for the baking dishes**
> **3 large egg whites**
> **½ teaspoon salt**
> **8 oz whole-milk ricotta cheese**
> **Minced zest of 1 lemon**
> **6 sticks Canderel**
> **Freshly grated nutmeg**
> **Raspberry-orange sauce, page 378**

Per Serving: Protein: 16.5 g   Fat: 16 g   Carbohydrate: 4 g

Preheat the oven to 375°F/190°C/Gas Mark 5. Have
ready 6 buttered ramekins or custard cups.

Beat the egg whites in a mixing bowl until you have
soft peaks. Mix the salt, ricotta, lemon zest and Canderel,
and fold the mixture into the egg whites. Pour the mixture into the ramekins and dust with nutmeg.

Bake for 30 minutes. The ricotta will rise, then settle
when the puff cools. Unmould and serve slightly warm or
at room temperature with raspberry-orange sauce.

SIMPLE RHUBARB

This basic buttery rhubarb is good on its own, as a sauce
or as a stand-in for syrup. SERVES 4

2 tablespoons butter
10 oz chopped rhubarb in ½-inch pieces
2 to 4 sticks Canderel to taste, or see Note below

Per Serving: Protein: 0 g   Fat: 5.5 g   Carbohydrate: 3.5 g

In a heavy saucepan over medium heat, melt the butter and add the rhubarb. Stew it slowly, stirring to coat
the pieces with butter. Stir again after 5 minutes and
check to see if the rhubarb is tender. Keep cooking until
it is. Add Canderel to taste. Serve warm with cream and
add a little minced ginger to the cream if you like.

Note: if you add ¼ teaspoon of baking soda, you can
cut the amount of sugar substitute in half. It will foam up
and turn the rhubarb a slightly different colour.

MELON WITH CARDAMOM

This refreshing melon dessert goes together in a moment. You can of course use different colours of melon – green, yellow, orange. It tastes best with chilled melon. The pepper is delicious here and the lime itself is sweet – but if you think you need it, you can add some Canderel. SERVES 4

> 1 cantaloupe, chilled
> ¼ teaspoon ground cardamom
> 1 tablespoon fresh lime juice
> A grinding or two of pepper
> Optional: 1 stick Canderel to sweeten, mint sprigs
>   to garnish

Per Serving: Protein: 0 g   Fat: 0 g   Carbohydrate: 6 g

Using a melon baller, cut the melon into balls – or just dice it if you have no melon baller. Toss with the remaining ingredients and serve in glass dishes with a sprig of mint.

How Sweet It Is . . .

In the sometimes bewildering world of aspartame, it takes a while to figure out what's what. It seems logical that Canderel would be in fact equal to sugar, but no, that's Canderel Spoonful, which can be used measure for measure to replace sugar. Canderel comes in sticks. Here's how they compare to sugar measures.

SUGAR	CANDEREL STICKS
2 teaspoons	1
1 tablespoon	1½
1¾ oz	6
2½ oz	8
3½ oz	12
5¼ oz	18
7 oz	24

AMBROSIA

The old classic from the Southern dessert table is always
in style. Don't bother segmenting the oranges — you're
just losing fibre in the name of refinement — but do slice
down the sides of the peeled oranges to be sure you've
got all the white pith removed. And take out the fuzzy
plug in the middle of the slices. Save any juice that accumulates while you're preparing the oranges and add it to
the ambrosia. SERVES 6

   4 Valencia or navel oranges, peeled, seeded and
        sliced thinly
   3 oz grated fresh coconut
   1 tablespoon brandy, optional

Per Serving: Protein: .4 g   Fat: 4.5 g   Carbohydrate: 8.5 g

Arrange the orange slices and the grated coconut in
alternate layers in a glass bowl. Sprinkle the brandy over
the fruit, cover and chill for at least 2 hours to develop
flavour.

PEACHES WITH AMARETTINI CREAM

The best peaches always seem to be the white ones, even when they come from as far away as Italy. But any peach that smells delicious is the one to choose. The amarettini cream dresses up this simple dessert. SERVES 4

> **4 perfectly ripe peaches, preferably white**
> **Sweetener to taste – Canderel**
> **8 fl oz double cream**
> **2 drops pure almond extract**
> **9 amarettini biscuits (the tiny ones in the Italian**
> **red tin), crushed**

Per Serving: Protein: 4 g   Fat: 22 g   Carbohydrate: 12 g

Peel and slice the peaches into a serving bowl and add sweetener. Mix gently to combine.

Beat the cream until it's nearly stiff, then fold in more sweetener, almond extract and the crumbed biscuits. Serve the peaches with the cream in a bowl to pass at the table.

BERRIES WITH TREMBLING CREAM

This rich, elegant, silky cream is sensational with fresh berries, even in winter with imported berries. It's a perfect dish to volunteer to bring to a party, since you can easily sweeten half a recipe with 2½ ounces of sugar for the other guests. SERVES 6

THE CREAM

15 fl oz double cream
1 envelope unflavoured gelatine
1 pint sour cream
16 sticks Canderel
1 tablespoon pure vanilla extract
A grating of fresh nutmeg, optional

THE BERRIES

3 pints mixed berries or all one kind
1 stick Canderel
Dash of balsamic vinegar for out-of-season
    strawberries, optional

Per Serving: Protein: 5 g   Fat: 45 g   Carbohydrate: 12.3 g

Pour the cream into a small saucepan and sprinkle the gelatine over. Let stand for 2 minutes. Heat very slowly over very low heat, whisking from time to time, until the gelatine dissolves, about 5 minutes.

Pull off any skin that forms on the surface of the cream. Add the sour cream, Canderel, and vanilla and mix well to blend. Pour the cream into a serving bowl and sprinkle with nutmeg. Cover the bowl with plastic wrap and chill for 3 hours before serving.

The berries: clean 2 pints of berries and mix them with the Canderel. Mash the third pint – strawberries or raspberries work best – to make a rough sauce.

Serve the cream in small bowls surrounded with berries and sauced with the berry sauce.

SPIRITED WATERMELON

It's hard to beat watermelon with crescents of lime to squeeze over it, but if you need something more exotic, try this: serve each guest a wedge of watermelon and pass a bottle of chilled Gewürztraminer at the table to splash onto the fruit.

Per Serving: Protein: 0 g   Fat: 0 g   Carbohydrate: about 10 g

PEACH AND BLUEBERRY CRUNCH
WITH ALMONDS

Ripe local peaches in season are so good served simply
with cream that it seems silly to mess around with them
and add more carbs in the bargain. But sometimes you
want a little crunch with juicy warm fruit – and this is the
answer. SERVES 6

FRUIT

Butter for the baking dish

4 ripe peaches, peeled and sliced

1 pint blueberries

2½ oz Canderel Spoonful

Dash of cinnamon

CRUNCHY TOPPING

10 oz almonds

3½ oz Canderel Spoonful

Pinch of salt

1 large egg white

2 teaspoons cornmeal, optional

Per Serving: Protein: 9.5 g   Fat: 23.5 g   Carbohydrate: 19.6 g

Preheat the oven to 375°F/190°C/Gas Mark 5.
Butter a 9-inch baking dish. Mix the fruit ingredients
together in a bowl, then arrange them in the baking dish.
Bake the fruit for 15 minutes.

Meanwhile, chop the nuts finely in a food processor.
Combine in a bowl with the sweetener and salt. In a separate bowl, whisk the egg white until it's quite foamy,
then pour the dry ingredients into the beaten white and
mix well, stirring in the cornmeal if you're using it. Rub

the topping through your fingers to be sure it's thoroughly combined. Spread the topping on a large plate and let it sit at room temperature until you're ready to use it.

After the fruit has cooked for 15 minutes, remove the dish from the oven and spread the topping evenly over it. Bake on the lowest oven shelf for another 25 to 30 minutes, or until the fruit is bubbling hot. Cool on a rack for at least 10 minutes before serving.

RUM-COCONUT BALLS

Bourbon would also be very good in these little nuggets
– a good thing to pass with after-dinner coffee. You can
easily double the recipe, to make four dozen.
MAKES 24, TO SERVE 12

    4 oz pecan pieces
    2¼ oz unsweetened dried coconut
    7 oz Canderel Spoonful
    2 tablespoons unsweetened cocoa powder
    Pinch of salt
    3 tablespoons butter
    2 tablespoons rum or bourbon, or more to taste
    2 teaspoons egg white powder or 1 egg white,
            beaten
    2 tablespoons warm water to dissolve egg white
            powder

Per Serving: Protein: 2.7 g   Fat: 10.6 g   Carbohydrate: 3 g

Preheat the oven to 350°F/180°C/Gas Mark 4.
Spread the pecans on a baking sheet and roast in the oven
for about 10 minutes, or until they begin to smell good.
Set aside to cool a bit. Meanwhile, in a large mixing bowl,
combine the coconut, sweetener, cocoa and salt. Melt
the butter.

When the pecans have cooled a bit, put them in the
bowl of a food processor and chop in several short bursts,
leaving a little texture. Add the pecans to the coconut
mixture. Mix the rum with the melted butter and stir
into the combined ingredients.

Put the egg white powder in a small bowl and add the
warm water. Beat with a fork for 2 minutes, until frothy

and dissolved. Mix the egg white into the combined ingredients.

Form the mixture into little balls – you should have 24. Leave the candies on a baking sheet to dry out a bit – about an hour. Store in a tin.

The Ice Cream Problem

Sugar isn't just another sweetener; it has complex roles to play in baking and even in ice cream making. If you try using your favourite ice cream recipe and just substitute aspartame for sugar, you'll end up with a rock-hard substance that's likely to break the plastic paddle on your manual ice cream maker – I ruined my Donvier this way. Sturdy electric models should be able to cope, though.

There are several ways around this problem: making soft ice cream in the food processor, making semifreddo slices (see page 347), adding a tablespoon of liquor to the ice cream mix or using gelatine. If you add, say, a tablespoon of rum to the vanilla ice cream, you can use a manual ice cream maker and it will produce soft ice cream in just a couple of minutes, not the usual 20 to 30 minutes it takes to make ice cream. If you go beyond the soft ice cream stage, though, you'll be jamming the paddle and producing the hard rocks. (By the way, adding egg whites, a traditional solution to the problem, doesn't work with aspartame.)

If you don't mind using gelatine, that will also work to keep the ice cream relatively soft. Just dissolve 1 packet of gelatine per 8 fl oz of cream this way: sprinkle over 8 fl oz of cream in a saucepan and let stand 5 minutes. Over medium heat, bring just to a boil before adding slowly to the eggs. Try this simple frozen custard recipe as your ice cream base. Sprinkle two packets of gelatine over 2 fl oz water in a small bowl. Let stand 2 minutes. Then microwave for 40 seconds to dissolve gelatine. Beat 4 eggs well with 1 tablespoon vanilla; strain. Add 5¼ oz Canderel

Spoonful and 15 fl oz double cream. Mix well with the gelatine and freeze in your ice cream maker. Or purée frozen chunks in the food processor for soft frozen custard. Serves 4.

If you really want pure ice cream that isn't soft, make the soft ice cream and then return it to the freezer for 15 minutes or longer until you have the texture you want. You'll have to experiment and see what timing works for your freezer. The more acid there is in the ice cream, the less problem with aspartame icing up.

PECAN MERINGUES

These are excellent – crisp, light meringues flavoured with finely chopped toasted pecans. They're good with ice cream or fresh berries, and you can even make the whole recipe into a pie shell to make a delicious base for an ice cream pie. Making meringues with aspartame is tricky; the key to producing crisp, dry meringues is using just a touch of real sugar and long baking in a low oven.

SERVES 8

2 oz toasted pecans, page 174, cooled to room
    temperature
3½ oz Canderel Spoonful
3 large egg whites, at room temperature
1 tablespoon sugar
Big pinch of cream of tartar

Per Serving: Protein: 1.8 g   Fat: 4.3 g   Carbohydrate: 5 g

Preheat the oven to 250°F/130°C/Gas Mark ½. Line a baking sheet with cooking parchment or brown paper. Chop the pecans finely with the Canderel in a food processor. Using an electric mixer, beat the egg whites until they start to gain some volume, then gradually add the sugar and cream of tartar with the mixer still running. Stop beating just when the egg whites hold firm peaks.

Sprinkle the nut mixture over the egg whites and fold in. You can spoon the meringue mixture into 8 little mountains on the baking sheet or shape them into little cups – good for holding berries or ice cream – by using a smaller spoon to make a depression in the centre of each mound.

Bake the meringues on the centre rack of the oven for
1¼ to 1½ hours; they should be a little brown and very
dry. Turn off the oven and leave them in until the oven
cools down. Or put them in another dry, warm spot for
a couple of hours. Peel them off the paper when you're
ready to serve them. Store in an airtight container.

Pecan Meringue Pie Shell

Pile the meringue mixture into a lightly buttered 9-
inch glass pie plate, covering the bottom and sides but not
the rim of the plate. Bake for 1¼ to 1½ hours, until the
pie shell sounds hollow when flicked with a finger. Let
dry completely in the turned-off oven.

ALMOND BISCUITS

These are a little like the traditional Mexican wedding cakes. They're somewhat crumbly, bite-size and quite addictive. MAKES ABOUT 20 BISCUITS

8 tablespoons unsalted butter, at room
    temperature
1 large egg yolk
7 oz Canderel Spoonful
½ teaspoon vanilla extract
¼ teaspoon almond extract
10 oz almond flour, page 44
¼ teaspoon baking powder
¼ teaspoon salt
¼ teaspoon cinnamon

Per biscuit: Protein: 2.8 g   Fat: 11 g   Carbohydrate: 3.6 g

Using an electric mixer, cream the butter, then blend in the egg yolk, sweetener and extracts. In a separate bowl, break up the almond flour with your hands, then mix it with the remaining ingredients. Add the dry mixture to the butter mixture and stir until evenly blended. Cover and refrigerate the dough for 1 hour.

Shape the dough into 1¼-inch balls and place them on a large baking sheet, evenly spaced. Refrigerate the biscuits on the sheet for 15 minutes while you preheat the oven to 350°F/180°C/Gas Mark 4.

Bake the biscuits for 20 minutes. Cool them on the sheet for a minute or so, then transfer to a rack to finish cooling.

PINCH PIE

This old-fashioned meringue pie shell can be filled with fresh berries or peaches or a combination of fruits and served with whipped cream. Or use it as the base for the delectable lemon Pavlova, page 340. But don't try it on a rainy day. SERVES 8

5 large egg whites
¼ teaspoon cream of tartar
2 tablespoons sugar
18 sticks Canderel

Per Serving: Protein: 2 g   Fat: 0 g   Carbohydrate: 5.5 g

Preheat the oven to 225°F/110°C/Gas Mark ¼. Beat the egg whites and cream of tartar in an electric mixer until you have soft peaks. Add the sugar a tablespoon at a time, then the Canderel one stick at a time as you continue beating the egg whites. When the whites are glossy and reach the stiff peak stage, the meringue is finished.

Generously butter a 9-inch pie plate, including the rim. Using a rubber spatula, spread the meringue over the pie plate, building up the sides about an inch above the rim. Smooth out the interior to make the pie shell and finish the rim by making little swoops with the rubber spatula.

Bake the pie shell on the middle rack of the oven for an hour. It should be firm and crisp on the outside. Let it stay in the turned-off oven for another hour.

Let the pie shell cool to room temperature before filling. If you're using a fruit filling, serve at once or spread with a layer of whipped cream before adding the fruit.

ORANGE CAKE

When you need a birthday cake that's low-carb, here's
a good choice. Serve it with clouds of whipped cream,
flavoured with a drop of almond extract and a little mace.
This is a variation on a cake developed by the NutraSweet
people. SERVES 16

    6¼ oz cake flour
    5 oz almond flour (page 44)
    24 sticks Canderel
    1¾ oz sugar
    1 tablespoon baking powder
    ½ teaspoon salt
    7 fl oz cold water
    3 fl oz vegetable oil
    4 large egg yolks
    1 teaspoon pure vanilla extract
    1 teaspoon pure orange oil, page 39
    2 teaspoons grated orange zest
    8 large egg whites
    ½ teaspoon cream of tartar

Per Serving: Protein: 4.7 g   Fat: 10.4 g   Carbohydrate: 16 g

Preheat oven to 325°F/170°C/Gas Mark 3. Have
ready a 12-cup Bundt pan, ungreased.

Combine the flours, Canderel, sugar, baking powder
and salt in a mixing bowl and beat in the water, oil, egg
yolks, vanilla, orange oil and orange zest.

In an electric mixer, beat the egg whites until you have
soft peaks. Add the cream of tartar and beat until they
stand in stiff peaks. Stir ⅓ of the egg whites into the flour
mixture, then add the flour mixture back into the egg

whites, folding in with a rubber spatula. Pour the batter into the pan and bake for 1 hour or longer, until the surface springs back when touched lightly.

Cool the cake in the pan on a baking rack for 10 minutes, then invert and release the cake onto the rack to continue cooling.

ALMOND POUND CAKE

This pound cake is excellent alone or with fruit and whipped cream. It has a pleasant grainy texture, and like the best traditional pound cakes, a dense, moist interior. The cream cheese gives the cake just a slight tang. The oat flour can be found in most health-food shops. SERVES 10

**8 tablespoons unsalted butter, at room
     temperature
4 oz cream cheese, at room temperature
10½ oz Canderel Spoonful
5 large eggs, at room temperature
1 teaspoon vanilla extract
6½ oz almond flour, page 44
5 oz oat flour
½ teaspoon baking powder
¼ teaspoon salt
¼ teaspoon grated nutmeg
¼ teaspoon cinnamon**

Per Serving: Protein: 7.4 g   Fat: 24.8 g   Carbohydrate: 12 g

Preheat the oven to 350°F/180°C/Gas Mark 4 and butter an 8½ × 4½-inch loaf pan. Line the pan with greaseproof paper, allowing about 4 inches of overhang on each of the long sides. Butter the greaseproof paper.

Using an electric mixer, cream the butter, cream cheese, and sweetener. Add one of the eggs and the vanilla and beat until smooth.

Put the flours, baking powder, salt and spices in a large sieve or sifter and sift them, breaking up any clumps by rubbing the mixture with your hands. Anything that can't go through the holes can just be dumped back into the pile.

Add the remaining 4 eggs and the dry ingredients alternately to the creamed mixture, beating until smooth after each addition, beginning and ending with dry ingredients. Scrape the batter into the prepared pan and smooth the top with a spoon.

Bake the cake for approximately 45 to 50 minutes, until a tester inserted in the centre comes out clean. Cool the cake in the pan, on a rack, for 30 minutes, then lift the cake out by the paper and place it on the rack. Peel down the sides of the paper and cool the cake thoroughly. Slice the cake after it has cooled. Store leftovers, wrapped in plastic wrap, in the refrigerator.

LEMON PAVLOVA

This is a bit like lemon angel pie and reminiscent of
lemon meringue pie – it's delicious, and deliciously rich,
a good dessert to serve after a relatively light meal. You
can gild this lily by adding a border of fresh raspberries
just inside the rim. SERVES 8

> **5 large egg yolks**
> **2 fl oz fresh lemon juice**
> **1 tablespoon sugar**
> **Zest of 1 lemon, minced**
> **3½ oz Canderel Spoonful**
> **8 fl oz double cream**
> **Dash of pure vanilla extract**
> **1 baked Pinch Pie, page 335**

Per Serving: Protein: 5 g   Fat: 14.5 g   Carbohydrate: 9.5 g

In the top of a double boiler, whisk the egg yolks until
thick. Add the lemon juice, sugar and lemon zest, and stir
together. Heat the mixture over simmering water, stirring frequently, until it's thick. Remove from the heat, let
cool for a few minutes, and stir in the sweetener.

Whip the cream until it's stiff, adding a little vanilla towards the end of the beating. Spread a thin layer of
whipped cream over the pie shell, then spread the lemon
filling on top. Spread the remaining whipped cream over
the pie, cover carefully with plastic wrap and refrigerate
for 2 hours before serving.

WARM BERRY COMPOTE

When berries are in high season, make this simple but delicious warm berry dessert. Serve it with plain vanilla ice cream, page 346, or with pouring custard, page 342. If you can get your hands on any lemon verbena, snip a few leaves into the warm custard to flavour it, then strain before serving. SERVES 6

5 oz blueberries
10 oz hulled and quartered strawberries
4 oz raspberries
1¼ oz Canderel Spoonful or more to taste
4 tablespoons butter

Per Serving: Protein: 0 g   Fat: 7.3 g   Carbohydrate: 8 g

Put 4 fl oz of water in a large saucepan and heat until it boils. Reduce the heat to a simmer, add the blueberries and strawberries, and cook for 2 minutes. Add the raspberries, the sweetener and the butter to the pan and stir well. The compote is ready when the butter is melted.

Remove the pan from the heat, stir one more time, and divide the compote among 6 small bowls. Top with ice cream or pass a pitcher of pouring custard at the table.

POURING CUSTARD

Variously called crème anglaise, stirring custard or the title it has here, this is a sauce for berries or other fruit that can be turned into frozen custard by using the method described on page 330. It's particularly delicious made with the seeds from a real vanilla bean; if you have one, slit the bean and scrape the seeds into the cream when it first goes onto the heat.

You're always on the verge of making scrambled eggs when you're cooking the custard, so be sure to keep it from boiling – whisk it constantly, and take it off the heat from time to time if it threatens to boil. But don't worry; even if you get a bit of scrambled egg in the pan, it will disappear when the custard is sieved.

MAKES 15 FL OZ, SERVES 6

    8 fl oz double cream
    4 fl oz milk
    5 large egg yolks
    6 sticks Canderel
    1 tablespoon vanilla extract

Per Serving: Protein: 4.5 g   Fat: 19.6 g   Carbohydrate: 4.5 g

Mix the cream and milk in a heavy saucepan and place it over medium heat. In a mixing bowl, preferably one with a spout, whisk the egg yolks together with the sweetener and vanilla until they're pale yellow. When the cream begins to have a bubble or two rising at the edge of the pan, take it off the heat and slowly pour it into the eggs, whisking all the time. Pour the custard back into the pan and return it to the heat.

Cook the custard at a bare simmer — don't let it boil — whisking constantly, especially around the edges of the pan. When the custard thickens, take it off the heat and continue to whisk for a minute or two. Pour the custard through a sieve into a glass measure. While still hot, place a sheet of plastic wrap directly on the surface to prevent a skin from forming. Let it cool, then cover and refrigerate until ready to serve.

RASPBERRY CRÈME BRÛLÉE

Here's the perfect dessert for a dinner party or a special brunch. Just remember to make the custards the day before – a plus for the busy cook – so they have plenty of time to chill. If no fresh raspberries are in sight, use frozen ones and defrost them for half an hour before using. Sweetened rhubarb makes a great alternative to the raspberries. SERVES 6

    15 fl oz double cream
    8 fl oz light cream
    5¼ oz Canderel Spoonful
    7 large egg yolks
    ¾ teaspoon vanilla extract
    1 pint fresh raspberries or 4 oz defrosted frozen
        raspberries
    2 packed tablespoons light brown sugar

Per Serving: Protein: 6 g   Fat: 40 g   Carbohydrate: 15 g

Put a kettle of water on to boil and get out 6 ramekins (these look like tiny soufflé dishes). Preheat the oven to 325°F/170°C/Gas Mark 3 and adjust the oven rack to the lowest setting.

In a medium-size non-reactive saucepan, bring the creams and sweetener to a near boil over medium heat, stirring occasionally. While that heats, stir – don't whisk – the egg yolks in a large mixing bowl until evenly blended. Remove the cream from the heat and cool briefly. Using about 2 fl oz for starters, stir the cream into the egg yolks. Add several more small batches of cream, then gradually stir in the rest of the cream. Stir in the vanilla extract. Strain the mixture through a sieve into a large jug.

Arrange a single layer of tightly fitting raspberries in the bottom of each ramekin. Slowly fill each one with custard. Don't be concerned if some of the berries float to the top.

Put the ramekins in a large roasting pan or shallow casserole, evenly spaced. Place the roasting pan in the oven, then carefully — so it doesn't splatter — pour enough of the boiling water into the pan to come halfway up the sides. Loosely cover with a sheet of tented foil.

Bake the custards for 40 to 50 minutes; when done, the custards will be just slightly wiggly and loose in the centre but not wet. Transfer the ramekins to a rack. Cool to room temperature, then cover with plastic wrap and refrigerate overnight. Just before serving, add brown sugar topping.

A quick way to caramelize the brown sugar on top is with a propane torch from the hardware shop. Just spread a teaspoon of brown sugar over the custard, then light the torch and wave it over the custard so the tip of the flame just hits the sugar.

Otherwise, spread the sugar over the custards and place them in a shallow casserole. Surround them with ice to protect the custard from the heat, then run the casserole under the grill. The tops should be about 6 inches from the flame. When the sugar melts and turns bubbly, they're done. Remove and serve at once.

VANILLA ICE CREAM

Here's a basic method for making soft ice cream, which
can be flavoured several ways. If you'd rather, instead of
soft ice cream you can serve what the Italians call a semifreddo — ice cream frozen in a loaf tin, then allowed to
soften slightly before it's sliced and served. Either way,
this ice cream is easy and delicious. Because the ice cream
is soft after it comes out of the food processor, be sure to
chill small serving bowls ahead of time to keep it from
getting too soft. SERVES 4

Butter for the tin
12 fl oz double cream, chilled
4 large eggs, separated
5¼ oz Canderel Spoonful
1 teaspoon vanilla extract
3–4 fl oz light cream, chilled

Per Serving: Protein: 8.7 g   Fat: 42 g   Carbohydrate: 13 g

Butter a 9 × 5–inch metal loaf tin. Line the tin with a
double layer of plastic wrap, leaving at least a 4-inch overhang on the long sides. Chill the pan for half an hour.

Using an electric mixer, whip the double cream until
it thickens. Beat in the egg yolks, sweetener and vanilla
until the mixture is not quite as thick as normal whipped
cream but close.

In a separate bowl, beat the egg whites until they hold
soft peaks. Fold the egg whites into the whipped mixture until uniformly blended. Scrape the mixture into
the chilled tin, cover with foil and refrigerate for 12 to 24
hours, until solid.

Note: unless you have a very large-capacity food processor, make the ice cream in half batches.

To make normal soft ice cream: chill your food processor bowl and blade. Put 1 inch of very hot water in a small shallow casserole. Lower the loaf tin into the hot water, wait 5 seconds, then remove. Firmly pull up on the plastic wrap and remove the ice cream loaf. Peel off the plastic wrap.

Cut the loaf into thick slices with a large knife, then cut each slice into 4 or 5 chunks. Immediately put these chunks in the chilled bowl of the food processor and begin to process in 5-second bursts, adding as much of the cream as needed to make the ice cream smooth. Scrape down the sides of the bowl as necessary. When the ice cream has a smooth texture, but before it's too soft, serve in chilled bowls.

To serve as semifreddo: unmould and slice the loaf into ¾-inch slices. Lay the slices flat on serving plates and let stand at room temperature for 5 to 7 minutes before serving. Garnish with fresh fruit.

To make strawberry or raspberry ice cream: halve a handful of frozen strawberries and add them to ice cream chunks. Process as above. Or use a large handful of frozen raspberries.

To make ginger ice cream: mince four ½-inch chunks of Australian candied ginger and stir into the soft ice cream just before you serve it.

To make coffee-hazelnut ice cream: add 1 tablespoon instant powdered espresso to the egg yolk/cream mixture. Toast 5 oz hazelnuts on a baking sheet in a 350°F/180°C/Gas Mark 4 oven for 15 minutes, or until they smell delicious. Cool slightly and rub between two kitchen towels to remove skins. Chop nuts coarsely and stir into soft ice cream before serving. For semifreddo, fold into ice cream mixture before it goes into the tin.

CRÈME FRAÎCHE ICE CREAM

Once you get into the habit of making ice cream, it's a cinch. This one is particularly delicious, with a subtle tang – good with berries or berry syrups.

MAKES 1³/₄ PINTS, SERVES 8

1⅓ pints crème fraîche, page 158
8 large egg yolks
5¼ oz Canderel Spoonful

Per Serving: Protein: 5 g   Fat: 31.1 g   Carbohydrate: 5.3 g

Put the crème fraîche into a heavy saucepan. Whisk the egg yolks and the sweetener together in a bowl, then pour the mixture into the crème fraîche. Heat the mixture over medium heat for 3 minutes. Use the directions on page 347 to freeze the ice cream.

RUM-COCONUT ICE CREAM

If you keep coconut milk on hand, you can rustle up this ice cream in no time. SERVES 6

> 15 fl oz single cream
> 1 (14-oz) can unsweetened coconut milk
> 5¼ oz Canderel Spoonful
> 2 tablespoons dark rum

Per Serving: Protein: 3.3 g   Fat: 20 g   Carbohydrate: 4.3 g

In a heavy saucepan, bring the cream to a boil, stirring occasionally. Remove from the heat and let cool.

Stir in the coconut milk, sweetener and rum. Follow the freezing directions in the vanilla ice cream recipe on page 346.

STRAWBERRY SHERBET

This is convenience food – if you have a packet of frozen unsweetened strawberries in the freezer, a few minutes' work will give you a fresh-tasting, refreshing dessert. If you'd rather have instant gratification, just throw the frozen berries into the food processor (hang on; it's a rough ride in the beginning) and add the lemon juice and sweetener to the strawberry slush to serve 3. SERVES 6

1 (1-lb) packet unsweetened frozen strawberries, thawed
1 tablespoon fresh lemon juice
1¾ oz Canderel Spoonful
4 large egg whites, beaten stiff

Per Serving: Protein: 4 g   Fat: 0 g   Carbohydrate: 7 g

Put the strawberries in the bowl of a food processor and purée. Add the lemon juice and the sweetener. Fold the berries into the egg whites and mix thoroughly. Spoon into a plastic container and freeze for 4 hours.

FROZEN COFFEE

Somewhere between granita and coffee ice cream, this is a great thing to have lurking in your freezer on a hot day. It's also the right thing to do with leftover coffee – just fill ice cube trays with it. You can sweeten it or not, add cream or not, serve it with clouds of flavoured whipped cream or just enjoy it straight. SERVES 6

4 cups strong brewed coffee, espresso or regular
Optional: Canderel to taste

TOPPING
7 fl oz double cream, whipped
½ teaspoon vanilla extract
Optional: Canderel to taste, 2 teaspoons brandy

Per Serving: Protein: .5 g   Fat: 10 g   Carbohydrate: .8 g

Pour the coffee and optional sweetener into ice cube trays and freeze hard. If you're using the topping, prepare it right before you're ready to serve the dessert. Whip the cream and blend in the other ingredients. Refrigerate. Empty the frozen coffee cubes into the food processor – you may have to do this in batches – and process until you have a chunky slush. Serve immediately with the flavoured whipped cream, if using.

STRAWBERRY-RHUBARB MOUSSE

The affinity of these two fruits (well, actually rhubarb's a
vegetable) for each other is an almost endless delight.
Once you have the fruit mixture together – before you
add it to the cream – you can purée it for a syrup. So you
might want to make a double recipe of the fruit part.
SERVES 8

1¼ lb diced rhubarb
Pinch of salt
1 pint strawberries, in small pieces
11 sticks Canderel
1 pint double cream

Per Serving: Protein: 1.2 g   Fat: 22 g   Carbohydrate: 7.5 g

Cook the rhubarb in the microwave until soft, then
add the salt – or add the salt to the rhubarb and stew it
gently, uncovered, on top of the stove. You may need to
add a tiny amount of water. Add 9 packets of Canderel.
Add the strawberries and put the mixture in the freezer
for 20 minutes while you whip the cream.

Whip the cream until you have stiff peaks. Mix in the
remaining 2 packets of Canderel, and gently fold in the
rhubarb-berry mixture. Pile the mousse into a serving
dish, cover with plastic wrap and refrigerate until ready
to serve.

CHOCOLATE MOUSSE

This goes together in just a few minutes and it can be made up to four hours ahead. Instead of the orange flavouring, you could use a spoonful of Kahlúa. SERVES 4

12 fl oz double cream
6 sticks Canderel
Minced zest of 1 orange
½ teaspoon vanilla extract
1 oz unsweetened cocoa powder

Per Serving: Protein: 1.8 g   Fat: 33 g   Carbohydrate: 3.7 g

Beat the cream in an electric mixer or by hand until it begins to get thick, then add the Canderel a packet at a time. Add the orange zest, vanilla and cocoa powder and beat until almost stiff. Turn off the mixer and scrape down the sides and bottom of the bowl. Mix again. Divide the mousse among 4 ramekins or small dessert dishes, cover and refrigerate for ½ hour or up to 4 hours.

PUMPKIN MOUSSE

This is the perfect Hallowe'en dessert — but it's so delicious that you'll find it works all year long. For a special touch, use mace instead of nutmeg, or just dust the top of the mousse with powdered mace (the outer covering of the nutmeg, which has a particularly delicate flavour).

SERVES 8

2 envelopes unflavoured gelatine
2 fl oz water
15 fl oz double cream
1 tablespoon vanilla extract
7½ oz canned pumpkin
1 tablespoon dark brown sugar
8 sticks Canderel
1 teaspoon cinnamon
½ teaspoon grated nutmeg or mace
⅛ teaspoon allspice
1 tablespoon bourbon
Garnish: a dusting of mace

Per Serving: Protein: 5.5 g   Fat: 22 g   Carbohydrate: 7.5 g

Sprinkle the gelatine over the water in a small bowl. Let stand for 2 minutes, then microwave for 40 seconds. In a small saucepan, warm 8 fl oz of the cream with the vanilla until it bubbles. Then stir in the pumpkin and sugar and cook for 3 minutes. Add the sweetener, the spices and the bourbon. Stir in the gelatine. Beat the remaining cream to soft peaks and fold into the pumpkin mixture. Scoop into a glass or ceramic serving bowl and refrigerate covered until ready to serve, up to 6 hours. Decorate the top of the dish with sprinkled mace.

POTS DE CRÈME

These intense little cups of chocolate are deeply satisfying, and just a few carbs more than a true diet dessert.
SERVES 6

    4 oz semi-sweet chocolate
    4 large eggs, separated
    1 teaspoon pure vanilla extract
    2 teaspoons very strong brewed black coffee
    Pinch of salt

Per Serving: Protein: 4.7 g   Fat: 9 g   Carbohydrate: 11 g

Melt the chocolate in the microwave and cool for 5 minutes. Beat the egg yolks slightly with the vanilla and coffee and stir in the cooled chocolate. In a separate bowl, beat the egg whites with the salt until they form stiff peaks. Using a rubber spatula, fold – do not beat – the chocolate into the egg whites. Pour into 6 small ramekins, cover and chill from 4 to 24 hours.

SPANISH CREAM

This is a classic dessert from the first half of the century but it's almost entirely disappeared, more's the pity. If you grew up in the forties, you may have had Spanish cream as a nutritious treat when you were sick. It's quite delicious: a glassy custard subtly flavoured with sherry supports little clouds of meringue. SERVES 6

    2 envelopes of gelatine
    2 fl oz water
    1⅓ pints milk
    3 large eggs, separated
    ¼ teaspoon salt
    1 teaspoon pure vanilla extract
    2 tablespoons sherry or madeira
    3½ oz Canderel Spoonful

Per Serving: Protein: 9 g   Fat: 6.8 g   Carbohydrate: 7.9 g

Sprinkle the gelatine over the water in a small bowl and let stand for 5 minutes. Put the milk in a saucepan. Put the egg yolks in the top of a double boiler and beat lightly with a whisk.

Mix the gelatine into the milk and stir to dissolve over low heat. Scald the milk, but don't let it come to a simmer (no bubbles). Off the heat, pour the milk very slowly into the eggs in the top of the double boiler. Heat the water in the bottom of the double boiler over medium heat and put the egg-milk mixture on top. Stirring almost constantly, cook until the mixture thickens enough to coat a spoon. Be sure to stir around the edges of the pot so the egg doesn't collect there and cook.

Take the custard off the heat and let cool for about 10 minutes. Meanwhile, beat the egg whites stiff. When the custard has cooled, add the remaining ingredients and stir well. Strain into a mixing bowl and fold in the egg whites, leaving little mounds of them on top of the custard. Pour the Spanish cream into a 1³/₄-pint serving dish and chill for 2 hours. Serve cold.

COFFEE GELATINE

Like all other gelatine desserts, this one seems to have
fallen out of our cookbooks. But it's an elegant, light
dessert and a good pick-me-up on a sultry afternoon.
You can use espresso or normal coffee; if you'd rather,
you can brew your own and use that instead of the 1⅓
pints of cold water. The cardamom is a delicate flavouring; you can also use sugar-free amaretto or normal
amaretto or sambuco, but they'll cost you a few more
carbs. SERVES 6

> 2 envelopes gelatine
> 1⅓ pints cold water
> 3 tablespoons instant espresso or coffee
> 3 to 6 sticks Canderel, to taste
> ¼ teaspoon cardamom, optional
> 2 tablespoons sugar-free amaretto syrup (page 40),
>   optional

Per Serving: Protein: 6 g   Fat: 0 g   Carbohydrate: 3 g

Sprinkle the gelatine over 8 fl oz water in a medium
saucepan. Let stand for 5 minutes. Add the remaining
water and stir well. Set the saucepan over low heat and
stir until the gelatine is dissolved, about 5 minutes. Add
the instant coffee and stir until dissolved. Remove from
heat and cool for 10 minutes.

Add the sweetener and the optional flavourings, if
using. Stir well and pour the mixture into a 1¾-pint
serving dish. Refrigerate for 2 to 3 hours to set.

The gelatine tastes best after it's been at room temperature for half an hour, to soften a bit and let the
flavours develop. Serve with vanilla-flavoured whipped
cream.

PASKHA

This is a traditional Russian cheesecakish spread made to serve with kulich, the tall Russian sweet bread. But mould it in a flowerpot, slice and serve it the next day as an enriched cheesecake, and you'll have no complaints. You can also make this moulded in a basket if flowerpots are out of the question. Just remember to make the cheese a day ahead. SERVES 16

> 1 lb cream cheese, at room temperature
> ½ lb butter, at room temperature
> 24 sticks Canderel
> 5 oz almonds, toasted and chopped
> 1 tablespoon vanilla extract
> Minced orange zest from 2 oranges
> 8 fl oz sour cream

Per Serving: Protein: 7 g   Fat: 27.8 g   Carbohydrate: 3.5 g

Push the cream cheese through a sieve and drain off any liquid that appears. In an electric mixer, beat the butter with the cream cheese until fluffy. Add the remaining ingredients and beat until thoroughly combined.

Line a clean new 5-inch clay or plastic flowerpot – or a basket – with a tea towel and add the cheese mixture. Fold the towel up over the top of the cheese, add a plate that just fits the pot, and weight the cheese down with a small can or other heavy object. Set the whole thing on the top shelf of the refrigerator and put a dish on the shelf directly underneath it to catch any drips. Let drain overnight.

Unmould the cheese and turn it out onto a serving plate. Let it ripen in the refrigerator, loosely covered, until ready to serve. Slice in skinny slices and serve on small plates.

CHEESECAKE

Forbidden on every other diet known to man, cheese-cake is the great reward of low-carb dieting. It's so good and so tempting, in fact, that I try not to make it too often, since I can easily eat several pieces without even noticing. To dress up this cheesecake, see the note on the chocolate drizzle below. SERVES 12

> **Butter for the pan**
> **2 lb cream cheese, at room temperature**
> **10½ oz Canderel Spoonful**
> **4 large eggs, at room temperature**
> **Zest of 1 lemon, minced, optional**
> **Zest of 1 orange, minced, optional**
> **2 tablespoons double cream**
> **1 teaspoon pure vanilla extract**

Per Serving: Protein: 8.2 g   Fat: 28 g   Carbohydrate: 4 g

Preheat the oven to 350°F/180°C/Gas Mark 4. Butter a 9-inch springform pan and set aside.

Using an electric mixer, beat the cream cheese well on medium speed until it's absolutely smooth. Slowly beat in the sweetener. Add the eggs one at a time and beat well after each addition. Add the remaining ingredients, scrape down the bowl and stir to combine.

Pour the cheesecake into the prepared pan and smooth the top. Bake for 10 minutes. Turn the heat down to 275°/140°C/Gas Mark 1 and bake for 1 hour, or until the edges are lightly brown. Turn off the oven.

Run a knife around the edge of the pan and return the pan to the oven to cool slowly. Don't worry if the centre of the cheesecake looks a little wiggly; it will firm up in the oven.

Cover the cooled cheesecake with plastic wrap and refrigerate overnight, or up to 3 days. To serve, run a knife around the edges again and remove the sides of the pan.

Chocolate-drizzled Cheesecake

Just before serving the cheesecake, melt 1 cup of semi-sweet chocolate chips in a glass measure in the microwave at 70 percent power for 1 minute. Stir every 20 seconds and stop the moment the chocolate is liquid. Drizzle the liquid chocolate over the cheesecake in a random pattern. Refrigerate for 15 minutes to set before serving.

Per Serving: Protein: .8 g   Fat: 4 g   Carbohydrate: 8.7 g

FATHER SARDUCCI'S CHEESECAKE

The origin of this cake is lost – as is Father Sarducci – but the cake itself has survived in books, cheesecake contests and the treasured recipe collections of home cooks. Have all the ingredients at room temperature. SERVES 12

Butter for the pan
1 (15-oz) container whole-milk ricotta
15 fl oz sour cream
16 oz cream cheese
10½ oz Canderel Spoonful
8 tablespoons butter, melted
3 extra-large eggs
3 tablespoons flour
3 tablespoons cornflour
2 scant tablespoons vanilla extract
2 scant tablespoons fresh lemon juice

Per Serving: Protein: 10 g   Fat: 34 g   Carbohydrate: 9 g

Preheat the oven to 350°F/180°C/Gas Mark 4 and set a baking rack in the middle of the oven. Butter a 10-inch springform pan.

Put the ricotta in the bowl of a food processor and process until smooth. Add the sour cream and cream cheese and process until smooth. Add the remaining ingredients through the feed tube and process until well combined.

Pour the mixture into the prepared pan and bake for 1 hour. Turn off the heat and leave the cheesecake in the oven with the door ajar for one more hour. Cool on a rack. The cheesecake can be made two or three days in advance and kept, covered with plastic wrap, in the refrigerator. You can also freeze it for up to three weeks; defrost before serving.

Note: if you forget to put out the eggs and cream cheese ahead of time so they'll be room temperature when you're ready to make the cheesecake, just drop the cream cheese in its foil packets into a bowl of warm water for a few minutes – same thing with the eggs.

Lemony Cheesecake

Add 2 teaspoons of minced lemon zest.

Lime Cheesecake

Use lime juice instead of lemon and add 2 teaspoons of minced lime zest.

THE RICOTTA DESSERT

Ricotta is one of the most satisfying homey desserts imaginable, and a 2-ounce serving of whole-milk ricotta will set you back only 4 carbs. Of course, the better the ricotta, the better the dessert, so it's worth seeking out a good Italian brand. For a velvety texture, whip the ricotta in a food processor briefly. Keep ricotta on hand and you have instant dessert — just add one of the following:

Raspberries

Minced lemon or orange zest

Warm Berry compote, page 341

A dusting of cinnamon

A dusting of espresso powder

A dusting of cocoa powder

Mini chocolate chips: 10 for 3 carbs

5 chocolate-covered coffee beans tucked inside

Chocolate sauce, page 366

CHOCOLATE SAUCE

When the lily — vanilla ice cream, for instance — needs
gilding, try this intense chocolate sauce, just 2 carbs for
a tablespoonful. MAKES 18 TABLESPOONS, SERVES 9

> 3 fl oz double cream
> 1 tablespoon butter
> 1 tablespoon sugar
> 4 oz semi-sweet chocolate, chopped
> 1 packet aspartame or more to taste

Per Serving: Protein: .4 g   Fat: 4 g   Carbohydrate: 3.8 g

Combine the cream, butter, and sugar in a small
saucepan and bring to a boil. Place the chocolate in a
mixing bowl and pour the hot cream over it. Stir well and
add the aspartame. Stir every 5 minutes until the chocolate is dissolved. Store in the refrigerator and serve at
room temperature.

CHOCOLATE PEANUT BUTTER DROPS

If you absolutely have to have a little sweet after dinner, try these, for just 2 carbs apiece. Not elegant, but not bad – these don't keep more than a day. Try them with homemade toasted hazelnut butter. MAKES 12

1 oz unsweetened chocolate

3 oz chunky peanut butter

2 tablespoons butter

1½ oz whole-milk ricotta

12 sticks Canderel

1 teaspoon pure vanilla extract

Per Serving: Protein: 2.8 g   Fat: 5.3 g   Carbohydrate: 2 g

Melt the first 3 ingredients in a bowl in the microwave. Stir well to combine. Add the remaining ingredients, stir again and drop by the tablespoon on greaseproof paper – you should have 12 drops. Chill until firm – at least 1 hour – and keep in the refrigerator.

THE CHEESE PLATTER

This popular finale to a great meal is as wonderful as ever. For your carb-eating guests, serve wholemeal biscuits and thin slices of dark nut bread. Low-carb crackers are fine with cheese. You need at least four different kinds of cheese to make this work, with contrasting flavours and textures. Serve them on a large board, a platter, a tray, whatever works. Real vine leaves — or the fake paper ones sold in speciality stores — look terrific under the cheeses. Serve the cheese with a mixed green salad. Or go in a different direction and add several bunches of grapes — again, different kinds — a couple of kinds of nuts and a jar of sweet celery sticks cut from the inner stalks. If your guests aren't sure how to cut the cheese, show them: in general, you follow the shape of the cheese for wedges; small rounds or squares are cut in wedges, and logs are cut in small circles. Using a real cheese knife — which has hollow areas in the blade — makes a big difference. Ask your cheesemonger for suggestions on felicitous combinations. Here are some possibilities:

Hard cheese: Gouda, cheddar
Blue cheese: Gorgonzola, Maytag blue, Roquefort
Goat's cheese: Boucheron, Montrachet
Soft cheese: Brie, Camembert, cambozola,
     St. Andre
Sheep's cheese: manchego, pecorino

Serve the cheese just slightly cool, with wine.

Breakfast

/////

In some ways, this is the most difficult meal of the day for low-carbers, even though there may be some extra leeway on carbs in the morning (see page 23). Juice has far too many carbs to spend frivolously – much better to eat the whole fruit and get the fibre too, unless you're such a juice nut that you're willing to spend all your carbs on juice. The traditional breakfast favourites – cereal, toast, croissants, pancakes, waffles – hit the carb budget too hard to enjoy, except for the low-carb whole-grain toasts. Then too, you need to remember to have enough protein.

For an on-the-run breakfast, which is what most everyday breakfasts turn out to be, you may turn to cottage cheese or one of the high-protein low-carb bars. More fun is the smoothie, made with soya milk and perhaps protein powder in the form of egg white plus some delectable fruit. Use the smoothie recipe on page 376 as a guide and play with the fruits and the flavourings. You can make a chocolate smoothie with cocoa powder and sweetener and vanilla, a mocha one by adding powdered espresso, or just have plain vanilla, with a little sour cream and grated nutmeg blended in.

Eggs and breakfast meats or fish (lox, smoked or kippered salmon, sable) are great solutions and there are a number of ideas here as well as in the Main Dish category. You can make skinny 2-egg flat omelettes and stack them with fillings like creamed spinach, mushrooms, rata-touille, etc. to make a big omelette cake. Top it with grated Parmesan and minced parsley; run it under the grill briefly to melt the cheese, and serve in wedges. Sausage patties or bacon or sliced ham is a perfect accompaniment.

For a big-treat breakfast, try the three-grain waffles with raspberry-orange syrup. They beg for some sausage or bacon – or both; add those and you've got a memorable breakfast feast.

Scrambled Egg Tips

- Add a little crunch by tossing in a few croutons briefly sizzled in butter for each serving.

- The great French gastronome Escoffier liked to scramble his eggs with a fork on which he'd impaled a garlic clove – good idea.

- Use half eggs, half crumbled soft tofu for a lighter version of scrambled eggs – good with hot pepper sauce. Add tofu during the last minute of cooking.

- To make a lot of scrambled eggs ahead of time for a crowd:

Preheat the oven to 225°F/110°C/Gas Mark $1/4$. Beat a dozen eggs with 2 fl oz of cream and add salt and pepper to taste. Melt 3 tablespoons of butter in a frying pan; when it's foaming, add the eggs. Stir well until the eggs are heated through completely but not cooked. Put the eggs in a buttered mixing bowl and set it in a pan of warm water in the oven. The eggs will finish cooking and hold well for about 15 minutes. Turn the bowl upside down on a round serving plate and unmould the eggs. Cover the mound of eggs with snipped chives and surround it with strips of crisp bacon and grilled tomatoes.

THE FORTY-SECOND OMELETTE

Howard Helmer is Mr Egg, the spokesperson for the
American Egg Board — and he really wants you to learn
how to make an omelette. This is his way. He likes cheap
10-inch nonstick pans with sloping sides and he uses
a pancake turner, so there's no specialist equipment.
Inside his omelettes can be half a cup of just about anything: grated cheese, vegetables, smoked salmon with
cream cheese and chives — whatever you can think of.
For each omelette, here's what you need to know.

SERVES 1

2 large eggs

2 tablespoons water or soda water

⅛ teaspoon salt

Pepper to taste

1 teaspoon olive oil or butter (I say butter)

Optional: ½ cup filling

Per Serving: Protein: 12.2 g   Fat: 8.6 g   Carbohydrate: 1.2 g

Break the eggs into a glass measuring cup. Add the
water, salt and pepper and beat with a fork until combined.

Put the oil or butter in the omelette pan and set over
medium-high heat. When the fat starts to sizzle, swirl
the pan to distribute it evenly. Pour in the eggs, which
will immediately begin to set.

Using an inverted pancake turner, push the cooked
eggs towards you to the centre and turn the pan so that
the raw eggs run into their place. Keep doing this until
the omelette has thickened and very little liquid egg remains. At this point spread the optional filling over half
the omelette. Using the pancake turner, flip the other

side of the omelette over the filling and slide the whole thing onto a waiting plate. Ambitious cooks can simply invert the omelette onto the plate with a quick flip of the wrist – a nice flourish.

KILLER SCRAMBLED EGGS

These are pretty exciting fare, considering that they're basically just scrambled eggs. They have chive or spring onion cream cheese folded into them and then they're topped with caviar or chopped smoked salmon. Perfect for a late-night supper or brunch. SERVES 1

> *For each serving:*
> **2 large eggs**
> **2 tablespoons cream**
> **Salt and pepper to taste**
> **1 teaspoon butter**
> **1 tablespoon chive or spring onion cream cheese**
> **1 tablespoon caviar or chopped smoked salmon**

Per Serving: Protein: 15 g   Fat: 17 g   Carbohydrate: 2.4 g

In a glass measuring cup, beat the eggs and the cream together with a fork and add salt and pepper to taste. Heat the butter in a frying pan until a drop of water sizzles when it hits the butter. Pour in the eggs and stir them around with an inverted pancake turner so that the cooked eggs come to the surface and the liquid eggs go to the bottom of the pan.

When the eggs are beginning to thicken, add the cream cheese and stir it into the eggs. When the eggs are firm but still moist, turn them out onto a plate and top with the caviar or smoked salmon.

BAKED EGGS WITH SPINACH

A good little informal supper or breakfast dish. It's worth making extra spinach so you'll have it left over to make these eggs. If you don't have individual ramekins, you can use a baking dish; just spread the spinach over the bottom, then slide the eggs on top. Try adding a little freshly grated nutmeg to the spinach. SERVES 1

For each serving you'll need:
2 teaspoons butter
2 oz cooked buttered spinach, squeezed dry
2 large eggs
Salt and pepper to taste
1 tablespoon double cream
1 teaspoon grated Parmesan cheese
Dash of paprika

Per Serving: Protein: 13.3 g   Fat: 24.8 g   Carbohydrate: 3.6 g

Preheat the oven to 325°/170°C/Gas Mark 3. Butter a ramekin and add a layer of the spinach. Put the ramekin on a baking sheet and into the oven to heat for a few minutes. Crack the eggs into a saucer and slide them into the ramekin, add salt and pepper to taste, and pour over the cream. Sprinkle the cheese and paprika on top and send the ramekin back to the oven for 5 minutes under a loose tent of foil. The whites should be set; the yolks won't look done at this point, but they will be by the time they get to the table.

MANGO SMOOTHIE

If you really miss mangoes, remember that your insulin
problems are at their lowest in the morning, so breakfast
is the time to indulge. This heavenly drink provides 23
grams of protein and satisfies the mango longing perfectly. SERVES 1

> 4½ oz diced mango
> 2 tablespoons sour cream
> 8 fl oz unsweetened soya milk
> 2 heaped tablespoons protein powder, preferably
>   egg white
> ½ teaspoon vanilla extract
> 1 stick Canderel
> Zest of 1 lime
> Dash of salt
> 7 fl oz water

Per Serving: Protein: 23.4 g   Fat: 9.6 g   Carbohydrate: 16 g

Mix everything together in a blender until smooth and
drink immediately.

THREE-GRAIN PANCAKES WITH RASPBERRY-ORANGE SAUCE

An excellent Sunday breakfast with bacon or sausage. Yes, these are a little high in carbs, but remember, your insulin is more sensitive in the morning and you should be able to handle the extra carbs with no problems – try these and see.

To save time in the morning, mix up the dry ingredients the night before and set them aside, mix up the wet ingredients and refrigerate them – the next day, all you'll have to do is beat the egg whites and mix everything together. SERVES 4

$2\frac{1}{2}$ oz fine yellow cornmeal
$2\frac{1}{2}$ oz oat flour
$2\frac{1}{2}$ oz barley flour (or use oat flour)
2 teaspoons baking powder
$\frac{1}{4}$ teaspoon salt
Large pinch of cinnamon
8 fl oz milk
3 large eggs, separated
4 tablespoons unsalted butter, melted

Per Serving: Protein: 10.2 g   Fat: 18.5 g   Carbohydrate: 28.8 g

In a mixing bowl, combine the flours, baking powder, salt and cinnamon – don't bother sifting. In a separate bowl, whisk the milk, egg yolks and butter. Make a well in the dry mixture, add the liquids and stir until evenly blended.

In a clean bowl, beat the egg whites until they hold soft peaks. Fold the whites into the batter, just until evenly blended. Using about 2 fl oz of batter each, cook the pancakes on a hot griddle, about 1 to 1½ minutes per side, flipping once. Serve hot, with the raspberry-orange sauce.

RASPBERRY-ORANGE SAUCE

SERVES 4

6 oz frozen raspberries
1 tablespoon grated orange zest
2 drops pure orange oil, page 39, optional
Canderel, to taste

Per Serving: Protein: 0 g   Fat: trace   Carbohydrate: 3.1 g

Combine the raspberries and orange zest plus the optional oil in a small non-reactive saucepan. Bring to a gentle boil, then reduce the heat slightly and simmer for 2 minutes. Stir in the sweetener and taste – you may need more sweetener or orange. Transfer the sauce to a food processor bowl and process until smooth. Serve the sauce warm to spoon over the pancakes.

SIMPLE WAFFLES

These crispy, delicate waffles can be served with sliced
strawberries and a dollop of sour cream or with butter
and berry syrup or ersatz maple syrup. If you don't have
a waffle iron, you can make them into pancakes – though
they're so light that turning them is a bit tricky. SERVES 4

> 4 large eggs, separated
> 4 tablespoons unsalted butter, slightly chilled
> 1¼ oz oat flour
> 8 fl oz sour cream
> ½ teaspoon pure vanilla extract
> ½ teaspoon salt
> Grating of nutmeg, optional

Per Serving: Protein: 7.9 g   Fat: 28.6 g   Carbohydrate: 7.3 g

Beat the egg whites in an electric mixer until they
form soft peaks. Set aside in another bowl. In the same
mixer bowl, cream the butter until fluffy and beat in
the yolks one at a time. Add the flour and sour cream
alternately, beating well after each addition. Stir in the
vanilla, salt and nutmeg. Fold in the egg whites. Bake in
a preheated waffle iron according to manufacturer's
directions.

RICOTTA PANCAKES

These high-protein, low-carb pancakes are at least reminiscent of the high-carb pancakes we all used to love. If you decide to leave out the powdered egg whites, the batter will be thin, so you should make little pancakes. If you're really hungry, two people can divide these pancakes for 33 grams of protein, 26.2 grams of fat, and 12.5 carbs each. SERVES 3

4 large eggs
4 oz ricotta
½ teaspoon vanilla extract
1½ cup oat flour
1 tablespoon melted butter or vegetable oil
Pinch of salt
Big pinch of grated nutmeg
1 stick Canderel, optional
2 tablespoons powdered egg whites
1 teaspoon butter for the griddle

Per Serving: Protein: 22 g   Fat: 17.5 g   Carbohydrate: 8 g

Set a griddle or a large frying pan over high heat. Put all the pancake ingredients (except the butter for the griddle) in a blender or food processor and blend well. When the griddle is hot enough so that a drop of water jumps when it hits the surface, grease the griddle with the butter. Drop the batter by spoonfuls, large or small as you like, onto the griddle. Turn the pancakes when the edges lose their shine and bubbles begin to appear. Cook briefly on the other side and serve immediately. Butter and Vermont Sugar-Free Syrup are the right accompaniments.

BLUEBERRY SYRUP

You can use fresh or frozen blueberries here. This is good
on pancakes or ricotta for dessert or just spooned over
cottage cheese when you want a little treat. SERVES 4

- 5 oz blueberries
- 4 fl oz water or more as needed
- 2 sticks Canderel
- Dash of cinnamon
- 1 teaspoon grated lemon zest or 2 drops lemon oil

Per Serving: Protein: 0 g   Fat: 0 g   Carbohydrate: 4.3 g

In a small saucepan, bring the blueberries and water to
a gentle simmer over medium heat. Crush the berries a
bit with a cooking spoon and add the remaining ingredients. Let the syrup thicken a little and take off the heat.
You can either purée it or serve it chunky.

MENUS

Christmas Menu

Smoked Trout on Watercress

Roast Turkey with Wild Rice Stuffing

Cranberry Sauce

Broccoli Purée

Spaghetti Squash with Roasted Pecans

Salad of Winter Greens with Pomegranate Seeds

Pumpkin Mousse

Celebration Dinner

Smoked Salmon Canapés

Standing Rib Roast of Beef with Horseradish Cream

Turnip Gratin with Blue Cheese

Wild Rice

Spinach with a Ton of Butter

Watercress Salad with Orange and Toasted Walnuts

Pecan Meringue Ice Cream Pie

New Year's Eve Supper

Caviar on Cracked Pepper Crackers

Radishes with Sweet Butter and Sea Salt

Oyster Stew with Mushrooms

Salad of Winter Greens with Orange and Avocado

Cheese Platter with Celery Sticks

Titbits: Chocolate Almonds, Chocolate Coffee Beans,

Candied Ginger, Cracked Walnuts

Casual Winter Supper

Aubergine and Pepper Dip with Endive

Sauerkraut Soup

Spicy Cheese Wafers with Caraway Seed

Big Green Salad

Ambrosia with Amarettini

Mexican Dinner

Mexican Prawn Cocktail

Carnitas

Tortillas, Large Romaine Leaves, Pickled Onions, Salsa, Sour Cream, Coriander Sprigs, Tomato Chunks, Lime Wedges

Mixed Melon Balls with Mint

Almond Biscuits

Texas Supper

Fried Cheese on Greens

Oven Barbecued Brisket

Tex-Mex Coleslaw

Potato Salad

Green Chilli Soufflé

Cumin and Courgette Pancakes with Salsa

Watermelon with Lime Wedges

Quick Dinner

Smoked Salmon Rolls with Hazelnut Cream Cheese

Nut-Crusted Swordfish with Romesco Sauce

Spinach with a Whiff of Garlic

Broccoli Purée

Chocolate Mousse

Elegant Spring Dinner

Walnut Parmesan Lace Crisps

Crudités with Cucumber Dip

Salmon with Garlic Cream Spinach and Chanterelles

Herb Salad with Lemon Vinaigrette

Raspberry Crème Brûlée

A Simple Dinner

Courgette Pasta

Crispy Chicken Cutlets

Green Bean Pie

Greek Salad, No Tomatoes

Father Sarducci's Cheesecake

A Grilled Dinner

Lime Scallops

Tuna with Mint, Garlic and Soy

Pan-cooked Watercress

Courgette Pancakes

Ricotta Puffs with Raspberry Sauce

A Southern Feast

New Orleans Spicy Prawns

Southern-Style Smothered Pork Chops

Country-Style Greens

Cauliflower Purée

Corn Crisps

Peach and Blueberry Crisp with Almonds

Summer Lunch

Vichyssoise

Salmon and Green Bean Salad with Dill

Spicy Cheese Wafers

Cherry Tomatoes

Berries with Trembling Cream

A Middle Eastern Dinner

Cheese Balls

Leg of Lamb with a Tapenade Crust

Slow-Baked Tomatoes with Feta Cheese

Tabbouleh

Melon Balls with Cardamom

Pecan Meringues

South American Grill

Provoleta

Steaks with Chimichurri Sauce

Potato Skins

Swiss Chard with Chillis

Peaches with Amarettini Cream

Italian Dinner

Olives / Caponata

Tricoloured Pepper Crescents

Roast Leg of Pork

Courgette Pancakes

Fennel and Orange Salad with Frico

Fresh Fruit: Cherries, Grapes, Forelle Pears

Pecan Meringues

Sources

To find the specialist low-carb products used in this book in the UK, please visit the following websites:

www.LowCarbMegastore.com
www.carblife.com
www.sugarlite.co.uk
www.sugarfreeuk.com

For information about low-carb diets in the UK, visit:

www.low-carb.org.uk

Index